TRABANT TREK

Crossing the World in a Plastic Car

TRABANT TREK

Crossing the World in a Plastic Car

Dan Murdoch

Signal Books
Oxford

First published in 2009 by
Signal Books Limited
36 Minster Road
Oxford
OX4 1LY
www.signalbooks.co.uk

A catalogue record for this book is available from the British Library.

ISBN 978-1-904955-50-4 Paper

Production: Devdan Sen
Cover Design: Baseline Arts
Cover Images: Dan Murdoch; istockphoto.com
Photographs: all photographs © Dan Murdoch

Printed in India

Contents

To the Trekkers: Anthony Perez, Brady Erickson, Carlos Gey, John Drury, John
Lovejoy, Marlena Witczak, Megan Calvert and Zsofi Somlai.
To the Trabants: Dante, Fez and Ziggy.
To the charities: Mith Samlanh and M'Lop Tapang.
And to the hundreds of people who helped us along the way.

Acknowledgements

Thanks to my family for putting me up, and putting up with me—my folks, Chris and Carol, and John and Tessa, and my grandparents, Lynn, Val and Pam.

Thanks to Claire for her support and affection and Dave for his encouragement. I'd also like to take this opportunity to unacknowledged Ben Chamberlain and Amit Tyagi.

Fat lot of help you two were.

Author's Note

Every Story has a beginning, but for each of the foolhardy souls that took on Trabant Trek, the beginning was different. Come to think of it, although we shared so many experiences, each of us had a different middle and ending as well.

To try and cover all of these would probably result in a terrifying mess and so I have little choice but to stick firmly to my side of the story. If it wavers from the recollections of the rest of the gang then I apologise.

You should know that this book started as a blog, scribbled in notebooks and on scraps, and then written up in cafés, bars and garages on the road. It is nigh on impossible to type in a Trabant—too cramped, too dark, too bumpy. The words and pictures were painstakingly uploaded using some of the world's most scattered and least rapid internet connections. There's nothing quite like the frustration of spending three hours trying to upload a couple of sentences on a steam-powered Uzbek PC running Windows 1905.

When I got home I rewrote the whole thing, checked the facts and sculpted the blogs, notes and memories into the work of epic importance you hold in your hands.

I hope you like it.

Dan Murdoch
July 2008

Introduction

Q) Why is the Trabant the quietest car in the world to drive?
A) Because your knees cover your ears.

WHY?

Even though he'd pulled us over, the policeman looked more confused than angry. He approached our convoy slowly in the snow, scratching his head and shining his torch along the faded, peeling panelling of the cars. The beam reached my face, making me blink away.

"Where are you from?" he asked in Russian.

"England."

"Where are you going?"

"Cambodia."

"Kaamboodyaa?" He rolled the word out, making it sound unfamiliar.

"Cam-bo-dia."

"Ahhh… Cambodia," he repeated, understanding the name, but not the answer.

"Why?"

Why? That was difficult.

The policeman shrugged and held up his camera phone, "Photo?"

THE EMAIL

I remember getting the email. Autumn 2006. I'd returned home late after a few post-deadline drinks, and sat on my bed with a laptop. The message was from

John Lovejoy. The subject line read: "Europe to Cambodia by Trabant."

Team USA

John Christian Lovejoy was a man of the world. Born in California, but raised at US Army bases in Germany, he had travelled extensively and boasted of friends across the globe. Tall, handsome, with a thick mop of curly hair and an occasional beard, he was a real charmer with a handy knack for getting people onside and a shameless approach to milking acquaintances.

His favourite word was "fuck". Used mostly for emphasis, it could be a noun, adjective, preposition, verb or anything he desired. As in: "What the fuck? Let's get the fuck back to that fucking place and get a fucking burger. I mean fuck. With that fucking sauce. Fuck me, man. It's fucking rad and it's fucking cheap. It's like what? Fucking two dollars?"

To maintain some sense of decency I have omitted many of these super-fluous curses from his quotes. Sorry, Lovey.

I first met Lovejoy with his friend Anthony Perez in 2002 in the sticky Thai jungle somewhere north of Chang Mai. Along with my travel buddy, Mr Al, I'd headed out on an organised trek into the bush. We'd noticed the two Americans when the group gathered earlier that day, but it took until a rest stop at a waterfall to make conversation. Mr Al and I had brought with us a bottle of the filthy local Mekong whisky; a vicious brown poison that cost next to nothing and doubled up as nail varnish remover. It was disgusting neat and, looking around for some inspiration, I noticed the Americans sipping from a bottle of Coke. From this whisky and Coke a partnership was born, and we bonded over three days of sweaty walks and cool waterfalls.

I was 19 at the time; Lovey, as Lovejoy was known, and Tony were a few years older. The pair knew each other from Washington DC, where they lived and worked, and had an easy rapport.

"You know," Tony would tell me years later, "Lovey's the only person I've travelled with where I can just go 'John, I'm going to go and do my own thing for a few weeks now. I'll catch you later' and he'll be absolutely fine with it."

Tony was half-Mexican, half-Italian but very American. Shorter than Lovey, but compact and dark, he liked to sport a Mohican and a moustache, which made him look a little Mongolian. The four of us got on well and when we waved our goodbyes I jokingly said I'd see them further on down the trail. Three weeks later and I was on the back of a Vietnamese moped, speeding through Ho Chi Minh City trying to flag down a bus to Cambodia. We were close up behind it, my driver honking manically and trying to get the bus to stop, when a rear window slid open and the dark head of Tony Perez popped out.

"Dan?" he said with a smile.

"Tony," I shouted over the traffic.

"How's it going?" he asked, cool as you like.

"Yeah great... er... I'm trying to get on that bus."

He looked around, dragged it out for a second, then grinned: "I'll get them to stop."

It turned out that Tony and I were heading the same way. We met Lovey in Phnom Penh, then continued to Siem Riep for a few days at Angkor Wat and the chance to consult a mystical shaman known as Burnhard Yungkermann.

One morning we decided to head into the jungle to visit the old temple of Bang Milia. I was tasked with hiring a moped for Tony, but rather than use a hire company I opted to borrow a scooter from a man in a bar, using Tony's passport as a deposit. The recklessness of this manoeuvre only became clear the following day when I went to return the scooter but couldn't find the man with the passport.

"So what did he look like?" Tony asked as we drove around town.

"Well he was a South East Asian chap, quite short, and he was in that bar there—or was it that bar there?"

As I had already booked a flight from Bangkok, I had to get a bus out of Siem Riep that afternoon. Lovey needed to get to Thailand too, so the pair of us set off, leaving Tony clutching a stranger's scooter, alone, documentless and without any way of leaving the country.

I wouldn't see him again for five years.

WORLD CUP 2006, GERMANY

Forward to 2006, and things seemed to be going well. I'd finished university in Brighton, got my basic journalist's qualification, the NCTJ, and settled into a job on my hometown newspaper, The Surrey Herald.

That summer I arranged to go to Germany with a few friends to follow the World Cup. Mr Al told me that Lovey would be there.

"He's going to pick us up from the airport," Mr Al said.

Great. I'd met Lovey for a drink in London the year before, but hadn't seen him properly for years.

I arrived at Munich Airport with Mr Al and my old friend Amit. Lovey met us there as arranged, looking healthy and casual in the sunshine. We hugged and made the usual noises as he led us to our transport.

"So what you driving?" I asked.

"A Trabant," he smiled.

"A what?"

Lovey pointed at this impish, quirky little car with faded blue-grey paint. Tiny but perfectly proportioned, with big round headlights, little wheels and small windows. There was something comic about it—it looked a bit like a clown car—certainly not a vehicle to be taken seriously. I couldn't help but laugh.

"What is that? Where did you get it?"

"It's a Trabant. I bought it for $60 in Hungary."

"It's ridiculous."

Lovey gave us a tour—the giant boot, the comically simple dashboard, the unique steering-column-mounted gear stick.

"It goes 80kph," Lovey said proudly, to emphasise its crapness, "and look, there's no fuel gauge on the dash. To find out how much gas you have, you pop the hood," he opened the bonnet, "and dip this ruler into the gas tank."

He did what he said and then held the ruler up in the sun, a thin high-tide mark rapidly evaporating on the surface.

"Four litres. We should be fine. But it's a two-stroke, so when you fill it up, you need to add oil to the mix," he waved a grubby little bottle of oil at me, "then you shake the whole car to mix it together." He planted his hands on each wing of the car and shook it from side to side. It was so light it looked like he could lift it.

"We can lift it," he said, laughing. "Wait until you meet OJ. Together we can lift up the back of it and shift it sideways. It helps with parking. It's made of plastic that's why it's so light."

"What?"

"Plastic," he tapped the panel, "it's made of plastic."

We were all laughing now. So it was half-car, half-lunchbox? No, it probably didn't even qualify as a car—it had a 600cc engine, just 25bhp. So it was half-lawnmower, half-Tupperware? Ridiculous.

Lovey explained that the Trabant was the East German competitor to the

West German Volkswagen. In the 1950s, when it had been designed, there was a steel shortage in the Soviet Union. So the boffins had to find a replacement material to build the panelling for the car. They used Duroplast, a mixture of polymer resin and leftover waste from the Soviet Union's cotton industry. The Trabant was the first car to be made out of recycled materials, possibly its only redeeming feature.

A small crowd of people had formed nearby to admire the car, which had a cult following in Germany. Some of the tourists were taking photos. We squeezed inside; it was cramped for four tall lads with tents and bags. In the front, my shins were bashing against a shelf that ran under the dash. In the back, Amit and Mr Al had their knees around their ears. We pulled away to the heavy revving of the little engine, basking in the laughter of bystanders. I loved it.

We spent the next week driving around in that thing. The Yanks had painted go-faster-stripes along the top and at our campsite, Brady, another American travelling with Lovey, knocked up a symbol, which he sprayed onto the doors. In the motif were the initials "MTP"—Mighty Tony Perez—a dedication to Tony, who was meant to be with us but had broken his ankle coming off a scooter in Cambodia earlier in the year and had to go home.

With Lovey and Brady was another Yank, John Bradford Drury, who knew Lovey and Tony from Washington DC and had been travelling with them. He had been dubbed OJ, or "Other John", being the second John on their trip. OJ was a giant of a man, a huge, towering, six-foot-three figure with bulging, twitching pectorals and a square jaw. His physique was almost ogre-ish, his muscles had muscles on them, but beneath that powerful exterior was a soft centre: he worked out, moisturised extensively and liked cooking.

I didn't spend too much time with OJ in Germany. My only real memory of him was one night, sitting around drinking with the group, seeing him alone by the campfire drumming furiously against his thigh with a pair of sticks.

"That's one weird kid," Lovey said, looking over. I would get to find out.

After a week in Germany we waved goodbye to Lovey, OJ and Brady and headed home. I occasionally thought of Lovey's little Trabbi, remembering the night we squeezed six large men in and drove around for an hour, lost in Munich. Or when we had to quickly empty the boot of counterfeit Thai football shirts because we thought we were going to be raided by German police.

Lovey and OJ carried on in the tiny car, eventually nursing it to the palace at Versailles, on the outskirts of Paris, before it broke irreparably and had to be abandoned. They managed six countries in that Trabbi, attracting attention, infamy and laughter everywhere they went, and sowing the seeds for what was to come.

Europe to Cambodia by Trabant

I remember getting the email. The title alone was enough to get me going and although the content was vague, it was enticing: "The route has yet to be chosen, but it would certainly involve parts of Central and Eastern Europe as well as parts of Central Asia, Mongolia and China. The question mark is whether to take the northern route through Ukraine and Russia or the southern route through Turkey, the Caspian Sea and other countries in Central Asia.

"I have written to the nine of you because I know you all to have the travelling spirit and the desire to do something different. I have travelled with most of you at one point or another and think for the most part each of you know one another, or at least one other person so it would not be completely random. This could be a great opportunity to get away from the hordes and see something we are not pushed to see, that the Lonely Planet hasn't put on the agenda for us."

The idea instantly resonated with me and I was excited. I had just turned 24, and forty years of work stretched out in front of me. Surely it was the time for an adventure, when I had no mortgage, no wife or kids, no unleavable job? I had been working hard for a few years, why not take a break?

And I was especially keen to get off the beaten track. When backpacking I'd come to the conclusion that guidebooks, instead of opening places up for exploration, set artificial limits on your experience. People tend to follow the recommendations and stick to the guide, resulting in hundreds of people following the same, weary paths. But this way we would be off the map. I didn't know of any guidebooks designed for people driving plastic Soviet relics across Eurasia.

I tempered my excitement with the thought that it might be an idea that sounds good at the time, but slowly drifts into nothingness. So I resolved to keep things under my hat—the whole thing could easily fall flat in the next few weeks.

But instead of drifting away, the idea developed, snowballed and gathered momentum as the emails kept coming. Should it be a race, or should the cars support each other? Do we need a theme? Maybe we should do it for charity? Should we stick to Soviet countries? Maybe we should film the whole thing?

As the plan morphed and developed it crystallised. The Trabants would be driven from the site of the old Trabant factory in Zwickau, Germany, to the home of the charities the group would be raising money for, in Phnom Penh and Sihanoukville, Cambodia.

Tony and Lovey worked out a route and chose not to go the quickest, straightest or easiest way. Instead they picked out things they wanted to see and places they wanted to go. They would take Trabbis where they had never been before: the Pamir Mountains, the Gobi desert, the Asian jungle.

The cars would go from Germany, south and east through the Czech Republic, Slovakia, Hungary, Romania and Bulgaria, full of Trabbi enthusiasts and easy repairs, then east through Turkey and the gateway to Asia. From there, north into the Caucasus, crossing Georgia, Armenia and Azerbaijan before getting a boat across the Caspian Sea into the forgotten world of Central Asia—the police state of Turkmenistan, the beautiful Silk Road cities of Uzbekistan, the stunning mountain passes of Tajikistan and Kyrgyzstan, and the endless flat of the Kazakh steppe. We would cross the forests of Russian Siberia and Mongolia's icy plains, then plough south through booming China before hitting the sun-speckled hills of Laos, the welcoming familiarity of Thailand and the jungles of Cambodia.

It would be a 15,000-mile journey through twenty-one countries. They reckoned it would take four months. The trip would be entirely self-funded, the trekkers paying for everything needed to get to across Eurasia. But they would also try to attract sponsorship to raise money for two Cambodian charities dedicated to supporting and educating children living in poverty, Mith Samlanh in Phnom Penh and M'Lop Tapang in Sihanoukville. And it would be filmed, at the very least for posterity, but hopefully we would get a TV network interested in the footage. We needed a website, press coverage, PR stunts, fliers, posters, a media presence, sponsorship, celebrity endorsement, T-shirts, bumper stickers and business cards. Lovey was nothing if not ambitious. He wanted this to be huge.

He called it Trabant Trek.

THE WAVERER

There were a lot of names on the list of people who were interested. Lovey was never able to tell me how many people he invited, but Tony guessed at about thirty or forty. There was plenty of correspondence between people who were committed in varying degrees and over the next few months the faint-hearted drifted away or pulled out altogether as further arrangements were made and realities dawned.

Lovey was the instigator and the driving force. He'd constantly be sending out fresh thoughts, guiding the development and explaining new opportunities and pitfalls that he'd come across. Sometimes we would get two or three emails a day from him and I admit to dreading opening my inbox for fear of what new horizon had been opened up.

I was sold on the idea of Trabant Trek, but wasn't sure if it was the right time for me. People were talking about leaving in May or June of the next year, 2007. At that point I would only be 15 or 16 months into my two-year training contract at The Surrey Herald. If I left then, it would be without my senior qualification, and would mean my time at the newspaper was wasted.

But as the New Year turned, fate intervened. Rumours were flying around that my paper was going to be bought out. This led to speculation that trainees like myself wouldn't be able to finish their course. So I took this to my editor and asked if I could take my exams in May, six months early. After some discussion, he agreed.

I got in touch with Lovey and told him I was in.

There was plenty to be done. Ironing out the minutiae of the route, working out what permissions were necessary in which countries, what visas and car papers would be needed, preparing different pitches for potential sponsors and TV companies.

In all honesty I didn't really do any of this stuff. I sent my passport with a load of visa forms out to DC, where the Americans got them all done together. I sent some money out to help cover start up costs, and wrote and sent out press releases and sponsorship letters for the UK, with little response.

It was a pitifully poor contribution compared to what Lovey and Tony were putting in, and I felt bad. Often Lovey would send out a long, rambling group email setting out just how much needed to be done, and just how much of it he was doing. This always made me feel guilty. "I think the rest of the group took for granted just how much work Lovey and I put into planning this thing," Tony said, many months later.

I told myself I had other things on my plate—a full-time job, preparing for exams and gigging with my band goldroom. Talk of special highway passes to cross the Pamir Mountains in Tajikistan seemed a little removed. It's hard to get home after a full day and set about chasing sponsors and media. That's what I told myself, but Lovey and Tony seemed to have no trouble.

TRABANT TREFFEN

By June 2007 I had passed my exams and handed in my notice. The initial plan was for the Trek to set off from the annual Trabant festival in Zwickau, the Trabant Treffen. But as the June date neared, and the to-do-list built up, Lovey decided to push everything back a month.

But we still wanted to go to the Treffen to spread the word about the Trek, as there would be tens of thousands of Trabbi enthusiasts there, and maybe some of them would sponsor us. I agreed to head to Germany with the only other Brit, a pretty blonde called Samantha or Sam, whom Lovey had met on his travels. Lovey flew from DC to Budapest to pick up the Trabbi that had already been bought. There he met up with our Spanish trekker and the pair drove to Germany to collect Sam and me.

We got the tent up just as the heavens opened in a storm straight out of a Hammer horror film. Forked tongues sliced through the sky, echoed by the steady murmur of rolling thunder. A small sea rained onto the campsite, turning everything to muck. We'd cleverly camped in the bed of a natural gully and as the field saturated a stream formed and began to flow through the tent, washing grass, litter and insects into our new home.

We used beer crates as stools and sat close together, wet and shivering but happy in the gloom. In those cold, damp and close quarters I got to know Carlos Gey, the Spaniard. His surname really was Gey, though he pronounced it "Hay", which always amused me. Often I just called him "The Gay" or "The Losbian" or "The Spaniard" or, occasionally, "Pedro", though I don't think he really liked any of those names.

The oldest of our group, Carlos was a Catalan and had been working in a hostel in Barcelona before we met, though really he was a marine biologist who had spent two years in Alaska counting fish. I never understood that.

Carlos had a perfect grasp of English, which he liked to demonstrate through the use of terrible puns, the sort of bottom scrapers that down-market tabloids would shy away from. These always made Lovey crack up. I never understood that either.

Shorter than me, but taller than Tony, Carlos was tanned and dark, with thick-rimmed glasses. The glasses disguised his most powerful weapon, the eyes. Oh the eyes, the glaring gateway to his Id, capable of firing fiery Exocets of foreboding at friend or foe. The "Spanish Eyes", as they were quickly dubbed, the brooding, faux sexual look he pulled for cameras (and women), the dark, angry Latino stare he used to show displeasure. It made everyone laugh: "Don't do the eyes at me. Not the Spanish Eyes. He's doing the eyes. Someone stop him doing the eyes."

Despite his smaller stature and girl's hips he walked a lot faster than me, often with his hands clasped firmly behind his back like Inspector Clouseau. I prefer to saunter around new places, slowly breathing it all in. But once Carlos has chosen his destination he puts his head down and gets there. Often that was exactly what we needed.

"Carlos gets things done," OJ once said, quite correctly.

The festival was a mud bath, but we made the most of it. Every conceivable Trabant modification was on show, like peacocks flashing their plumage. Stretch Trabbis, jeep Trabbis, lowered Trabbis set on alloys with tinted windows and chrome rims. Some had one-litre engines, some had no engines, others had tents on their roofs, one was turned into a trike, another into a boat, one Trabbi was mounted on a 4x4 chassis, most had four wheels, a few had six wheels. My personal favourite had a garden table and benches mounted on its roof. Six large German men sat atop the moving vehicle spilling frothy lager onto passers by and jeering in Teutonic unison.

A week later I got a phone call from Sam. She was pulling out. Her weekend at the Treffen had been characterised by running arguments with Lovey. She was an accountant by profession and had an orderly mind. But Lovey was light on facts and specifics, as we all were, and it is fair to say that the two didn't combine well. She expressed the fall-out a little differently and entirely un-printably.

So we were a man—or a lady—down. Sam was the third female to pull out and there was a danger that the Trek was going to become a little cock heavy. We were down to five guys and two girls, though Lovey was still working on a few people, and there was a chance that some folk would travel with us for a few weeks here and there. No official departure date was set, but the call came in to assemble in Budapest in the second week of July. The Hungarian capital would be our base camp. The Trabants were there, and Lovey knew a Trabbi specialist who would be making modifications to the cars and sourcing spare parts.

There was a lot to be done, I was told; we needed to assemble and start doing it. Once everything had been organised we would drive to Germany for the official start of Trabant Trek.

Setting off on that sort of journey always gives me butterflies. That feeling of nerves and expectation in the pit of your stomach—who knows what will happen next? There were new people to meet, new friendships to form, and a car to be driven across Eurasia. How do you really prepare yourself for that? I guess you can't. You just go ahead and do it.

Four months, it'll take four months. Over by mid-November? I told my friends and family I would be home for Christmas, just to be on the safe side.

On 9 July 2007 I flew out of England.

TRABANT TREK HEADQUARTERS

Carlos and Megan met me at Budapest airport. I hugged the little Spaniard, who was sporting a new Trabant Trek T-shirt for the occasion, and gave Megan a peck on the cheek. I only knew a little about her, and I'm not sure what I expected, but she wasn't it.

American and about my age, she was blond, unmade-up, casually dressed and, like Lovey, had spent some time growing up on US military bases. Maybe I had imagined more of a straight-laced, all-American do-gooder, which she certainly wasn't, and I mean that in a good way. Opinionated, forthright, hands-on, emotional, tough and no shrinking violet, she said what she thought and never hesitated to denounce a plan that she saw as flawed, a trait which occasionally provoked other members of the team. She had a great sense of humour and a natural instinct for physical theatre, often annotating her stories with actions, strange songs and dances. She could throw a tantrum at a border guard in the blink of an eye, and return to normal in a few breaths. But that was all ahead of us.

The pair had come to collect me in one of the Trabbis, the same one Carlos and Lovey had driven to Zwickau for the festival the month before. In the short time that it had been sitting in the car park it had somehow managed to discharge its battery. So, appropriately, my first job on the Trek was to flag someone down and ask for a jump-start. This was a role I would become accustomed to.

I was taken back to the home of the delightful Angyal sisters, Zoe and Melody. They were friends of Lovey, who once worked in Budapest, and ever since opening their door to Carlos a month before they'd had played host to a Trabbi invasion.

"So how many other people are coming? It would be nice to know when someone else is going to be staying here," Melody said, to no one in particular, by way of a welcome. Tony gave me a hug, asking "What's up, Danno?" which was a relief as he had every right to thump me for leaving him passportless in Cambodia five years before.

Also at the house was our Hungarian trekker, Zsofi Somlai. Pretty, well-kept and brunette, she'd spent a year in the States so spoke faultless American. At 21, she was the youngest of the group, and had never travelled for more than a few weeks before, but you wouldn't have guessed it from her confidence and organisation in those early Budapest days. It was her home town, she was a part-time tour guide and always seemed to know what was going on. Zsofi was still studying at the time, but was so enamoured by the trip she was ready to take four months off. She told me that her friends and family thought she was crazy to be heading across the world in Trabants with virtual strangers. And when put like that, I guess she was. But she could be determined and single-minded and had her heart set on the Trek.

Over the next few days we gradually turned the place into Trabant Trek Headquarters, known locally as TTHQ. Boys were stationed downstairs in the dungeon, an unfinished apartment with the grimy ambience of a squat party. We slept on mattresses pushed together on the floor between various pieces of upended furniture.

The ladies were nesting in the loft, normally used as a storeroom. They bedded down among dusty vases, dodgy TVs and old rollerblades.

From that luxurious base we plotted global dominance, assembling resources and contacts ahead of our departure, scheduled for 17 July—or the 18th or perhaps the 19th. Nobody was really sure, the dates kept shifting and swirling. Do you need any sense of organisation to travel the world? I was soon to find out.

PICKING UP THE REST OF THE FLEET

We woke up at Zsofi's apartment in the centre of Budapest. Megan, Tony, Carlos, Zsofi and I were a little the worse for wear after an exuberant evening, but we immediately dared the midday sun to pick up the last two Trabbis and the Mercedes that would act as our support vehicle. All of the cars had been bought and modified by Gabor, a Trabant specialist who ran a garage in the city. He wasn't around, but said we could go and collect them from outside his place. Despite our physical condition, we were all excited to get a look at the cars we'd be spending the rest of the year in.

On arrival things seemed bad. The lock was jammed on one Trabbi, so Carlos had to break in through the boot. He smashed off the parcel shelf and slid his scrawny Spanish butt over the backseat, only to find the little tyke had a flat battery.

There was no trouble getting into the other Trabbi, although it too had a dead battery, and once we jump-started it and tried to drive off we found the rear wheel had completely seized and we could only drag it along the road.

There was a brief interlude where it seemed things had truly fallen apart. Dehydrated and sweating in the heat, we cursed and considered the possibility that Trabant Trek might amount to little more than a four-foot skid mark made by that jammed rear tyre. Apparently a man known only as The Bear had been working on the cars with Gabor. Zsofi got in touch with him and he claimed the wheel seizure was no big deal—the car had just been sitting still too long.

"These are Trabants, these things happen," was the gist of the phone call.

We had little choice but to leave the seized Trabbi for The Bear.

In his younger days Tony had spent a couple of years training to be a mechanic. Although he now managed a bar and restaurant, this qualified him as the official team mechanic, a vital role if we were to coax the old cars across two continents.

"Well we've got the worst cars in the world, so it only seems right that we have the worst mechanic in the world," Tony told me comfortingly.

On further inspection by The Mighty Tony P, the prognosis was raised to "good". It seemed the Merc had a fairly new engine, and new wiring, and the Trabbi ran fine. Tony fixed the broken door and later that night we found a couple of headrests in a pile of discarded junk.

"This car will get us to Cambodia, I have no doubt" was Tony's analysis as he stooped over the engine. Time would tell.

The year 2007 was the fiftieth anniversary of the first Trabant, the P50. Plenty of newspapers ran features on the car, with fond accolades such as "the rattle-trap cars that have become perhaps the most enduring symbols of the former East Germany" (New York Times) and my personal favourite, the headline from The Times (London): "Party time as world's worst car celebrates 50th birthday." The story went on to describe the Trabant as "the smoke-spewing communist car whose coughing two-stroke engine has been compared to a death rattle."

We'll take three.

All of our Trabbis were from the 1980s. One was a Kombi model from 1987 with a big boot, like an estate car. The others were limousine-style 601 models, from 1985 and 1986. Although the cars were only twenty years old, the design was exactly the same as the original 1963 model. Very little had been changed or added over the years, and so, although the parts weren't frighteningly old, the design and technology were. The engines were simple things—air-cooled, two-cylinder, two-strokes—which, we reasoned, was good because there wasn't too much to go wrong, and they weren't too difficult to fix.

But spare parts would be pretty much unattainable once we were out of Eastern Europe. This was where the Mercedes support vehicle came in; it was a big old station wagon with a huge boot and a hydraulic suspension. We planned to fill the thing with enough spares for three cars for four months on the road—we pretty much wanted to take an entire spare Trabant in the back of it. A spare engine, spare gearboxes, clutch plates, A-arms, transaxles, carburettors, bulbs, engine mounts, fan belts, spark plugs, exhausts, batteries, bearings and anything else that could go wrong. The larger, more powerful Mercedes would bear the brunt of this extra weight.

We also needed to take enough two-stroke oil with us for all three Trabbis for the entire trip, as we weren't sure whether it would be available on the road. Lovey and Tony calculated that to be about 120 litres. So we had two giant barrels of oil along for the ride too. We were able to fit these in the Kombi by removing its rear seats, and to save more space in the Trabbis Tony bolted spare wheels onto the car's wings, giving them a rugged, rally look.

To prepare them for the terrain ahead, Gabor made a few alterations to the Trabants. He reinforced the leaf springs that acted as suspension, and made thick, removable metal plates that bolted on under the Trabbis' engines to protect them. The Trabbis themselves cost us between £150 and £350 each. The metal plates were £250 a piece.

The Mercedes was our biggest expense, tipping the scales at a hefty £1,500.

But for that price we couldn't find anything else with enough space in it to do the trick. Strange to think we could probably have bought a dozen Trabbis instead.

Although the Trabants could be taken up towards 100kph, Gabor said we should avoid it. If the cars were to make it, he said we should consider 80kph our maximum speed, and on bumpier, rougher roads, we should take that right down to 30 or 40kph.

This was difficult, especially early on, when we were on decent European roads. Sticking to 80kph on the German autobahn, where there is no speed limit and BMWs doing 160kph overtake you, is a challenge. But then, when it takes 21 seconds to get from 0-95kph you are pretty much resigned to going at a gentle pace.

An unspoken decision was made to do everything in kilometres, and most of the speeds and distances in this book reflect that. Only the Brits and Americans really use miles, most of the distances on road signs across the world are in kilometres, as were the Trabants' speedometers and odometers. So we got into it, and it became second nature to only think of things in kilometres. And besides 70kph sounds quicker than 50mph, and managing 450 kilometres in a day sounds better than 280 miles. (In case you're struggling, there is 1.6km to a mile.)

That night it was Tony's birthday, 23 he claimed, though that statistic didn't bear close scrutiny. We went to Zsofi's folks' house for a party. I think her parents were keen to check out what type of hoodlums were taking their daughter away. I made a fool of myself during a brief altercation with a mosquito net, but other than that we came through the event unscathed.

OJ arrived the next day. The more I got to know him the more I liked him. He'd initially seemed a little aloof, but over the next few weeks that fell away and I grew a genuine respect and affection for the Oj. Sometimes we called him by his middle name, Bradford, and often we called him The Slav, as he claimed to have Slavic ancestry. Smart, educated and good-looking, he liked to cook and had a passion for languages, things we knew would help. He also had the Strength of a Thousand Men special ability, which would surely come in handy.

They were strange days. We were treading water really and the period was characterised by an utter lack of organisation. Megan set about trying to find hostels along the way that might put us up for free. Carlos looked for people who could do the same thing on websites like Sofa Surfers and Hospitality Club. Zsofi worked on sponsors and Tony tinkered with the cars while OJ learned Russian. It was sweltering hot, and we all invested a lot of time in staying cool.

To the mix were added Justin Rome and Marlena Witczak. The pair were friends of Lovey and had been travelling around in Europe that summer so decided to come and meet us. Marlena was Polish, but had an American passport and was studying in Boston. She was great fun, always laughing and giggling and never taking things too seriously. She got on well with everyone, and formed a close friendship with Megan. We were all keen that she come along with us, and she wavered for a bit but eventually agreed to tag along, taking the place of Sam and bringing our numbers back up to eight—five chaps and three ladies. Four Americans, a Hungarian, a Spaniard, a Pole and a Brit. An eclectic mix of nationalities and near strangers.

Lovey arrived on 20 July, adding even more hair to the trip. Tony and Megan had already been in Budapest for a fortnight, I'd been there slightly less, and I guess we were hoping that Lovey would provide the answers and the impetus we needed to get things moving.

There were plenty of meetings and discussions, but they could go on for hours and we weren't always pulling in the same direction. It was pretty much the antithesis of a military operation. Lovey was the best informed, but he had a penchant for drama. He rarely mentioned things, instead he announced them, and sometimes I felt uncomfortable getting involved in the decision-making, especially when I'd done none of the planning and wasn't really up to speed on a lot of the details.

There was so much going on, things became what the Americans called a "cluster-fuck". I was never sure of what that meant, but the term was bandied about aplenty and seemed to sum up the general vibe.

Trabant Trek was a cluster-fuck.

DANTE, FEZ AND ZIGGY

We always planned to paint the cars, and Montana Colours in Barcelona had kindly donated forty cans of spray. But none of us really knew how they worked. Luckily, living with us at the Angyal house was a graffiti artist named Johnny who agreed to bring his crew in and do the job. So Johnny and his mates, Nandi and Luca, showed us a few sketches, discussed a few designs and then went at the cars. We plied them with beer and they worked into the early hours on the street, listening to hip-hop and smoking.

The results were fantastic. Suddenly the cars, which had previously been dowdy, Soviet murky-grey or blue, were vibrant and alive. Three distinct designs, but clearly part of the same team.

One was a deep sky blue with a rising sun coming from the front wheel arches, its orange and yellow rays streaming down the side of the car. This was the same car that Carlos had taken to Zwickau and back, then driven around in Budapest for a month. He felt a real kinship with the thing and named it Fez.

The Kombi model was mostly black, with psychedelic, abstract, eye-like shapes swimming in a fiery finish. Tony took to it straight away. "I think it looks like little devils burning in hell," he said, and named it Dante. Each to their own.

The last car had a clean, geometric design with plates of brown and cream colour divided by sharp, jagged bolts of gold. As the car in the best condition, Lovey had always had his eye on it. It was named Ziggy.

The Mercedes, which we didn't bother painting and always looked rather clapped out, had a variety of names, mostly insulting, but Gunter and the Merkin seemed to stick. A merkin is a pubic wig.

Painting the cars was a seminal moment, it forged them into a unit and with their names each seemed to develop a distinct personality. Fez was unreliable and childish but fun, normally inhabited by Megan and Marlena. Dante was slow and heavy and constant, carrying Zsofi and Tony and his assorted tools. Ziggy was quick and messy and always keen to lead the way, particularly with Lovey behind the wheel. Gunter was a disaster on wheels and driven in a rota, except by Zsofi, who refused to go near it. All four of the cars were a little sporadic. There were plenty of dead batteries and jump-starts and getting into one was always a bit of a lottery. But we were getting to know them and it was all good preparation for the months ahead.

Z-PLATES

The next day we got a new recruit. The TV deal that Lovey had been working on came to fruition and the production company sent a cameraman to join us. His name was Istvan, he was Hungarian and he spoke next to no English. Quite how they thought he would cope was beyond me, but from day one it seemed like it was going to be hard work. We re-christened the poor bloke Melvin and tried to work around him. We were also lent three mini cams to use in the cars for our own personal filming.

There was still a long list of things to do, but time was bearing down on us. We had already received a lot of our visas, so we had set dates to be in certain countries, and needed to head off soon. Unfortunately we made the mistake of putting export plates, or Z-plates, on Dante, Ziggy and the Mercedes. This allowed us to take them out of Hungary and not bring them back again. But it was a one-way deal—once the cars had left the country, they could not return—and seeing as we were planning to drive to Germany for the official start of the Trek, then head through Hungary on the way back, this was a problem.

After a lot of debate we realised there was nothing we could do, it was just a cock-up. So only one Trabbi, Fez, could make the journey to Germany for the start of the Trek. Lovey, Tony and Zsofi wanted to stay behind to finish various jobs. So Carlos, OJ, Justin, Istvan, Megan, Marlena and I would go to Germany in Fez and Istvan's car.

The group was gelling well. A few people had bickered with Megan over her occasional negativity, I had attracted some flak for overindulging in the vino, and

Lovey's attitude of infallibility had drawn the odd murmur of discontent. But, although I can't speak for everyone, I thought it was a good bunch. Lovey had chosen well.

We didn't pack the cars properly when setting off. We knew we'd be back at TTHQ in a week so we just threw in overnight bags. It would be a little excursion ahead of the big event, a dummy run to iron out the issues, and the first real test for Trabant Trek.

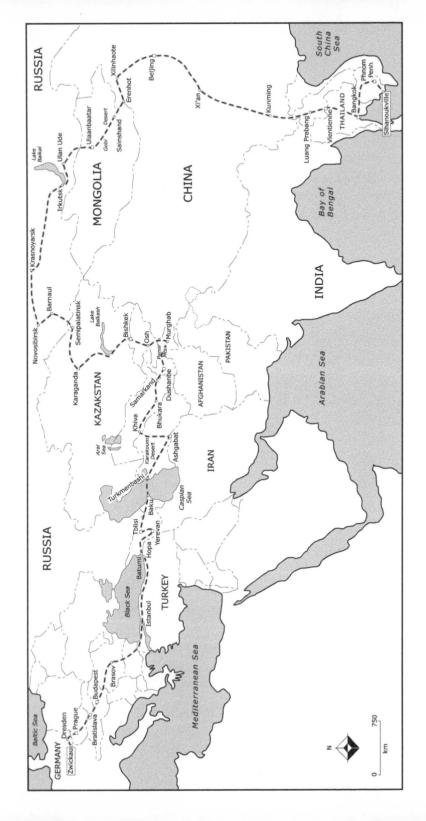

1

THE BEGINNING
Europe to Turkey
24 July – 13 August 2007

Man pulls up at garage.

"I'd like two wiper blades for a Trabant, please."

Short pause.

Garage owner replies, "OK—it's a deal."

ZWICKAU

It is hard to say when Trabant Trek began. Probably with the fizz of a synapse in what Lovey called his "dusty, unused grey matter" at some point in 2006. A year later, there we were, Trabant Trek in Zwickau, Germany, at the start of something big.

Only we weren't all there. In fact Lovey wasn't there at all, nor Tony or Zsofi. And our only Trabbi was the stalwart Fez, never likely to miss the big day, but Dante and Ziggy hadn't bothered.

We had arrived in Zwickau just before midnight that Tuesday, 24 July 2007.

For the record, we were Fez the Trabbi, Carlos, OJ, Justin, Megan, Marlena, myself, Istvan the cameraman and our German contact Mike, who was a native of the city and had agreed to find us somewhere to stay. After a few drinks and a bite to eat, Mike kindly showed us to an overgrown field sloping down a windswept hill, and by the headlights of our cars we pitched camp for the first time.

Quite fitting to our ragtag half-team was the inauspicious location that, unknown to any but that small handful, would mark what we hoped would be the start of the greatest journey ever undertaken by the Trabant. A Pulp line came to mind: "Somewhere, somewhere in a field in Hampshire, all right."

We opted to throw up the big, eight-man main tent and, as it was a new experience and it was dark and windy and we were a little lubricated, the result was a chaotic hour of mismatching poles to the sound of Megan barking instructions that the rest of the group happily ignored. The police turned up and eyed us curiously for a while, but thankfully were in no mood to move us on

The Trabbis blend seamlessly into the crowd

from that odd location.

OJ slept in Fez, Mike in his car and Istvan in his. The tent had two sections, so Marlena and Megan took one, while Carlos, Justin and I took the other. It was a moment I will always remember, huddled up together in our sleeping bags for the first time, Justin passing round a flask of some filthy devil brew that we gagged on while laughing and joking like we were on scout camp. It felt like the first day of holidays, like arriving at the Glastonbury Festival two nights early and relaxing in the calm before the storm.

The following grey, murky, dewy morning, waking up and packing up, wearing the poncho and swigging from Justin's flask, staring out over the fields and suburbs of outer Zwickau, I could taste the start of the Trek. After all the delays and debates, we were now Trekking and I was happy. It's impossible to be unhappy in a poncho.

On 25 July 2006, we began the drive to Cambodia. Four months. It'll take four months.

Mike took us to his mechanics' workshop to check out a strange noise coming from Fez and to change the spark plugs. The little car was making a coughing noise when idling and had been caught farting at some traffic lights a couple of days before. As Carlos said, "Fez is like a baby. When baby farts you must change her nappy. When Fez farts you must change his spark plugs." Strange Catalan wisdom.

We had a wander around the Trabant Museum before trying to film our departure from the old Trabant factory nearby. Unfortunately the security guards weren't too happy with the arrangement and the official start of Trabant Trek was marred by having to flee the marauding security, but I suppose it was a fitting warm-up for what lay ahead.

We made the short drive in convoy to Dresden where we were put up for free by the kind people at Lily's Homestay. By complete chance one of the themed rooms had a Trabant inside which had been stripped out and turned into a bed. In the months ahead I would sometimes dream of that Trabbi bed.

Prague, Absinthe and Punctures

I love Prague. The city oozes its history and culture from every alley, even if the latest trend seems to involve stag parties and their associated excesses. The medieval old town square is a web of narrow cobbled streets with the buildings leaning in on them, as if trying to shut out the light. Charles Bridge stands in all its opulent, if weather-beaten, glory, and the epic castle dominates the skyline.

Quality beer, cheap absinthe, beautiful women, stunning architecture: I could see what attracts the revellers.

We met up with a friend of Justin, an English lad called Rich, and he took us out to a well-priced beer garden with a bunch of his mates. As seasoned travellers and intrepid explorers determined to experience all manner of diverse cultures, we had little choice but to experiment with the local absinthe.

There are many different ways to drink absinthe, but in that particular beer garden they recommended dowsing half a teaspoon of sugar in a shot glass of the spirit, then removing it and setting light to the sugary spoon. The absinthe acts as an accelerant and once the sugar is bubbling in the spoon you stir it into the shot and drop an ice cube in to cool the mixture down—then neck it.

Making the potion was half the fun and the results were good. It tasted far better than the absinthe I'd tried in France, England and Germany, and was only £4 a pop. It had various effects on the group. OJ accidentally knocked back the ice cube that was in his shot glass, almost choking himself and seemed distinctly uncomfortable afterwards. Megan loved it, demanded more, became very excitable and then threw up. Istvan suddenly became lively and began speaking confidently in Magyar interspersed with his favourite English phrases: "no problem", "big problem", "please" and "fuck".

Justin ended up asleep in the bar, sitting bolt upright with his underwear exposed through a tear in the crotch of his jeans. We decided the best option was to take photos of him. As I said, Prague is a beautiful country, oozing history and culture from every alley; it would have been rude of us not to partake in that sophisticated and elaborate way of life.

The following morning OJ, Justin, German Mike and I headed east to visit the town of Sedlec. A wealthy family bought the town's ossuary, graveyard and chapel a couple of hundred years before and began to get creative with the skeletal remains of the 40,000 people buried there. What possessed them I don't know, but the results were a heady brew of the vaguely interesting and frankly disturbing. They had the family crest made out of human bones, with a skeletal bird picking at the eye of a human skull. Chandeliers made of skeletons hung from the ceiling and the chapel was cornered by four ten-foot high pyramids of human bones. What strange perversion. Perhaps the family were Satanists or some kind of twisted worshippers of the dead. The area, formerly known as Bohemia, certainly had its fair share of alchemists and weirdoes.

The plan was to stop off in Bratislava, the Slovakian capital, for lunch *en route* to Budapest. But Istvan blew a tyre in his supposedly superior car on the way, setting us back a couple of hours and forcing us to miss out on lunch. It was the first such incident of the trip and I wrote in my notebook, "I suspect this will be a theme of the next four months."

If only I'd known.

PLOTTING A COUP

Back in Hungary we were reunited with Tony, Zsofi and Lovey. Our Budapest base camp was the usual chaos, with Lovey always frantic about something. He was juggling a lot of balls, so he was rather stressed out and made sure we all knew about it.

Getting anything done with that many people took time. With eight Trekkers and a cameraman even sorting out minor details was a horribly drawn out process. A decision might need to be made, but, coming from democratic countries (except the Americans), everything first had to be put to a committee. Everyone had to be rounded up for a meeting, which invariably meant explaining the whole situation again and again *ad nauseam* as we took it in turn to stick our oar in.

Often these meetings took hours and nothing actually came of them—after all the discussion we often didn't even reach a clear decision. I guess we really were operating a true democracy.

Some of us did have permanent roles. Carlos was treasurer. Istvan was the cameraman. I was writing the story. Tony was the mechanic. But maybe we needed a leader?

Perhaps there should have been weekly presidential elections; once someone had been selected they would have absolute authority for the week, before facing a vote of confidence.

Or we could have divided the countries among ourselves, and each taken control in our own chosen nation. It would certainly have helped with planning if we had specific countries allotted.

Or maybe I should have instigated a coup? Seized power, put trusted lieutenants in positions of authority and crushed dissidents. After all, we were in the former Soviet republics. I could have put photos of myself in all the cars, slowly developed a personality cult, set five-year plans and insisted on collectivising resources in my own car, from where I could distribute them as I saw fit. Anyone who discussed the plan or schedule, or questioned my judgement, could easily be exiled to the support vehicle. Either way, decision-making needed to be streamlined. For the sanity of all of us.

THE SECOND GOING

Zsofi had arranged a departure party at a popular Budapest haunt called West Balkan. They kindly gave us a 5,000 florin (€20) bar tab each, let us put up sponsors' signs all over the place and give a press conference to a bunch of local TV and radio stations.

The press conference was excruciating. We foolishly didn't start the thing until gone ten, and everyone had made a decent stab at the bar tab by then. We paraded onto the stage in front of the cameras and a moderator interviewed Zsofi in Hungarian while we stood looking sheepish and uncomprehending in sponsored polo shirts.

Lovey then had the opportunity to address the attentive journalists in the manner of all great captains setting off on long journeys—think Neil Armstrong before Apollo 11. Unfortunately Lovey wasn't at his optimum and the moderator's attempts at opening him up were met by one-word answers. I'm not sure what the Hungarian public thought of us, but I sensed people didn't rate our chances of reaching Cambodia too highly.

Everyone kicked back and partied, culminating in a great performance by Brains, a local reggae/drum 'n' bass act that Zsofi persuaded to play for free. We had all the Trabbis parked in the courtyard of the club so most of us ended up falling asleep in them at the end of the night. I can't quite see the practice catching on at Ministry of Sound, but it gets my full endorsement.

The next morning OJ and I, feeling a little the worse for wear, returned to Bratislava to get the footage we had missed when Istvan's tyre blew out. It seemed a nice enough old place, with a similar feel to Budapest, sitting along the Danube with its attractive Habsburg architecture. I discovered that it's possible to squeeze a Trabant along the public footpaths in the centre of the city to gain easy access to a beach by the river. Security weren't as impressed with this manoeuvre as I was, but they let us film on the beach for ten minutes before moving us on.

Our journey from Zwickau through Dresden, Prague and Bratislava to Budapest had gone smoothly and routinely. With good roads and an easy path, we had pretty much partied the whole way. It felt like a dummy run, a test flight, and other than a few minor adjustments—the tent is crap, there is no cigarette lighter in Fez etc—all was good.

Back in Budapest there were a good few days of repacking the cars and pulling together all the last details, which inevitably took longer then expected. One day turned to three, with the departure date pushed back again and again. Megan started to get frustrated, Justin ran out of time and went home to Philadelphia, but Marlena opted to stay on, which was a welcome decision—it was good to have more female company.

Eventually we all felt as ready as we would ever be, except Lovey who was still negotiating with a TV company in Budapest. He decided he would stay behind to finalise a few things, then catch us up in Romania by plane.

So again we set off, and this time we almost had a full team, all three Trabbis, the Mercedes, Tony, OJ, Carlos, Zsofi, Megan, Marlena, Istvan and me. Four cars, eight people, and more instant noodles than I ever care to carry again.

ROMANIA

Entering Romania from Hungary was like entering another world. The border town we drove through was crumbling, windswept and dilapidated, full of beggars, chancers and street urchins.

But as we got into the countryside the scenery, and my opinion, slowly shifted. Driving through the Carpathian Mountains, there is a real Alpine feel. Tall evergreens cover the hillsides, with streams, rivers and dams along narrow valleys. But the houses are different; fewer of the sturdy looking log cabins pre-ferred by the French, more rickety wooden shacks.

The old women in the countryside genuinely looked like storybook gypsies—sturdily built, leathered faces, large bosoms and shawls wrapped around their heads. They always seemed to be carrying a wicker basket, child or animal. The old men, too, seemed like caricatures, often wearing worn, old fedora hats on top of tanned, wrinkled faces that lifted into a gurn when they offered a gummy grin at our passing cars.

The manicured main roads were a kind of living museum for modes of transport past and present: livestock and horse and cart mixed with up-to-date Western and clapped-out Soviet vehicles. Dogs barked as we passed, and plump, ripe looking cows stood casually in the road to admire our paintwork, showing scant regard for road safety. You can't outstare a cow and nor is the horn an effective weapon in such cases. There must be some kind of bovine warning that will get the damn things to move, but perhaps centuries of fenced-off domestication have left the modern agri-cow too thick to get out of the way of oncoming traffic.

We got a lot of attention as we passed through. Cameras snapped and kids waved. Older folk stopped and stared as if to ask whatever next would come through their country.

We'd been on Czech and Hungarian TV, and the message was obviously out because twice we were recognised at petrol stations by middle-aged Hungarians who'd seen us on the news. One of them, wearing the smallest shorts east of the Danube delta, helped us negotiate for petrol after we foolishly ran out of gas without any local currency or knowledge—a situation that would frequently recur.

We had always planned to try and visit some children's charities along the way, and we found our first in the city of Bacau. I brought along a football, thinking the best way to bond with the kids would be through the beautiful game, but I wasn't prepared for the reception. The kids were crazy, full of all the energy you'd expect of excitable ten-, eleven- and twelve-year-olds, clambering on you, shrieking, jumping about.

We had a kick about and then took them for a spin in the cars. They loved it, screaming, squealing, grabbing the wheel and honking the horn. It was a great visit and filled me with energy and optimism. I also found it inspiring to see good work being done on the scarcest of resources, something we could probably have learned from.

Trabbi Clubs in Romania

Navigating the Carpathian Mountains was fun. The Trabbis could only make the steeper climbs in first or second gear—they would rev like lawnmowers and hit 20kph if we were lucky. So we ascended at this horribly noisy and frighteningly slow pace, normally with a long line of traffic behind us. I'm sure the other motorists would have been honking if it weren't for the sheer ridiculousness of our convoy.

The way down was easier, as the Trabbis handled well, even if the brakes were a touch weak, and when the road was dry you could carve the little beauties round the turns like rally cars. Carlos and I were overcome by the spirit of Fernando Alonso and Lewis Hamilton and took to racing each other down the steep, winding paths.

Transylvania may be best known for its vampires, but the region is also famous for its hospitality, and it didn't let us down. Everywhere we went people insisted on feeding us, housing us and taking a look at the cars.

We had arranged to meet the Trabant Club of Udvarhely as we came through the town, but we were characteristically late and unsure of how to contact them. They must have had spotters around because within a few miles of entering Udvarhely a suped-up Trabbi swooped down on us, overtaking and flashing its lights. It led us to a nearby petrol station where another four Trabbis greeted us with their owners and a woman from a newspaper.

The Trabbi owners swarmed around our cars. Lifting the bonnets to examine the engines and tinkering with the lights, they looked like little nanobots scurrying over the vehicles. They had opted to stick with the original Trabbi exterior, but beef up the interiors and stereos. The cars looked classic, original, and were clearly the labour of an intense love—a noticeable contrast to our battered old Trabbis.

We left Fez with the Trabant club members, who spent a couple of hours removing and adjusting the engine, and fixed the lights. Transylvanian hospitality.

Despite the maintenance, Fez wasn't too happy, and much of the next day was written off by breakdowns. This was a regular occurrence. We spent a couple of hours stuck high in the mountains in a quiet old town beautifully named Homorod. It was a long, stop-start day, with Gunther proving a lot of trouble, and to top it off we forgot to close the bonnet properly before a test drive along the potholed mountain road and the hood duly leapt up and smashed the windscreen. We finally limped in to Brasov late at night after covering just 150km in eight hours.

On the outskirts of the city we were met by a Trabbi club very different to our previous hosts. While the Trabant Club of Udvarhely had stayed loyal to the original shape and colour of the cars, the Trabant Club of Brasov had no qualms with modifying to suit their own rather camp tastes. The three cars that met us were neon pink, lime green, and bright orange convertibles with animal print seat covers and novelty gear sticks. They were drag queen Trabants.

We stopped by the airport to pick up Lovey and do a few TV interviews with some very camp reporters. Were we being used for gay propaganda? It was impossible to tell.

Members of the Brasov Trabant Club kindly let us sleep on their floors and put on breakfast the next morning while Tony went to get the Mercedes repaired. Our Romanian hosts had a thorough look at our Trabbis and returned with a less than enthusiastic conclusion.

"You'll be lucky to get 5,000km in those Trabants," was the expert verdict, as interpreted by Zsofi, "those cars are terrible. Who did this work for you? You should have brought the cars to us. No way will you get to Cambodia. Maybe if you leave them here for a month and we work on them. But now? No. 5,000km maximum."

This was worrying. The guy owned three Trabbis himself and had a garage crammed with spare parts. I was pretty sure he knew his stuff. 5,000km would get us to Turkey. Pitiful.

But Tony was characteristically cool. "They're snobs," he said, and he had a point. Their cars did look impeccable, they were clearly perfectionists. "Our cars aren't perfect like theirs, but they'll get us there."

I trust Tony. Fez, Dante and Ziggy may not have had all the spit and polish, all the replacement parts and careful maintenance. They were rough, but they were ready. We hoped.

VLAD THE IMPALER AND COUNT DRACULA

The medieval market town of Brasov was once visited by one of Transylvania's more colourful characters—the fifteenth-century prince, Vlad III, more commonly known by his nickname, Vlad the Impaler.

The Impaler earned his moniker from the brutal way he executed his enemies. The victim would be seated on a long, sharpened stake and a horse tethered to his legs. Then the horse pulled away, gradually bringing the stake upright. As the victim's full weight came onto the stake it impaled him, via his anus, through his body and out through his mouth.

Vlad's cruelty was infamous. According to legend he went to Brasov in 1459 and had 30,000 of the city's merchants and officials impaled for refusing to accept his authority. An old Romanian story claims people were so afraid to commit crimes in Vlad's time, you could leave a bag of gold in the middle of the street, then return and pick it up the next day. On one occasion Ottoman emissaries failed to remove their headgear after entering his court, so Vlad ordered their hats nailed to their heads. That'll teach them.

To be fair to Vlad he had a tough upbringing. His father was executed by the Hungarians, who "scalped" him—they sliced a line around his head, then literally tore his face off while he was still conscious. And his older brother Mircea also fell victim to his political opponents, who blinded him by jabbing hot iron stakes into his eyes and then buried the poor bugger alive. Vlad himself was held hostage for years by the Ottomans, who kept him in an underground cell and occasionally brought him out for a good flogging. So you can understand why he had a few issues.

Despite his indiscretions, Vlad is regarded as a folk hero by Romanians for driving off the invading Turks. Historians believe he impaled 100,000 Turkish Muslims, and legend has it that Mehmed II, the famously ruthless Ottoman king, turned back from invading Vlad's capital when he saw the impaled remains of 20,000 soldiers outside the city gates.

He was so successful at protecting Christian Europe's eastern frontier that the Holy Roman Emperor appointed him to a secret sect called the Order of the Dragon, *Societas Draconis*, and it is from the Romanian translation of Dragon that Vlad takes his most famous title: Dracula.

It is probably from the Vlad legend that Bram Stoker took the name for the famous vampire count in his 1897 novel. What's strange about Count Dracula's popularity is that he's the creation of an Irish theatre manager who wrote an English horror novel after being inspired by a visit to a Scottish castle. Yet this entirely fictitious count is now Transylvania's most famous figure, and draws legions of tourists to Bran Castle, commonly known as Dracula's Castle. We were no exception. Well you have to have a look don't you?

Dracula's castle

In fact, the castle has few links to the real Walachian Prince Dracula aka Vlad the Impaler, or the fictitious Count Dracula. But why let the facts get in the way of the tourist industry? It isn't a particularly impressive castle: pretty, ornate and overlooking an important pass in the mountains, but just outside the gates there is a full-on Dracula market cashing in on the legend with all manner of tat.

Unsurprisingly we arrived too late to get in, so decided to camp overnight and visit in the morning. We found a great spot by a church, near a graveyard, overlooked by the castle. A couple of gypsy families lived nearby and, when the police turned up to try and move us on, the families intervened to let us stay.

We drank Hungarian moonshine while OJ knocked up some pasta over the campfire. We had set off with such ambitious ideas of luxurious camps that we had even packed a picnic table and a few chairs. But in fact these were rarely used, and we only made campfires on a handful of occasions. We tended to either drive well into the night, or stop to eat at a café ahead of camping. We were all thirsty for coffee in the mornings, but making a fire seemed an over-long process when we were keen to get back on the road. Eventually we picked up a gas stove that did the trick. We could set the thing up in the boot of Dante, so it was impervious to wind or rain, and boil hot water for coffee or pasta. OJ settled into the role of group chef; he loved to cook, even if it was instant pasta in powdered sauce.

That evening we had a merry, giggly time. Megan drank a little too much and regaled us with streams of nonsense. Istvan lightened up and started offering head massages. Later on we overheard the sound of bass lines pounding in the distance, so a few of us set off into the night and eventually stumbled across an outdoor party where we danced with locals and tourists, before stumbling back by moonlight under the disapproving gaze of Dracula's Castle.

It was a good bonding session. Istvan in particular had opened up for the first time, ignored the language barrier and got involved, which was important. Already people were reluctant to ride with him because he didn't really speak, and the only person he could communicate with, Zsofi, flat out refused to share his car. But if there was trouble brewing, and the demonisation of our cameraman could only spell trouble, then hopefully the new relaxed Istvan would get through it.

BULGARIA

Although we had planned to stop off along Bulgaria's Black Sea coast, we reckoned that we were already running about a week behind schedule—quite a feat considering we had only been on the road for twenty days.

In these situations we had to weigh up what we wanted to see the most, in this case a bit of Bulgaria, or more of Turkey. One would have to be sacrificed and in the end we opted for Bulgaria. We would drive day and night for 450km to get through the country, our first real stab at all-night driving.

There was quite a feeling among the group that I was a crap driver. People always get defensive about this sort of thing, and of course I would stick up for myself. But it occurred to me on one of the long, idle roads through Bulgaria that prior to Trabant Trek the longest stint I had ever done behind a wheel was three hours stuck in traffic trying to get across London. Hardly ideal prep for our mission. I'd only passed my test 18 months before we left, and in that time I'd managed to frighten most of my friends, not, I would argue, through driving dangerously, more through their miscomprehension of my unique roadside manner. I would always chime in that I'd never had an accident, though really I imagined an accident was the sort of thing that should improve your driving, or at least help you grasp your limits.

England is a small country and there are few excuses for long drives, from London it is an easy few hours to Manchester or Bristol, and I can get down to Brighton beach in fifty minutes. But America is a hugely different story and the Yanks would talk about short nips down to mysterious places like The Lake or The Cabin that took seven or eight hours, an automotive odyssey in my world.

So really there could be little argument that in terms of time spent driving and miles covered, the Americans were far ahead of me. Obviously I had an innate inner talent for motoring that few else on the planet share—just witness my parallel parking—but yes, I was low on experience.

Carlos would get particularly worked up by the Yanks' cocky assertion of highway superiority. "Yes, well, Americans are the best at everything," he would tell me, trying to etch sincerity across his face but giving the game away with the cheeky Spanish eyes.

But, for me at least, Bulgaria was my first stab at driving through the night, and it wasn't an easy experience. Being stuck cruising at 80kph on long, straight, dark roads is the purest sleep inducer. The headlights in Fez were so poor that only a few feet of road was really visible, so it was better to follow the taillights of the Trabbi in front. And in the depths of the night how those lights mutate and twist and fade and trick. They draw close to each other and join the number plate to form the eyes and mouth of a ghostly visage. They fade apart and appear like traffic lights on either side of the road and as you are lost in the vision the eyelids droop and sag and weigh so heavy. Then a jolt, a jump, something comes at you from the side of the road and you sit bolt upright swerve the wheel and snap out of it, but there's nothing there. I look over at my passenger, see they haven't been woken by the commotion, and carry on. And again the lights are off and dancing and taunting and the vision clouds and fades and my eyes are open but I can't see and the head rocks and again the jump, the brake, the swerve and I come to.

On these night drives I tried all sorts of things to keep myself awake. I would wind my window right down and hang my face in the onrushing air. Once I tried holding my arm out and rolling it in circles—I got to 2,000 before tiring of the game. Music helped, but the stereo in Fez was a fickle beast and my MP3 player had broken before we had even set off. Singing seemed to work, though initially I felt for my passenger with me belting out Adem at the top of my voice. This concern was overcome when I witnessed Carlos singing his favourite Spanish love ballads as he drove—an emotional and upsetting performance.

Often in those early days I took to slapping myself around the face to keep me going, a hard, firm right-hander across the cheek. But as the lids gained weight the slaps became more frequent until I was permanently beating myself up—not a lasting solution.

I would take to playing my own game with the odometer, breaking down the distance we'd covered into fractions and percentages and working out how much further we had to go: "... so we've done seven kilometres, out of 450, so seven goes into 45 what six times? No nearer seven? No somewhere in between, say 6.4, okay so seven goes into 450 maybe 64 times? Okay, so just sixty three of those journeys left. And how long did that take? About ten minutes, no, nearer twelve minutes, okay so 64 times 12, bugger, okay 60 times 12 is 720, 720 remember 720, 720. Now 12 times four is 48, add that to 720, okay, 760, 768. So there's 768 minutes to go, so what's that? 10 hours is 600 minutes, so 12 hours is 720 minutes so that's about 12 hours and three quarters left of driving... bollocks... well how far have we gone now? Right ten kilometres, okay, so that's..."

On and on this game would go, although I'm not sure if mental arithmetic speeds time up or slows it down. Another challenge was to avoid looking at the odometer for as long as possible, but at night with nothing but blackness and those taillights it was a pretty fruitless exercise.

The general consensus, at least in Fez, was that you drove until you started seriously hallucinating, then you woke your buddy. I hated waking my buddy, it always felt like a cop out and I avoided it as long as I could. But if you were the one sleeping and you were told it was your shift you had no choice. The worst time to be woken would be about 2am. You may have had three or four hours broken sleep, then you were expected to drive through the night and into the sunrise, a time of day that plays havoc with your night eyes.

Thankfully it rained throughout our Bulgarian drive, giving no one much inclination to leave the cars, but a bout of the shits hit the group, only adding to my desire to leave the country. In our tightly packed Trabbis diarrhoea was an unwelcome guest.

The Bulgarians were mostly unpleasant and inhospitable; though I don't mean to sully an entire nation, that was my feeling after twelve hours in the country.

Late that afternoon, when looking for somewhere to fill up, we realised Gunther had a flat. The petrol station we were in didn't take credit cards, and once again we had cleverly neglected to exchange any currency at the border. On discovering this, the husband and wife team in charge seemed genuinely appalled that we were in their petrol station with no money to buy gas, despite being clearly unable to leave the place due to one horribly flat tyre. They gesticulated, shouted and generally looked angry.

Seeing that we were trying to navigate four cars through 24,000 treacherous kilometres we had attached plenty of spare wheels to the vehicles. But we didn't bring a tyre iron or wrench that would fit the Mercedes. No tool to actually replace a tyre. The intellectual vacuum in our preparations was almost unfathomable, I mean really, who forgets a tyre iron? That day's note reads: "If we get through this I'm sure we'll have disproved Darwin's theory of the survival of the fittest. Utter stupidity."

The obnoxious couple who ran the petrol station refused to help us, instead waving the international hand gesture for piss off. After an hour of begging and searching among the few nearby stores open on a quiet Sunday in some long-forgotten path through the Bulgarian hills we came up with a tool and repaired the Merc.

I'm not sure what was said, but when we drove away the owner of the petrol station threw a handful of stones and gravel at us and mimed a couple of uppercuts into the air. Bulgarians...

Late that night, at a truck stop, I had the worst chicken soup known to man. The joint was a filthy fleapit, filled with overweight truckers smoking incessantly and scratching their balls. We ordered from what appeared to be a gremlin. He stood blankly behind the counter with a trail of snot running from his nose to his mouth. The soup was covered in a thick film of unshiftable grease and lurking in the bottom were the random odds and ends of a chicken that would have been unservable if they weren't shrouded in the mysterious milky liquid. I limited myself to two spoonfuls and filled my stomach with bread.

Entertainment was provided by a plump, aged prostitute who repeatedly tried it on with OJ. After attempting to chat him up, then insisting on serving him food, she danced on a bar stool in what she must have assumed was a seductive manner. She looked agonisingly pathetic, and I couldn't help but wonder which of the truck drivers in the room were turned on.

Lovey left his wallet in the car while we were in the café, and later he realised it had gone missing. In it were his bank cards, but also $300 of group money.

Well into the night, we pitched our tents half a kilometre from the Turkish border. By that time only Americans were driving.

We entered Turkey on Monday afternoon, 5 August 2007, after a six-hour nightmare crossing the border.

"Where you go?" asked the border guard.

"Cambodia."

"Where?"

"Kam-boh-dya," I tried pronouncing the word in a dodgy kebab shop voice.

"Cambodia? You funny. Have nice Istanbul."

Immediately I noticed a major difference between the skylines of Eastern Europe and Turkey. While the Bulgarian and Romanian cityscapes were dominated by huge chimneys reaching out from usually derelict factories, the Turkish horizon was punctured by the minarets and spires of thousands of mosques reaching for the clouds. The Soviet investment in the industrial contrasted with the Ottoman affection for the spiritual. Or something like that.

Istanbul was a true wonder. Every corner I turned, my breath was taken away by another convergence of history, culture and religion, lying like geological formations with telltale signs of their period. I spent the first day walking with eyes fixed firmly at the sky, so stunned by the architecture that I kept bumping into passers-by. After a collision I would instinctively touch my wallet through the canvas of my shorts before offering my apologies. Istanbul is amazing—but entirely human.

We negotiated a good price to sleep on the roof of a hostel, and set up a bar tab on the promise of a group discount. It turned out two beers cost the same as our accommodation, but we didn't discover that till many, many beers later.

It is claimed by some that in advertising sex sells, but in Istanbul's Grand Bazaar, the merchants have gone so far as to insist that buying some knock-off copy of Calvin Klein aftershave will ensure you cop off with anything that moves.

"You want perfume—this best, you like it. Good price. Where you from? Make you good jiggy jiggy. I love England. Take this, have perfume, you like it—best jiggy jiggy. You lots jiggy jiggy this," claimed a hawker exchanging a knowing wink with another trader and trying to thrust perfume into my hands.

Unimpressed, we ploughed on, not an easy task in the bazaar's crowded aisles, but the pimp followed us, uttering his sales pitch like a hermetic chant, rising to a crescendo as he finally got frustrated: "good for jiggy jiggy, Good For Jiggy Jiggy, GOOD FOR JIGGY JIGGY."

The products of globalisation were fully on show—Adidas, Nike, Christian Dior *et al*. I had no idea whether it was fake or real and avoided eye contact where I could.

"Where you from?" seemed the traders' favourite opener.

"Er… Surrey…"

"Ah, Surrey very nice place."

"So you've been?"

A blank stare.

"Surrey very nice place. You like T-shirt?"

Wherever I said I was from, I was always told it is a very nice place before having something cheap and badly labelled waved at me.

By the evening I was sick of company. Travelling in a group that size meant constant compromise and debate, and I wanted to go at my own pace. So I made a vague excuse and split from the group. I ate a meal alone at my table, past midnight, surrounded by locals, and it was refreshing to have a few beers with my thoughts.

An old man with a cigarette-strained voice played the sitar gently and a drunken Italian woman giggled loudly, as if being courted, though I didn't turn to look. It was comforting not to have to make any more group decisions and I retired early to the roof, where the sea breeze cooled me to sleep.

A few weeks later I learned that my non-appearance with the others had led to a sort of group bitching session. Over the preceding few days I had made a short video for the web called "Searching For Bulgaria" about our attempts to find the border with the help of a couple of Romanian kids on a scooter. In the video Carlos is seen giving a cigarette to a fourteen-year-old. This didn't go down too well with the group, who were insistent that it should be removed because of the charitable nature of our trip—we were meant to be helping kids, not poisoning them. This wasn't the first time the group had tried to censor me; earlier in the trip I had used the term "squirrel fellatio" in a blog and had again been widely derided.

I think the general problem was that I was writing most of the blogs, I was doing a lot of the stuff on camera, and now I was making videos for the website. But not everyone agreed with my style, or what I had to say, and there was a worry that the outside world was only seeing my representation of Trabant Trek, which maybe didn't suit sponsors or charities. Lovey said that Google lost interest in sponsoring us when they read my mildly critical blog about Bulgaria. I had also signed off the video I made with my own name and email address, which seemed to upset some people. But I was always taught to sign your own work—otherwise someone else will.

Anyway, whatever was said that night, and I'll never really know, I felt a detachment from the group occur. Maybe it was just a low ebb—I'd been away from home for a month—but I consciously decided to stay away from the camera a bit and focus more on writing. I also decided to start my own website to host the more risqué posts, while the more sponsor-friendly stuff could still go up on the group site.

This was the first post on my new website:

CENSORED: AN ANGRY RANT AGAINST CENSORSHIP AND SPONSORSHIP

The 'doing it for the kids' thing is pissing me right off.

So we're supposed to be raising money for charity. So we need to attract sponsors. But the sponsorship thing is a giant chain around our necks—oh you can't mention squirrel fellatio in your blog, that might scare off sponsors; you can't have a three second scene of Carlos giving a 14-year-old a cigarette on your website, we're doing this for the kids remember, it might scare off sponsors.

Bolox to sponsors—there aren't any anyway—what've we got from sponsors? Three useless GPS from Nav'n'Blow to wear their shitty T-shirts, a box full of aspirin from some pharmaceutical company in exchange for a bumper sticker—fuck all that, wish we hadn't got involved.

How am I meant to portray what happens when we're travelling if it gets censored by the rest of the group because we're meant to be raising money for kids? Or because some giant corporate company gave us a couple of SatNavs that won't even work for the majority of our journey.

What a load of shite.

We should never have done this for charity—instead we should have done it for a TV show. We should have filmed it, edited a pilot and then tried to flog it to anyone who was interested.

I've even been told that I can't mention how terrible Günter the Mercedes is in case I worry Zsofi's parents. If that's the precedent I may as well never mention a day on the road.

At the moment we're catering for our 'sponsors' and 'donators' so can't show any of the interesting or funny stuff that's happening—"Ooo, mustn't offend anyone…"

Where will this end? Am I allowed to mention that we're using illegal number plates to cross borders? Should I say that we camp where we shouldn't? That we're planning to film in Turkmenistan without a licence? That we smuggled a camera into Bran Castle? These are the highlights of the trip, strip them out and we're a bible camp.

THE AYA SOPHIA

The next day I wandered alone in my new spirit of detachment, but was happy to embrace the beauty of Istanbul and its vibrant atmosphere. The city straddles the Bosphorus, making it the only city in the world on two continents, Europe and Asia. Its history is linked to the great empires of both continents, particularly the Romans, Byzantines and Ottomans, all of whom have ruled and left their own fingerprints.

The place is crammed with mosques; like pubs in English cities there's one on every block. Spires and minarets reach out majestically from the base of elegant hubs to pierce the sky and inspire the heart.

Perhaps the best symbol of that great city is the Aya Sophia—the Church of the Holy Wisdom of God—a building so magnificent no conqueror could bear to sack it, instead consecrating it for their own religions. The colossal sixth-century domed church had been used by Byzantine Orthodox Christians, Roman Catholics and Muslim Ottomans over the years. Now it was in the hands of secular authorities and, fittingly, had been turned into a museum. Much of the Ottoman plasterwork had been stripped away, revealing the stunning mosaics, hidden for five hundred years.

I could have stayed in Istanbul for a week, but visas wait for no man. Two nights there was all we had. So grudgingly I left, promising myself that I would return with greater freedom.

IZMIT

"Do you ever feel like we're duping these people?" OJ asked me. "I mean, I want to be good, I want to seem professional. But we are all such fucking idiots."

Wise words as we arrived at an Izmit hotel room, paid for by a local charity, after managing to turn a simple 60km journey into a three-hour nightmare. I sometimes felt the same. Should we be accepting the charity's hospitality? We were not raising money for them specifically, though I guess the press attention we were attracting may have helped in some way.

They were certainly very keen to help us, arranging for us to meet the city's "president" or mayor, Halil Yenice. Mayor Yenice is an important man, we were told, and he runs a city of two million people, bigger than Budapest, and one of the richest cities in Turkey. As we were already running late to meet this dignitary, and on a tight schedule, Dante's battery decided it was a good time to throw in the towel. After ten minutes of trying to defibrillate the thing Tony decided to change it. We were in a tiny back alley while this was going on, with trucks trying to weave past, the Trabbis facing in opposite directions and a growing crowd forming to point and laugh.

Maybe it was because we were holding up so much traffic, possibly it was because we were aiming the wrong way down a one-way street, whatever the reason, the police showed up to escort us to the meet the mayor. They closed off streets along the route and when we arrived we were greeted by a mob of photographers and journalists, snapping away enthusiastically, and the big man himself, Yenice, who came down to shake hands, pose for pictures and look over the engine.

We were called up to his office for more photos, a press conference and a chance to quiz him about the city. He explained that Izmit was the former capital of the Eastern Roman Empire and in the fourth century was the fourth biggest city in the world. Then called Nicomedia, it was far more important than nearby Constantinople (Istanbul) as a staging point for Roman armies and navies heading along the Bosphorus. It was a perfectly placed administrative centre, and, surrounded by what was known as the "Sea of Trees", it had a prolific shipyard.

But, explained Yenice through an interpreter, eighty per cent of the Roman architecture remains buried underground. Yenice wants to bring it to the surface to attract tourists and help re-establish the city. As a mark of how big a job he has, I told him that, despite Izmit's imperial past, the city did not even get a mention in our guidebook—not so much as a paragraph. He nodded and said he hoped our presence in the city would help attract attention to it. For a moment I felt like a British emissary at the court of a far-away king, rather than a scruffy, slightly malodorous crackpot on a hair-brained folly across the world.

I mentioned to Yenice that I fancied a kick about with some kids—maybe from the charity that was putting us up. I'd imagined a friendly footy game, a bit of exercise for me, fun for the kids and shots for the film. But Yenice can obviously pull a few strings. We were taken to a full-blown football academy, where forty or fifty kids were training. They were involved in a practice game, and it was clear when we arrived that we were going to be horribly out of our depth, but there was no backing out.

After two minutes of being hounded by the little Turks, who seemed to be everywhere, my lungs burned and I felt sick. OJ had given away a penalty with a hand-ball, and I'd equalised directly from a corner.

Just when I thought I might faint, they subbed on a fresh team. Then after ten minutes another one. Then another. We were shattered, and by the end were being run ragged by ten-year-olds. Only some goalkeeping heroics from Lovey stopped us getting slaughtered. He reminded me of Sly Stallone in *Escape to Victory*.

Our pre-teen tormentors eventually equalised to make it an honourable 3-3 draw, suitable for both sides, and the whistle went. Damn that Yenice, I was knackered.

MORNINGS

It was nigh on impossible to leave anywhere early, a situation that really began to rile some people. Istvan in particular would despair at our lazy morning progress and the amount of good light we missed. It was always going to be difficult to get going with that many people, but broadly there were two camps: the folk who struggled to get out of bed, including Lovey, Tony and me (strangely also the drinkers), and those who struggled to get moving, mostly OJ and Zsofi.

I justified my lie-ins by pointing out that once I was up I was ready to drive in a matter of seconds. But others seemed to take an age to sort themselves out. Zsofi always seemed to find something to do just as we were all about to leave. Everyone would be in the cars, engines started, ready to go, and then the shout would go out: "Where's Zsofi?"

She would be in the toilet, brushing her hair, or she had decided to repack her bag. It seemed to happen every time and she eventually earned the nickname "Kamaz", after the slow Russian lorries that we passed. Further down the trail we would get to know just how much faffing about OJ was capable of too.

Megan and Carlos were always the first up and the Spaniard normally stood by a car looking pissed off and waiting for everyone else to get ready. It used to really wind him up, but by the end he just took the micky out of us all:

The phone call home

"So OJ can we go? Or do you want to take your top off, do some press ups, watch a film then moisturise?"

We all knew that if we set off earlier we wouldn't have to drive until so late, and by spending more daylight time on the road, we would get to see more of the world. But despite this being raised frequently, it took months for us to fall into a better routine.

Asmara

We drove from Izmit through the night, aiming for the Black Sea. As we were slowly finding out on those winding mountain passes, the Trabbis did not enjoy the steep inclines and the little engines would scream in pain.

"Shh shh shh, come on Fez, you can do it."

We would nurse the cars to the top of a hill, then be at the mercy of the Trabbis' brakes as we free-wheeled down. Every few hours the smell of smoking brake fluid would waft into the cabin, and we'd stop on the side of the road to let the plates cool.

We found the sea shortly before 3am, drove right up to it and the team pitched our tents in a stony car park while I went to hunt celebratory beer in the small coastal town of Asmara. We had a few drinks before bedding down, but the moment we had settled, and the swishing of polythene sleeping bags being adjusted had died down, our silence was broken by a cacophonous call to prayer. It was 5am. We had to laugh.

I always prefer to breakfast alone. I'm not at my best in the morning and small talk makes me irritable. Witnesses to my morning ire can wrongly take it as a personal affront, which sets out a bad stall for the rest of the day. I prefer to shake off the sleepy remnants of my subconscious with a coffee, plate of eggs and newspaper.

Of course, in little Asmara few people speak English, there are no British papers and they do breakfast their own way. So I settled down at a café with a beautiful view over the small, cliff-ringed bay and admired the ambitious bushes and trees that clung to the rocks, surviving on the surplus of sun despite the weakness of the thin, stony soil.

I had a traditional breakfast of wrinkly olives, a hard-boiled egg and salty feta with fresh bread, sticky honey and a salad of tomato, cucumber, peppers and onion, washed down with bitter, black tea.

It felt like any town on the English coast—souvenirs and hawkers on the seafront, overpriced cafés with wonderful views, holidaying families splashing in the water.

We drove the Trabbis onto a rocky section of beach and made a shelter from the wind and sun so that we could play a board game and unwind from the last two weeks of perpetual motion. OJ swam across the bay, I read and wrote, Megan and Marlena had a few drinks, Tony checked out the cars. Only Istvan was unhappy, suffering from a sickness of sorts and reluctant to get out of the Mercedes. I think his patience was wearing thin. But out of sight in the Mercedes he was out of mind and everyone enjoyed a lazy, sleepy day, and most retired early following a few late afternoon drinks. We expected it to be the last beach before Cambodia.

SOCIALISM IN TURKEY

Driving through the Turkish night to try and hit the Georgian border, Lovey and OJ noticed some kind of festival and pulled over. I had been asleep in Fez and felt groggy.

An amphitheatre had been created in some urban wasteland, with four rough wooden stands set up for the crowd. An old man at the front played sitar and chanted in a deep voice that carried down my spine and earthed through my feet. The organisers had faced the stage lights towards the crowd, so the singer was impossible to make out behind the dazzling brightness.

It was a lot like a festival—damp, crowded, with loud music and men and women in a state of ecstasy, looking ridiculous in rain macs, arms aloft, singing at the top of their voices. The smell of tobacco smoke hung in the air, but there was no alcohol on sale.

I separated from the rest of the group but quickly attracted the attention of the locals who first attempted to interrogate me in Turkish, then wheeled out an English speaker. Anil Yenigul, a nineteen-year-old English student, told me that we were at the fourth annual socialism festival, organised by the local communist party, an occasion to celebrate and spread socialism, which was strangely popular in that small border town of 20,000. He acted as a translator as I quizzed the leaders of the party.

What are people here for?

"They believe in a society in which socialism lives. They are not a party, they are a movement, a group, but still they want to govern society. They want revolution. Their main aim is to achieve revolution, to organise Turkey into a socialist society."

But how will you achieve that?

"With the fire of revolution."

I tried to get an explanation but I looked up from my notes and saw I was surrounded by angry, spitting, young men, shrieking in Turkish demanding that their voice be heard. My translator was overwhelmed.

"We are Mao's people," I heard above the melee, and a Turk thrust his face into mine. "We are Mao. China's people. Mao, Mao, Mao."

I could tell that the finer points of Turkish socialism were beyond my translator, so I asked what the music was.

"Ahhh," he said, a broad smile forming across his spotty top lip, "Nurettin Rengber. Traditional Turkish folk music. I love him."

Never before had I seen communists attempting to foment revolution through the power of traditional folk. Firebrand socialist folk activism—quite a sight.

The police were out in force, young recruits wearing full body armour, looking primed for action. They had formed a blockade with trucks near the entrance to the square. "They are protecting us," my guide explained, "because fascist attacks may happen. But also, they are the fascists you know," he grinned.

One of the police carried an AK47. The army were there too, carrying what looked to my naive eye like sub-machine guns.

"MP5," Lovey told me later, "Heckler and Koch."

Americans know about guns.

I moved through the crowd with a growing entourage. They wheeled out the local girls and suddenly I was dancing. Everyone joined hands, insistent that I form a circle with them—not my forte—but I smiled and tried to hide my embarrassment.

"Are you a socialist?" I asked one of the girls, in an effort to gauge the political activism of the women.

"What?" She leant in closer, and I hunched down to meet her ear.
"ARE YOU A SOCIALST?" I shouted above the twanging sitar and booming voice.

"Thank you," she replied, fluttering her lashes and retreating to giggle with her friends.

"Where are you staying tonight?" one of the braver girls stepped forward.
"Err… Georgia." We were planning to cross the border, thinking it would be quicker late at night.

"Yopra?" More giggles.

My new friends left me with a traditional Turkish goodbye—touching each cheek against mine, an intimate and welcome gesture. I withdrew just in time from kissing Anil's oily skin; we're not in France.

As we left the police appeared ready to break the place up—riot gear and shields at the ready, standing in formation near the blockade. They were only kids, late teens at most, but you could tell they were ready to crush what ever they were aimed at: socialists, fascists, liberals, Islamists.

It's illegal to film the military in Turkey, and they shouted when I tried to photograph them. A local journalist, Sener Aslibay, saw my clumsy attempts, and took my arm: "It's better that you leave now. I think there could be a problem with Gendarme."

"Why"

"They are on opposite sides you know," he replied, meaning the socialist festival-goers and the "fascist" police and army.

"What will happen?"

He shrugged and declined to elaborate, but the growing roars of the departing partiers, and the sight of the gendarmes armed and primed for a clubbing was enough.

My new friend offered me a place to stay, and a meal, but I told him we were heading to Georgia that night. "You know in Georgia it is not safe?" It was a statement phrased as a question from Sener, who looked unsure about us leaving.

"Why?"

He shrugged. "They are poor. They are thieves. You just be careful."

"Have you ever been to Georgia?" I asked.

"No. I know nothing of Georgia."

Just another scare merchant. If I had listened to all the people who gave me similar advice I would probably not have got out of bed in Shepperton.

There was a split in the group over crossing the border. It was late, nearing midnight, the ground was soggy and we had made many socialist friends who, with typical Turkish generosity, had offered us food and shelter. Why cross into an unknown and possibly dangerous country late at night, with nowhere to stay, only to pitch a tent on the side of the road?

We're behind schedule and they're just scare stories ran the counter argument. It won. We crossed the border in the early hours and headed into the Caucasus.

2

THE CAUCASUS
Georgia, Armenia and Azerbaijan
14 August – 31August 2007

Q) How many workers does it take to build a Trabant?
A) Two, one to fold and one to paste.

BALLROOM DANCING, HANDGUNS AND THIEVES

The Caucasus exists in a sort of limbo between Europe and Asia. A thin strip of land between the Caspian and the Black seas, the north the home of warring nationalists, Chechens and Abkhazians, while to the south were the old empires of the Ottomans and Persians, Turkey and Iran. I considered our group to be made up of Caucasians—white Europeans and North Americans, and although the term was out of fashion, people looked a lot like us in Georgia, more so than the Turks we had passed.

Georgia was the south-westerly limit of the old Soviet Union, and although the country was now looking west, we expected people to speak a bit of Russian. I'd had a stab at picking some up, but OJ had a natural talent for tongues and had absorbed enough words on-line to see us through most situations. On reflection I wish I had learned more. Despite the fall of the Union, a huge swathe of the globe still spoke Russian as a first or second language, and our route would take us through seven such countries. I comforted myself with a vague apprenticeship in the more important words for the road—yes, no, please, thank you, car, petrol, mechanic and beer.

We crossed the border late, drove for a few hours, then stopped at the Black Sea-side town of Batumi. Our random drive around town only revealed areas of run-down homes with an impressive church and nicely lit synagogue. There were no hostels willing to let our band of motor nomads in at 3am, but we'd learned that if you drive brightly coloured cars in circles around a city long enough the police will eventually pick you up and find you somewhere to camp. If you're lucky they'll check on you throughout the night.

Fez hits the Caucasus

We pitched on a tyre-strewn and heavily littered tarmac car park to the sound of bass rolling out of the distance. After circling the wagons, Lovey, Carlos, OJ and I followed the music in the hope of getting some refreshments. We were surprised to find a Brighton-esque sea front pit of hedonism, shamanism, voyeurism and alcoholism. The clubs were closing, emptying whacked out zombies and worked up punters onto the neon strip, but I managed to find an open beer shack.

It was there I met George.

As was Trabant Trek custom, we had yet to find any local currency to pay for drinks, and a long, mostly incomprehensible dispute with the drunkard in charge of the stand was only curtailed when a young lad intervened and insisted on paying. He introduced himself as George and we got chatting. He was Georgian, but had a Texan drawl, a symmetric, youthful face that should mature to become handsome and the confident, assured manner of the privileged.

I never did work out what his father did, but five years ago young George had gone out to Texas to visit his sister. He ended up going out with the daughter of the "multi-billionaire" owner of an American football franchise, so he stayed in the States to study.

He claimed to be the number one ballroom dancer in Georgia, and when he arrived in the US he quickly established himself, coming sixth in the US Ballroom Dancing National Championships.

As the police had found us a place to stay, we asked George if they were ok.

"The police are fine," he said, "They're not really corrupt anymore. They want to encourage tourists, so they protect them. Anyway if they bother us we tell them to piss off. We have the Georgian FBI with us."

He gestured towards a short stocky guy in his thirties who was at the hotdog stand. I took a closer look. He was a thuggish troglodyte, with arms like a gibbon, a disturbing smile and a frighteningly large bottle of rum resting neatly beside a small handgun. Phil Mitchell meets Mad Frankie Fraser. He was taking a backseat, but I could tell he was part of the group.

"My friend's father is a minister, so he has a guard," said George.

"Right," I said, wondering what state the country's security was in when politician's families needed bodyguards, and whether George had drunk a little too much. I think he sensed my scepticism.

"Hey, come over here," George beckoned the guard. They conversed in

Georgian, then George turned to me: "Dan, do you want to fire a gun?"

Words to excite the most flaccid cock. I have mixed feelings about guns. I'm pleased we don't really have them in England, and that state of affairs seems to work—in order to kill someone you have to do something far more primal than just squeezing a trigger. You need to knife them or bludgeon their life away, which I imagine is quite a hard thing to do. But I'm still fascinated by firearms. Maybe their inaccessibility adds to their allure.

The burly guard pulled out his handgun, loaded a round into the chamber, removed the clip, then pushed the thing towards me.

"What, here?" I looked around the beachfront park, filled with homebound revellers. We were a hundred metres from the emptying clubs and metres from an open hotdog stand.

"Yeah, just fire it in the air, dude."

I took the gun. It felt lighter than I'd imagined, though the clip wasn't in. The metal was chipped and the paint had flecked off. It still felt robust, but the cosmetics had faded. Was this guy really in the secret service? Or the mafia?

"Point it into the air, dude."

"Ok."

I waved it towards the sky. How do you hold a gun? In two hands, as common sense would suggest, or a daring one hander, as Hollywood has taught me? I opted to grip the thing double-handed at arms length like a floppy but threatening sausage, locked my elbows, closed my eyes, pulled a face like a nine-year-old who knows he's about to fall off his bike, then squeezed.

A jet of fire shot out the end accompanied by a loud, airy, champagne cork pop and, I imagine, a bullet. Who knows where that ended up? I'm sure Newton mentioned stuff coming down.

"Fucking hell," was the best I could do.

The guard quickly took the gun away, reloaded the clip and slipped the thing into his jacket while my new Georgian friends cheered. I was strangely affected. My heart pumped adrenaline quickly round my body, I felt a little light-headed and very excited. Maybe it was the danger, the stupidity or the illegality, I don't know, but it felt good and I wore an inane grin for the next hour.

The drizzle we were loitering in grew into a downpour and George insisted we return to his friend's hotel rather than our dirty campsite. We dried off then George, Carlos, the bodyguard and I went to get drinks.

When I saw the bodyguard's car—a top of the range BMW, with dark tinted windows—I genuinely believed he worked for the secret service. But as he sped off, pulling donuts in the car park where we were camped, I again had my doubts, and put my seatbelt on, much to the amusement of the Georgians.

George was a good host, and the bodyguard was fun. You wouldn't want to piss him off, but he laughed easily and did what George told him to do. Night turned to day, and the beer and wine flowed, interspersed with dips in the warm Black Sea and traditional food at various eateries, all paid for by George's considerable hospitality.

"George, please, let me buy this round."

"Dan, stop it." He'd throw his arm round me: "in Georgia we look after our guests, stop asking."

"Well I'm getting the next one."

And of course I never did. It got to the point where I took it for granted that I was being taken around Batumi on an epic bender with my own armed bodyguard at the expense of the Georgian National Ballroom Dancing Champion.

By 4pm George was done in, and wanted to head back, so we arranged to meet again in five hours and I headed to a beach café to sober up with some light beer, maybe a snooze and some time to write.

I chose the wrong café.

The local men, with seemingly nothing to do but drink on a damp Wednesday afternoon, inundated me with questions in Russian about my country, my Mac, my girlfriend, my travels, whether I would go to see women with them, and finally demanded that we drink vodka together "like brothers".

This was the prompt for a valuable cultural lesson in the art of boozing Russian-style. Where folk back home might sup a pint, these guys knocked back shot after shot of vodka with salted slices of cucumber, hunks of bread and beer chasers. The effect was exactly as you would expect—rapid tipsiness. The Georgians weren't immune, but they were hardy. I watched an elderly gentleman, perhaps in a show of bravado, down a half pint of vodka then casually eat of chunk of cucumber. That's serious drinking. Despite our language barrier we had a grand old time, it was a perfect introduction to the former Soviet Union, and I would come to know those vodka-based bonding sessions well.

As the sun set I stumbled back to the campsite waving a large reed at passers-by and muttering piecemeal Russian. The rest of the gang had slept off their excesses and were gearing up to go out and meet George again, so I made an about-turn and headed back onto the beach front for a full dinner with more vodka and then VIP seating at a strobe-lit club with a seemingly limitless bar tab.

We drank cocktails and went dancing, but something went wrong with George. Maybe Marlena or Zsofi rejected his advances, maybe he drank too much, but he disappeared without a goodbye, and the bodyguard brusquely ordered the girls out of the club.

In the early hours of that morning, 24 hours since I had met George, and 42 hours since I had last slept, I found myself riding a small quad bike that I had commandeered from a youngster near the beach.

I had just finished speeding around the car park where we were camped when I noticed a fat skinhead looking our cars up and down. It was a sight we were all well used to, and I went to explain to him what we were doing. I was surprised when he grabbed the car door and shook it violently, as if testing its durability. I thought him odd, but was in no state to make a firm character assessment and so let him be.

A few minutes later Lovey turned to me. "That guy's stealing our cameras," he said, matter of factly. I was standing with Megan and Marlena and we all looked up in unison. The skinhead was sprinting flat out across the car park towards an old abandoned shopping mall.

"So he is."

We stared at him for a while, an incongruous sight, his stumpy legs furiously propelling his squat, fat body while clearly holding our cameras out to one side.

"Let's get him," said Lovey without a hint of panic.

The girls sprinted after him and Lovey and I jumped in Ziggy, but he had been sleeping and took a few precious moments to start. Eventually we sped off towards the old mall, which was surrounded by a couple of acres of overgrown wasteland.

We did a few circles but couldn't see the thief, so jumped out of the car and made our own separate searches. From behind me I heard Lovey shout and turned to see him sprinting after fatty. I gave chase and it dawned on me that I was barefoot and sporting boxer shorts.

"Where are my trousers?" went through my head as I saw Lovey tackle the skinhead to the ground, kneel over him and start laying into his face. When I arrived the guy had clearly had enough and was cowering, so we pulled him up and demanded our cameras, which he was no longer holding.

He knew what we wanted, but I could see him looking for an escape route, so I threw a right cross into his face and felt the bones in my knuckle crack and fracture as they connected with his eye and nose. He looked stunned but started scouring the ground for the cameras.

From the darkness Megan appeared. She had given chase on foot and arrived high on anger and adrenaline. She flew straight into him in a tangle of curly blonde locks, knocking him to the ground, punching and slapping. Then Marlena appeared and gave him a kicking with her bare feet. It was vigilante justice, mob rule and I felt, and still do, a little bad.

We found the cameras on the floor near where we had got fatty; one of them was broken, and I wonder where the story would have gone if the police had not arrived *en masse*. The fat thief seemed relieved they were there.

Initially we thought he would be able to buy his way out of trouble, but like George had told me the previous night, the police wanted to encourage tourists and protect them. The guy was a pathetic sight, sitting awkwardly on the ground, hands cuffed behind him, breathing heavily though a broken nose, puffy eyed and split-lipped, his giant gut hanging over his shorts.

None of the cops spoke English, but after half an hour they brought out a young lad who worked at a local hostel to interpret for us. By 6am things seemed to have reached a conclusion, but they insisted we go back to the police station to give more statements.

"Three hours maximum," they told us.

Liars.

The police headquarters was more of a complex than a station, with a couple of checkpoints to get in, and a mix of military and police uniforms inside. We were shown to a large, almost empty building that felt like an abandoned school—one long echoing corridor with rooms coming off it. With just a couple of computers in the whole place and not a thing on the walls, it felt barren, unused and unloved. Plug sockets were heavily overloaded and the toilet had a leaky roof, the sound of water dripping into buckets reverberating along the hallway.

Nothing was moving quickly so I had the chance to explore. The offices were devoid of any personal effects, as if all the cops were hot-desking. Not a picture or decoration in sight. I found the armoury and counted at least twenty AK47s in a rack and a cupboard with maybe forty side-arms.

I tried to sleep, but they wouldn't let me put my feet up on the sofas (I think it's a Georgian thing) so I ended up pacing, numb with exhaustion, and examining my swollen hand.

After eight hours of bureaucracy they said they would let us go, but they were keeping our cameras as evidence. We couldn't believe it, they wanted to keep our cameras? No way. We kicked up a fuss, threatening to call the embassy, telling them I was a journalist and anything else we could think of. We didn't go through all that to lose our cameras to Georgian police.

After an hour of telephone calls we came to a compromise. We would provide them with a couple of photos taken with the cameras to prove that they were ours, then we could keep hold of them. So I downloaded a smashing picture of me in my underpants onto the police computer. There's your evidence.

They finally dropped us back at our car park campsite at 3pm. I hadn't slept in days, since before the Turkish socialist festival, and was feeling it, so I lay in the back of Fez and quickly lost consciousness. I woke up deep in the Georgian hills.

THE OIL PAN: EPISODE ONE

We planned to head from Batumi into Armenia. Marlena didn't have an Armenian visa and we were only planning to be there for a few days, so she opted to stay behind. She hitched a lift to the capital, Tblisi, from a random guy we met near our campsite, which in retrospect probably wasn't the safest thing to do. We planned to meet her in the capital later in the week.

The "road" we took to the border barely warranted such a description. Unpaved, pockmarked with craters, strewn with rocks and covered in loose sand, it would have been better suited to 4x4s than our little Trabbis. It could probably have been avoided, but we opted to go against local advice and take a more direct route to the border, rather than the more circuitous but I imagine better quality road we'd been recommended. Luckily, though unsurprisingly, there were few other vehicles on it, and we had the "road's" full width to weave around the trenches and chasms.

Somewhere along the way Dante lost a number plate. I was driving the Mercedes with Istvan at the time and as it was the fastest car, I said I'd go back down the road to have a look for the missing tags.

Thinking speed was of the essence, I may have driven a little recklessly, and at some point we took a hit to the oil pan beneath the engine, tearing a hole in it and depositing the lubricant in a dark trail along the road.

Istvan didn't seem pleased. Though we didn't share a language, I gathered from his arm waving, eye rolling and head shaking that he was angry and he blamed my piloting. This was probably a fair reaction. He'd never trusted me behind the wheel.

"No Playstation," he once told me.

After a considerable wait the others found us. We flagged down a passing minibus and the driver agreed to give us a tow. We still didn't have a towrope, a situation I'll never understand, but Tony improvised by removing a couple of seatbelts and tying them together. We would have to go back on ourselves for a few hours to find a town with a mechanic who could fix it. The delay cost us a day.

LOVEY THROWS HIS TOYS OUT OF THE PRAM

"To cross the border it is $255 for each car."

Stunned, we asked the Armenian customs official for a breakdown of the costs.

He looked up from his peeling lacquer desk and grinned: "That's $180 for the bank and $75 for me."

Welcome to Armenia.

We'd hit the border late in the evening to be confronted by three hours of passport stamping, document checking and bribery. So once again we arrived in a strange new country in the early hours and pitched on the side of the road.

When day broke we found we were camped on some sort of industrial wasteland covered in odd metal scraps, and the Mercedes had a flat. Our pitiful cross-iron bent when we tried to use it, so we had to scout out the area for a garage with some tools before we could continue towards the capital city of Yerevan.

Thankfully we had contacts there. Carlos had made a friend, Gohar, through a networking website and she found us an apartment to rent. The next day we visited a couple of children's charities, Zortak 89 and Orran, then went out to meet another friend Cheryl, whom the boys called Cherkyl. She had travelled with Lovey, OJ, Tony and Carlos in South East Asia the year before, and was working in Armenia as a volunteer in the Peace Corps.

Cherkyl explained to us that the Armenian national dish was barbecue and took us out to try some. Now I don't really see how barbecue can be considered such a culinary treat that it is the national dish. I mean you're grilling chunks of meat over a fire, much as cavemen used to do. It's not cooking, it's heating things up, which is surely no more than a start. Hardly gourmet is it? There were such delicacies on the menu as brain, tongue and lamb's testicles, but I opted to play it safe with pork.

Dinner took a surprising turn when Lovey announced, after some protracted questioning from me, that he was going home. I've slipped that bombshell into a small segment on barbecuing because that's exactly how he did it. The gist of his reasoning was that the project was not what he wanted, no one listened to him, we hadn't got any donations and no one cared about "the kids". He gave a stream of truth and half-truth that thoroughly enraged me and left me feeling distinctly distrustful of him.

"I just don't think people care about the kids," he told me, like he was Mother Theresa. "Where are the donations?"

We had had very little corporate sponsorship and the personal donations I'd managed to attract amounted to £20 from my old colleagues at The Surrey Herald. Up to that point we had raised just $5,000, though he hadn't raised an extravagant amount himself.

The decision must have been playing on his mind for some time, though I wasn't even aware of any rumours or rumblings. He had been complaining of being unwell for a while, struggling with a chest infection that had left him drained and surly. The Trek had been getting steadily more difficult, with Georgia the hardest part yet, and breakdowns were now a daily occurrence. But no one else was talking about giving up and I thought our day-to-day follies were at the very least becoming more streamlined.

After we'd eaten I walked with two of the people who'd travelled with Lovey before, Tony and Cherkyl. They told me he always threatened to go home.

"He's a drama queen," Cherkyl said. "One night when we were in Asia last year, he told us not to be surprised if he was gone when we woke up. Don't take him seriously. He just wants people to tell him he's needed."

But it is not in my nature to pander to drama; I find extravagant but empty threats infuriating. He was the instigator of the whole trip and he was threatening to dump us all out in the middle of Asia. He should surely have been offering some kind of leadership, instead of threatening to turn tail and run when things got a little difficult.

That night he continued laughing and joking with the group, but I skulked. OJ was unhappy too, and went off to phone his girlfriend. Later, at an Irish bar in the city, Lovey told OJ he could get cheap flights from Almaty, so he'd be staying with us till Kazakhstan. His outburst saw him sink drastically in my estimation. Up until then I had occasionally found him arrogant and stubborn, but I thought I could cope with that, and when he was on form he was great to be around. But that night I completely lost trust in J Love.

I was genuinely worried, so the next day I spoke to Tony, who had known Lovey since school. But Tony didn't seem too bothered, he wasn't letting the situation get to him, he wasn't taking Lovey seriously. It was a welcome knack of the Mighty Tony P to remain unfazed, and that day I resolved only to be as concerned as the little Mexican—I would use him to gauge just how much nonsense Lovey was talking.

Bribery and Corruption in Christianity's First Nation

Armenian women divided opinion: tall with slender legs and curved chests, but broad shouldered, with large, strong noses. Ladies with full moustaches were a common sight and some of the older women folk sported freak-show beards.

I spent a day driving around town looking for a garage that could weld a protective plate under the Mercedes to shield its oil pan and petrol tank from the Caucasian roads. I met a lot of Armenian mechanics and I tell you they are big into gold teeth. Extreme bling.

Armenia is proud to be the first country that declared Christianity its state religion. It converted in 301, and claims to be home to the world's first Christian church. The country is fiercely Orthodox, despite the attentions of neighbouring Muslim Turkey, and the cities and countryside are littered with old churches and carved stone crosses. Our days in Yerevan were lent a biblical bent by the vague and hazy lump of the distant Mount Ararat, where Noah grounded his ark.

We went on a day trip to the city of Echmiadzin, famed for its many churches. Gohar was our guide, and brought with her Albert Poghosyan, a 27-year-old Armenian who had spent the last three years studying in Salford, England. An impressive and stout character with a full stomach, a jet-black beard and a shaved head to make the best of the receding hairline he inherited from his father, he was studying eCommerce in Manchester, but had broad interests and a confident grasp of English—I found him stimulating company. In the sweaty, crammed bus ride to the city, I told Albert about our experience of bribery at the border and asked about corruption in Armenia.

"Oh yes, the corruption on a low level is very high. Here is an example: I want to set up an organisation here. I fill out the paperwork and go with the $20 fee. But the officials demand another $250 to stamp the paperwork. If I do not pay then they say there is a problem with the paperwork, that I have not done it right and they send me back to do it again. I come back with it, but again they want money, and I don't pay so they send me away. This will carry on for ten months or so and they let me know that if I don't pay, they will never stamp the paperwork. So I pay, and it takes two days, not a year.

"The problem is people don't care, they don't want to finish corruption. They understand that the corruption is practical. If you pay then things are ok. When I say I will not pay, people are amazed. I say 'why should I pay? I pay my taxes, you should go by the rules.'"

Don't people go to the police to complain about corruption?

"No, people don't trust the police. The mentality is the same as in the Soviet times when there was the mafia so nobody spoke to the police. Back then all the money came from Russia, so if you stole the money you were a hero. Mafia were heroes. People loved these guys and these guys protected them. Intelligent guys you know, speak many languages, can talk to you about Da Vinci, about Tolstoy, very clever people.

"Things were ok. Ordinary workers got two holidays a year, they could go to England or see their family anywhere. People were happy. But a free state had always been a dream, people wanted to be free from Moscow. Then in 1991 when the Soviet system collapsed, the teachers and professors came to power in Armenia. They gave the mafia bosses three days to leave the country. But these mafia were so powerful they don't believe them. But then these guys with automatic weapons come and just kill the mafia leaders, maybe a dozen of them. But the mafia used to run the city, so it leaves a hole.

"And now who runs the city? The police. In a small country like this it is the police people are scared of. The police can take you away. They can take you to prison. The police are the new mafia. The state is the new mafia.

"Then the war with Azerbaijan and for five years we have a blockade. No electricity, no proper food. I had to read by candlelight, and I read a lot. It was like the nineteenth century."

So what can be done?

"I don't think there can be a revolution, there must be an evolution. We need to change the minds of the young people. Engels and Marx's revolutionary theories are complete shit. They're not working. Marx made his theory so good, so clever, with everything in it, Kant, Hegel, everything, but it is shit."

I suggested that Marx only had a theory, it wasn't a practical solution, it was Lenin who put it into practice. Albert nodded: "And Lenin was a German spy, sent by the Kaiser to cause a revolution in Russia."

I hadn't heard that one before. "So you're saying the Bolshevik Revolution of 1917 was planned and funded by the Germans to try and end Russian involvement in World War One?"

"Yes."

I thought I'd best leave that alone.

We arrived at the church where they claim to have the spear that a Roman soldier used to stab Jesus when he was on the cross. I was entranced by the rusty, old spearhead. Did it really pierce the Son of God? It felt very strange to look at.

Deep in the bowels of the church is a door that leads to an underground pagan temple. Apparently the church's architects decided to hedge their bets, just in case the old gods tried to reassert themselves.

"Err... and Please, Big Problem"

On our last night in Yerevan our cameraman announced he too would be leaving us. Old Istvan pulled the plug, threw in the towel. At least he gave it a decent go. He tried, but eventually he lost faith in such a disorganised rabble.

Our routine over the preceding weeks was almost embarrassing. We woke up late, drove through the night, spent an hour refilling petrol, made painful progress through the hills, broke down constantly, stuck to our schedule intermittently, changed plans every few hours, discussed much, resolved little. So now our leader and our cameraman were abandoning us. It had been a tough few weeks.

Istvan was almost the perfect candidate to follow us. He had a military background, he was a hardy chap with bush skills who could sleep anywhere and drive well into the night. He'd filmed for news channels during the Kosovo conflict, and done big budget feature films. He had a good eye for a shot, and would climb up crumbling buildings to get an angle. He liked a drink, a smoke, had a sense of humour and some crazy left-wing conspiracy theories. The problem was that he didn't speak more than a dozen words of English.

"Problem", "Big problem" and "No problem" were his most common phrases, helping us judge the scale of our balls-up.

"Errr... and no light, filming, why? Please. No light. Why? No filming. Big problem. Please. No filming, big problem."

That means that we've wasted the day by being disorganised and lost the light just when we hit the good scenery.

"Errr... and please, Dan, please, speaking, please."

Means I should do a piece to camera.

"Errr... and benzene and no and why? Why and no? Fucking problem."

Means we've run out of petrol again.

"Errr... and fuck and Zsofi, FUCK. Big problem, Andrew, FUCK, and telephone, FUCK, (garbled Magyar), no speaking, FUCK, big problem."

Meant he couldn't get through to Andrew, his boss.

"Errrr... and fuck and fuck, big problem, please, Zsofi, Zsofi."

Meant he couldn't adequately express his displeasure using his English vocabulary and he would wait to rant at Zsofi, our Hungarian trekker, so she could interpret.

The main problem was that not only could we not understand him for some help and direction with his shots, but he couldn't understand us to film the dialogue. When someone was telling a good story, or there was a little bit of comedy, he didn't know when to jump in and start shooting. Plenty of important side stories were missed because he didn't know what was going on. Plenty of potentially good narration was wasted because he didn't have his camera out. To be fair to the poor guy, he tried to learn English in Ireland. Not sensible.

After announcing his departure, Zsofi translated while Istvan gave us a three-hour tutorial on how to use the cameras, what he thought of the film and how we could make the best of the rest of the show. He wanted us to succeed, but he couldn't be a part of it. He was a good man, even though we may have demonised him. He said he missed his two young children.

Istvan gave me a powerful hug and walked away. I didn't know where he planned to fly to, but he told us he was not welcome in Hungary, where he had somehow upset some important people with his work. Maybe he went back to Ireland to wait tables and scrub pots. Who knows? I missed him—the crazy Hungarian camera guy.

From then on we would be filming that caper on our own, with OJ now chief cameraman. We discussed it and agreed it could work in our favour. The end result might have fewer scenic, cinematographic shots, less stunning camera work and sweeping imagery, but more dialogue, more story, more chat. And shots are useless without a story. But if we had a good story, and we felt we did, then we should be able to find the shots.

SIGHTSEEING AND WAR ON THE ARMENIAN BORDER

Tony's voice crackled over the walkie-talkie: "Um, guys. This village is not abandoned. I can see people."

We were driving in glorious sunshine through the lazy Armenian hills towards the border with Georgia when we noticed the derelict villages. Dozens of houses were stripped bare, their windows and doors gaping lonely holes in crumbling brickwork, the roofs long collapsed. Were these the remains of some ancient city?

Fascinated, we decided to divert for a closer look and some filming. Our convoy left the highway and slipped onto a cratered road that turned into a rough dirt track leading towards the overgrown ruins of the ghost town.

"I say again I can see people," the walkie-talkie burst into life, putting me on edge. Tony, in the lead car of the convoy, was 50m ahead but I couldn't see any people.

"There are people here," the voice from the walkie distorted, paused, then came across loud but calm, "and they have guns. There are people coming with guns. Back up. These guys have guns."

The voice didn't betray a hint of panic, but I slammed on the brakes and squinted through the windscreen. In the distance I could see a man in scruffy shirt and trousers, with someone behind him wearing all green. Are those fatigues? What is he carrying?

"They are waving at me, they want me to go to them," warbled the walkie, "one of them has a gun. I think we should go back."

I began to panic. There was a man with a large machine gun hurrying towards the lead car. I rammed the stick into reverse with a horrible scraping sound and looked out of the back window. The guys behind were already reversing, but I could see Carlos was out of the Merkin and filming the whole thing.

"He has a gun and he wants me to go to him," said the walkie, with a trace of panic.

"Reverse, mate, let's go, come on, let's get out of here. Let's go," was my advice.

But his car sat motionless as thoughts raced through my head. Do we leave Tony here? Do we stay and face up to this with him? The adrenaline flowed fast in the panic.

"Tony, let's go. Come on."

Still no movement from the lead car. I watched as the man with the gun reached it and then broke into a run as he went past. He was clearly in my view now. Wearing a metal helmet, green fatigues, body armour and carrying a machine gun.

Terrorist? Insurgent? Revolutionary? Hostage taker? The thoughts flew by and he was nearly on us. I've never been run at by a man with an automatic weapon before. It is truly frightening. Fear-induced paralysis set in. There was going to be a confrontation, we were in a lot of trouble, but best it be a verbal onslaught than a bullet-based exchange.

Megan and I looked at each other: "Hide the laptops."

Where do you hide laptops in a tiny plastic car? Under the seat would have to do, that'll fool them, they'll never look there. The man ran past us, past the next car, and it became clear who the focus of his attention was—Carlos and the video camera. I saw the impish Catalan trying to stash the thing but it was too late, the man with the gun was on him, we were busted. We got out of our cars and we went to face our fate.

It quickly became clear they were Armenian military—a huge relief. There was a lot of shouting and radioing and I was worried they were about to bring their cohorts down and march us off.

But a battered old car arrived and three men stepped out. They too were from the military, but you could immediately tell the difference between them and the squaddy who'd chased us. They wore loafers, not boots, had beer bellies instead of armour plating, caps instead of helmets, side-arms on their hips and stars on their shoulders. They were officers, and I didn't know if that meant we were in more trouble or less.

Initially there was shouting, but OJ used his simple Russian:

We saw these abandoned villages and thought we'd investigate.

We're driving to Cambodia.

After a lot of gesturing, OJ translated their reply. We had stumbled onto the Armenia-Azerbaijan border and—just our luck—the two nations were still at war. The villages weren't ghost towns, they were a war zone. They didn't crumble under the ravages of time, but were blown apart by Azeri shells. The hills were fortified by both sides' militaries in a tense stand-off.

The officers said that if we had gone further up the dirt road we would have crossed the disputed Armenia-Azerbaijan border. He said the Azeris would have shot at the cars if they had seen them coming over the hill. I tried to imagine what threat our battered convoy would seem to present. A new-fangled Armenian weapon disguised as a band of gypsies?

The filming was the biggest issue. It turns out that the military don't like their front lines being filmed. We showed the head honcho what we'd shot and he demanded it be erased, or else he'd start shooting something else. So we pointed the camera at the ground and filmed over the offending footage, but when we showed him the result—a five-minute film of Armenian rocks—he went into a rage and demanded it be erased. So we closed the lens cap and filmed blackness. Anything but give him the tape, which had some good shots of us driving through the countryside.

Tony passed cigarettes to the officers and they seemed to relax. They looked through our passports and laughed at our stamps, inquired about our Azerbaijani visas, but seemed to accept we were just stupid foreigners, not enemy spies. We'd lost our footage, but Megan couldn't resist taking a sneaky picture of the military in our wing mirror.

After an hour of interrogation we were escorted back to the main road. One of the officers gave Tony a peach as he sent us on our way, another brush with disaster under our belts.

THE RETURN OF LOVE

Back in Georgia we headed to Tblisi to pick up Marlena. With Istvan gone, there seemed less pressure on the group. We no longer had to maintain the pretence of sticking rigidly to the phantom production schedule, and we could take more enjoyment from filming, knowing it was for ourselves, not anyone else. We could go where we pleased and shoot for fun, without concern for a channel's audience.

Morale was also helped by Lovey regaining some sanity. His health had improved, his conversations were no longer accompanied by a hacking cough, and he didn't look so tired, drawn and miserable. At a group meeting I asked him pointedly when he was planning on leaving us.

"I'm not definitely going," he replied, getting defensive, "that was just an option."

I shrugged and thought it best not to push the point, but back in Yerevan he had sounded like his mind was made up. I just hoped his good mood held—he would have been a sad loss to the group.

In a sign of the new peace, I rode in Ziggy with Lovey as we headed out of Tblisi towards Azerbaijan. We hoped to cross the border before nightfall, and vaguely along the way was Davit Gareja, a famous old monastery out in the hills that we'd heard was worth a visit. Looking in our patchy guidebook map it only looked like a short detour...

LEAVING GEORGIA: HOSPITALITY, DAVIT GAREJA AND ST GEORGE

I guess England has its fair share of industrial wasteland, but in the plains east of Tblisi we passed failed industry on an epic scale. Enormous factories with shattered windows and semi-collapsed roofs loomed up from the flats. Twisted metal, broken fencing and rusted pipes adorned the slumping ruins of Five Year Plans. Whole industrial towns had been left to rot.

There was some activity in there—a towering chimney belched yellowish gas high into the atmosphere. Up close I hardly noticed the clouds, but from 50km away I looked back and saw that thick smog was lying over the whole area, all emanating from that one industrial minaret.

As we continued the scene became more natural and the land turned to pastures, miles of fertile grazing, sandwiched between rolling mountains. Bright green foliage followed the basin of a once powerful river now reduced to a trickle.

After stopping for directions at a strange shack that served as a shop, we turned off the main road onto a maze of dirt tracks that we ended up following through the fields for three hours. The dusty paths were better suited to horse, cart and cattle, but the landscape was spectacular, we met some interesting shepherds and driving the Trabbis in those conditions was fun. The little machines handled like rally cars, and because they only went at 80kph, I could try and drive Ziggy flat out, cackling as he skidded through the dust.

Our path was often blocked by herds, crossing the road in huge groups like pedestrians in cities. One horse tried to race us, despite having its front legs bound loosely together to stop it running too far. It was a surreal moment, gunning the Trabbi across the dirt with a horse in full flight alongside.

It was nearly nightfall when we arrived at Davit Gareja, and the old monastery was locked up, so we scrambled up a steep rock face to try and get a look over the walls.

"So now you're breaking into churches?" OJ asked, unimpressed, but after driving all that way we had to peek inside.

After half an hour of clambering about, a monk appeared and opened the doors. He asked us to cover up exposed shoulders, legs and feet, then took us on a tour in the fading light.

He said St David had founded a Christian church in a cave at the site in the fourth century, and it had been an important shrine ever since. The stunning and remote centre was carved out of the porous rock—a cave system surrounded by high walls and steep cliffs. At its peak 6,000 monks lived there, but in the sixteenth century the Shah of Iran took an army to the place and slaughtered them all.

When we arrived, just 45-year-old Padre Antimoz lived there with three other monks and a few guests. A bridge engineer during Soviet times, twenty years ago he joined the spiritual academy and became what he called an "air monk". He had lived in a cave for the past four years, just as St David did.

Padre Antimoz showed us around the main church by candlelight. The grave of St David lay in a cavern near a fresco dedicated to the 6,000 slaughtered monks. I was stunned when he explained that one painting depicted St George slaying the dragon. The dragon wasn't the winged, tailed beast of English legend, but an armoured man of Asian descent. According to Padre Antimoz, this "dragon" was a Byzantine soldier who was loyal to pagan Rome at a time when the Roman Emperor Theocritian worshipped Zeus and hated Christians. He had killed "many, many Christians", the priest said, and so earned the name "Dragon". In 303 AD a Turk from Kapadoccia named George slew the Dragon, earning sainthood. It was strange to hear the story of England's patron saint told by an air monk over candlelight in an ancient Georgian cavern. Padre Antimoz had no idea what linked St George to England.

It was late when we'd finished our tour and the priest said we could stay at the monastery. But we were keen to press on to the border, so said our goodbyes. Within a few hours Fez had broken down; he would run, but wouldn't start. It was no big deal as push starting the light little fellow was a simple process (in fact we had got to the stage where we could reverse push start a

Trabbi against traffic up a hill).

As we were standing by the side of the road while Tony checked Fez's engine, tired and hungry in the Georgian night, a passing truck saw us and pulled over. The driver stepped out, reached into the back of his lorry, pulled out three giant watermelons, handed them to us and drove off into the darkness. The gift raised morale, brightening everyone's mood as we messily divided the fruit with a penknife and gorged ourselves in front of Ziggy's headlights. Out there such a simple gesture meant a lot to us.

A couple of hours later, Gunther the Mercedes got a flat, his fourth in a month. Tony mentioned that the car was overloaded, but there wasn't too much we could do about it.

We had a lot of trouble jacking up the heavy load on the uneven ground, but every passer-by stopped to help despite it being the early hours of the morning. Then, when we'd finally replaced the wheel, the hydraulic suspension failed. We decided to limp on to the border and try to tackle the problem there, but it took us two and a half hours to crawl the last 80km.

We rolled into the checkpoint and the guards slowly came to life. One went around kicking lampposts to get them to work. We showed our papers, chatted a while, then a dark-haired official in his early thirties called me to one side conspiratorially.

"Hey, Dan, come here."

For a second I thought he was going to demand money to let the Merc through—old Gunther was clearly broken—but from somewhere he conjured up a giant, dusty, plastic container of syrupy, brown liquid.

"Take this," he said as he slid it towards me in the shadows, "Georgian wine. My friend in Kakheti made it. It is the best around."

I was overwhelmed. We had always planned on tasting the famous delicacy, but ran out of time. "I'm sorry we only have five litres to give you. Drink it. Drink too much, you will be drunk."

Maybe he knew we had a long night ahead of us. We made it through the Georgian border without a hitch. But the Azeris had closed up for the night, leaving us trapped in no-man's-land. We had no choice but to wait it out. We were stuck there for seven hours, but that tub of sweet moonshine made it all bearable.

Georgian hospitality had lived up to its reputation, from George in Batumi to the old monk offering us a bed, the watermelon man and those generous border guards. I will always have fond memories of the country.

Roadside Manner

When on the road we tried to stay in a convoy, but it wasn't always easy. Generally, if you lost sight of the car behind you, you flashed whoever was in front and then pulled over to wait. We soon learned that any more than a five minute wait probably meant a breakdown, so we'd turn back to help.

But sticking together in congested conurbations could be difficult, particularly in some of the Asian cities, where motorists followed unconventional and unpredictable rules. Often it was worth stopping even if a traffic light was green to make sure we could get the entire convoy through in one. We regularly spent a couple of hours trying to get into or out of a city, constantly losing each other or our way.

To help co-ordination, each car was equipped with a walkie-talkie. When they were charged, these were genuinely helpful, though we occasionally got carried away and took them out on the town with us.

"Is Tony at the bar?"

"Yeah, I think so."

"I need a drink."

"He's got a walkie on him."

"Perfect."

The walkies only lasted half the trip, but if we did it again, I would get CB radios installed in all the cars.

In Fez, the backs of both the passenger's and driver's seats were broken, so they constantly fell backwards. We could stuff bags and blankets behind the driver's seat to keep it upright, but the passenger seat was more difficult. Eventually I just tore off the back of it. This only left the seat of the chair, but the passenger was now able to sit in the rear of the car and use the remains of the seat in front as a footrest. This was a far more comfortable arrangement, particularly for sleeping, and although the rest of the group thought we were idiots, I never regretted the decision.

Fez and Ziggy had roof racks full of excess stuff, but Fez's was a nightmare—it came off constantly, normally on bumpy roads during the night. You would hear a pop, a lot of bumping and scratching on the roof, then the tent would droop down over your windscreen and blind you. Screeching to a halt would project everything from the roof onto the bonnet, and then the arduous search for the little rubber suckers needed to reattach the whole bloody thing would begin. Eventually we lost so many of the parts to it, that it stopped functioning.

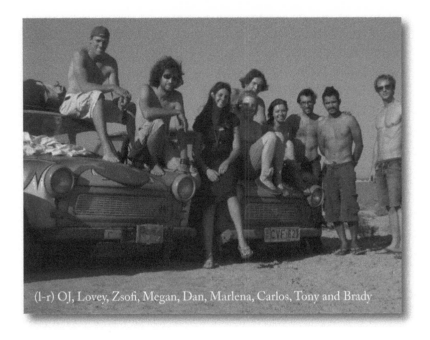

(l-r) OJ, Lovey, Zsofi, Megan, Dan, Marlena, Carlos, Tony and Brady

ONE IN, ONE OUT?

We picked up a new recruit, Brady, in the Azeri capital of Baku the next day. I'd met Brady the previous summer in Germany and was looking forward to the extra company. He was from LA, a talented photographer and designer, and the front man in a cool band, The Sunday Drivers. He planned to be with us for a month, which was a welcome addition—fresh blood. We met him at the airport shortly after 3am, took him for an expensive beer at the terminal, then treated him to his first night as a trekker—camping on a patch of debris yards from the runway.

One in.

But our joy at collecting a new trekker was tempered by the terrible news that Tony had lost his passport somewhere on the 500km drive through Azerbaijan. He knew it was loose in Dante and guessed it had fallen out along the way. He'd narrowed the spot down to a few miles of road where everyone got split up late in the evening. OJ went back with him the next day to retrace their steps and they spent all morning searching, but came back empty handed.

It was potentially a major blow. From a social perspective Tony was a steady hand, a calm, easygoing character who got things done. He was someone I found easy company, and he knew how to handle Lovey. He'd struck up a particular friendship with Zsofi—the two of them got on well and usually travelled in Dante together. We joked that it was harder to get into Dante than China. You needed a letter of invitation and a visa, and even then you were unlikely to get more than a day in the car.

And TP was our mechanic. Over the preceding six weeks he had got to know each of the Trabbis intimately. While we'd been out filming, he'd often stayed behind to work on the cars and knew the nuances and character flaws of each. It was rare that more than a couple of days would go by without him fixing one of them, and his expertise would be sorely missed, possibly jeopardising the entire trip. And it had happened at the worst possible time, just when we were about to head into the unknown of Central Asia.

It was possible to replace the passport, but not the visas. So Tony had little choice but to contemplate heading home.

One out?

Mud, Oil and Bribery in Baku

The cop pointed his red flag at our car and blew his whistle hard. I felt like I'd been pulled over while go-karting. Our entire convoy had just followed Lovey into a U-turn on the motorway, a manoeuvre that would be illegal in most civilised countries, and Azerbaijan was proving no exception. Ziggy and Gunther the Merc had managed to get away, but Zsofi and I in Dante were left to face the music with the occupants of Fez.

My experiences in Azerbaijan over the preceding day and night had all been good. The people seemed friendly; one family had flagged us down on the motorway to insist we join them for dinner, and in the foreigner-friendly capital of Baku I expected the police to be reasonable.

The cop ambled over in his own time, so I took my sunnies off, grabbed my identification and left the car to meet him with my best silly but harmless foreigner smile.

"Salam," I offered my hand, which he took firmly. The bones in my knuckle had yet to heal from our incident with the Georgian camera thief and I winced as the pain shot through my palm.

"Alaikum Assalam."

He seemed affable enough, but spoke no English, and I used my handful of Russian words to explain what we were doing. He let me know there was a problem and led me back to his car where he sat me down in its relative privacy.

He took my details and made a great show of writing out a ticket. The BMW felt shiny and new and smelt of leather—it was strange being in a proper car after so long in Trabants. The cop sucked the air in through his front teeth, making a gurgling sound. He seemed to be weighing me up.

He casually flipped over the ticket and wrote on the back: $150.

Three cars, fifty dollars each, he communicated through the universal language of hand. He obviously didn't realise that the Mercedes was with us, but he knew Ziggy had got away. I pulled a face which I hoped conveyed confidence in my position but respect for his, and shook my head.

"Nyet dollar. Nyet."

There was a silence at this impasse. He looked more disappointed than angry.

"Ya rabotayu journalista v'London"

I work as a journalist in London, I told him as casually as I could, hoping the latent threat would come across without sounding challenging.

"Journalista?" He raised his voice, then tried to work out my age from my passport.

"Twenty-four," I tried to help him, raising my fingers.

Again using sign language, he asked whether I was married or had children, and was surprised when I said no. Then he asked if Zsofi, who had been in Dante with me, was my girlfriend. I said no and he made a crude gesture to ask if I was sleeping with her. I laughed in a laddish way and said no but he nudged me and winked all the same, apparently adamant that two people could not share a car without fornicating. He looked down at the back of the ticket where $150 was neatly written.

"Ya rabotayu journalista v'London," I repeated, pulling an old The Times press card out of my wallet and handing it to him. He grunted, and shouted out of the car window to a colleague who had a few more stars on his shoulder. He showed him the card and they exchanged words.

$50 was written on the back of my ticket.

It seemed ridiculous that he was writing the amount he wanted as a bribe on the back of the official ticket and, to hide any compliance on my part, I scrawled $10 in my notebook. He seemed to give up.

"Ok, Daniel." He waved me away and I left the car.

Dan 1 Cops 0

"Baku is oil. That's why everyone's here," the man shouted into my ear, spraying the side of my face with spittle. He was northern and drunk, but it was late and I was in an Irish bar—what could I expect? The only locals in Finnegan's Irish Pub in Baku were hired hands: barmen, doormen and whores.

A live band was playing and an Azeri was singing Dancing in the Moonlight, but he clearly couldn't speak English because evabadey waz danswing in da moonliy. The Trabbi girls didn't seem to care, frolicking, laughing and having drinks bought for them.

"It's boom town. The oil's bubbling out of the ground. Everyone wants a bit. It's the English that have got it though."

I wiped my cheek. There are a lot of ex-pats in Baku, enough to warrant two English language newspapers, and British Gas has a large interest in the city. Oil platforms hover just off the coastline and stretch out into the Caspian Sea. Pipelines crisscross the surrounding countryside.

People have been going to Baku for oil for their lamps for thousands of years. Marco Polo said there were different coloured oils in different areas, blue, red, green and yellow, with yellow being the most popular. The world's first offshore well was drilled there in the mid-nineteenth century.

The city is a strange mix of neo-classical, neo-neo-classical, and dilapidated. But you can tell the money's there—construction is everywhere, McDonalds is everywhere. The next day I was sitting on a step in the shade of a birch tree, reading and waiting for Brady and Zsofi to finish in a shop. I heard shouting and looked up to see a cop demanding I move. I stood up, put my bag back on my shoulder and moved to the side of the pavement. There'll be no sitting on the street in Azerbaijan.

Dan 1 Cops 1

The departing cop was pulled over by a well-dressed local at the restaurant I had been sitting near. They argued, the cop left, then the man called me over. "You can sit there," he said, then gestured at the policeman, "he doesn't know the rules."

I sat down and the cop glared at me as he shuffled off.

Dan 2 Cops 1

My defender was dressed in a well-fitted suit, with gold cufflinks and an expensive watch, and dining with men of similar attire.

"Why did he move me?" I asked.

"He thinks it is still Soviet times. Beggars used to sit on the ground," he shrugged, "but it's ok."

I guess I looked a little like a beggar. Dirty stained shorts rolled up over my knees, a sweaty, creased shirt and long, unkempt hair that had taken the shape of a thatched roof.

"Are you a tourist?"

I explained my mission.

"What was Armenia like?"

"They told me all Azerbaijanis are evil," I said in a horribly miscalculated comedy gambit that only served to get his back up. The two countries are old enemies.

"We are all Caucasian. We are the same people."

And he returned to his business.

Baku is hung with pictures of the country's former president Haydar Aliyev, and its new one, his son Ilham. Despite Azerbaijan being a democracy, arrangements were hastily arranged for a hereditary transfer of power when Aliyev Snr became ill a few years before our arrival. His son was quickly promoted to prime minister and thrust into the public eye. When old Aliyev popped off, the power of his political and electoral machine was handed to his son, who waltzed into the hot seat at the subsequent presidential election.

Images of the two of them were all over Baku: paintings in shops and homes, billboards on buildings, signs in police stations, shrines by the road. Another personality cult. But stability in oil-rich Baku is vital to the West, and world leaders seem willing to overlook the Aliyevs' abuses of power to ensure their fuel supply remains uninterrupted.

MUD VOLCANOES

We drove out of the city to visit the mud volcanoes, where liquid mud bubbles and belches from the peaks of glutinous mounds. The fractured landscape looked like the moon; the mud had been erupting for hundreds of years, forming a dry, cracked skin of mudflows and deltas. It was a pleasant day trip and Megan was on great form, lying in the burping pools of mud and jumping around covered in gloop.

Carlos had made contact with a student named Parvin through a social networking website, and he'd kindly lent us his front room to sleep in, another random act of kindness from a genuinely friendly guy. We left the cars parked outside the apartment and when I went out to check on them I found a gaggle of police in attendance. One of them, Captain Sayeed, asked to be taken to our host's apartment for a chat.

"That's the nicest policeman I've ever met," our host reported once the cop had left, "he didn't ask for money. Six years ago they were like beggars—they went round always asking for money. That was the system, even with the big guys. But now they make the salary higher so they don't have so many problems."

But they still ask for money?

"If you make a little mistake then yes, they make you pay. But before, whether you made a mistake or not, they would ask for money. Everyone pays, I pay, my father pays. People do not know any better—this is how it has been for years. People don't know how much a speeding ticket should cost, so they pay whatever they are told."

Lovey enjoys the terrain near Baku

55

The day before we planned to leave Azerbaijan, news came from the American embassy that Tony's passport had been handed in. Relief swept through me, and Tony was pretty chuffed too. Things would have been a lot tougher without the little man.

Partly because of the tense international situation, it was difficult to get permission for the Americans to drive through Iran. So to avoid the country we planned to get a ferry from Baku, across the Caspian Sea, to the port of Turkmenbashi in Turkmenistan. We didn't know too much about the ferry, and there were no fixed prices on display at the port, so we were resigned to entering into negotiations.

Four cars and nine people. How much to Turkmenbashi?

The price started at an extortionate $1,350, but OJ and I negotiated it down to $1,100 over two sweaty hours. It felt infuriatingly expensive so we took a break to talk about it, and phone the British embassy for advice. I got through to a charming Azeri woman, who agreed that the fee seemed expensive. "But this is a private matter, we cannot get involved."

"Do you think I'm being bribed?"

She laughed. "Of course. This is Azerbaijan. This is how it works."

"Well, is there anyone I can complain to?"

Another giggle. "No, this is Azerbaijan."

"So what should I do?"

"Do you have any other way of getting to Turkmenistan? Do you have any other choice?"

"No."

"Then you pay. This is Azerbaijan, this is how things work."

We grudgingly paid up, but on our way into the dock we got hit for a random $30 "road tax fee", presumably for using the 50m strip of tarmac between the port gates and ferry, a $44 bridge fee for a goon to open a gate onto the ferry, and a $10 per car loading fee. They told us the boat would take twelve hours, so we packed appropriate supplies, mostly beer and crisps. What could go wrong?

SHIPS IN THE NIGHT: CROSSING THE CASPIAN

The ferry would have been a perfect setting for a horror film. A large, looming cargo ship with a dozen cabins for passengers seemingly added as an afterthought. Although only twenty years old, the vessel was in a terrible state of disrepair, all smashed panelling and flaking paint, furnished with dusty, stinking chairs. A crewman reassuringly informed us it was the ship's last voyage before she would be docked for an extensive service.

Azer the cabin boy showed us to our grimy, four-berth rooms then demanded $5 from each of us. We refused to pay. There were no sheets on the grubby, stained mattresses, which had clearly been gnawed at by vermin, and Azer wanted another $3 from each of us for bedding. We refused.

I tried to close the door, but the lock was smashed where the room had been broken into. Everywhere peeling linoleum revealed the oily hull. I watched a cockroach sneak across Lovey's laptop when his back was turned.

The Azeri customs officer had told us the crossing would take twelve hours, but a day and night passed with no sign of land, and every time we asked our arrival time in Turkmenbashi was pushed back.

The ship was designed like a labyrinth, but as I explored I got to know the thing. I was thrown out of plenty of areas—the Captain's mess, the bridge, a strange stairwell into the bowels of the vessel. But things became more accessible at night, when we would sneak into the kitchens to boil water for instant soup.

The second night I slept on deck on a broken plastic chair beneath a lifeboat, a few metres from the cool Caspian. The crew moved me on in the morning and I found a dusty row of chairs in what looked like an abandoned cinema. I noticed that we weren't moving and looked out of a porthole to see Turkmenistan stretching out across the horizon. We were told that the ship had to wait for a berth to dock, that it would be a few hours. But another day and another night slipped by. Supplies dwindled, the meagre rations we'd bought at Baku went quickly, and we began drinking the discoloured water from the taps.

Where were we? Lying a few miles off the Turkmen shore, pulling against our anchor as the wind and current shifted. We had checked out of Azerbaijan, but had yet to check into Turkmenistan. Someone on the boat had our passports. We were document-less, identity-less. No nation held our registration; we floated in the international ether, untraceable, uncontactable.

At night jets of orange sparks shot from one of the boat's twin exhausts.

57

It was a pretty if disturbing sight—as if someone had stuck a catherine wheel in the pipes. Tony suggested they were burning the bodies of the passengers who hadn't made it through the intense heat of the day.

The distinction between passengers and crew was unclear. There were no uniforms, but there may have been a dozen Azeris or Turkmen along with the nine of us trekkers and the crew. A crowd formed around the sparkling exhaust, though I couldn't tell if they were officials or just idle spectators like me.

Deep inside the ships underbelly felt like a level from Doom 2. All rusted metals, greasy chains, scrawled graffiti, half open hatches and metal grilles. The echo of my flip-flops chimed against the splash of the sea on the stationary hull, mingling with the disconcerting sound of water flowing beneath me. The Trabbis were parked alongside giant trains that I guessed were filled with oil or gas.

Is the Caspian a sea or a lake? It is an important question of interest to more than just geographers and academics, as the answer determines how the Caspian's abundant oil deposits are to be divided among the countries around it—Azerbaijan, Iran, Turkmenistan, Kazakhstan and Russia. If it is a sea, each country owns the stretch of water off its coast. If it's a lake, then the resources of the entire body of water must be shared out evenly. I suspect the arguments will continue until the oil wells run dry.

When we finally got a slot to dock, the wind changed, making it impossible and again we sat and waited. The following morning we got off the ship, having been at sea for three nights and four days. Good riddance to the good ship Azerbaijan; I was delighted to get off the thing, but the crossing had eaten into our patience and our short visa for Turkmenistan. At the time none of us appreciated the consequences of the delay.

3
CENTRAL ASIA
Turkmenistan, Uzbekistan
31 August – 13 September 2007

Q) How do you double the value of a Trabant?
A) Fill up the tank.

TURKMENISTAN

Reaching Central Asia felt like a major achievement for the Trek and at the same time the beginning of a new challenge. Europe and Turkey had been perfect places to cut our teeth, with good roads and facilities, even though we'd made things as hard as possible by rigidly repeating our mistakes.

The Caucasus was more difficult, there was a marked reduction in the quality of the infrastructure, but to me it still felt pretty European and accessible. But Central Asia was a major step into the unknown, not the sort of place you normally go on your summer holidays. And that was exciting.

These were a different people from the Caucasians we'd left behind, and a different landscape from the rolling greens of Azerbaijan. This was a place of deserts, mountains and nomads that we knew as "the stans"—Turkmenistan, Uzbekistan, Tajikistan, Kyrgyzstan and Kazakhstan. Names that hardly roll off the tongue or get much attention back home in Blighty, and before the trip I would have struggled to place any of them on a map. But this was our chance to explore.

Over the last few millennia Central Asia has been overrun by pretty much whoever was dominant in the region—Parthians, Macedonians, Huns, Scythians, Mongols, Seljuk Turks and Ottomans all marched through. The region's heyday coincided with the rise of the medieval Silk Road when local kings and khans used their military power to control the trade that crossed to and fro between the Mediterranean and China. But these routes dried up when Europeans discovered a sea route around Africa, and trading power shifted to the seafaring nations—the Portuguese, Dutch and British.

Since the late nineteenth century Central Asia had been consumed and hidden by the Russian Bear, a thick cloak thrown over the region so that the West had almost forgotten the centre of its own map.

Ziggy and a yurt in Uzbekistan

Turkmenistan, possibly the most secretive and isolated of all the Central Asian countries, was our first stop and nobody really knew what to expect. It sits on the east coast of the Caspian Sea and is divided from Iran to the south by the Kopet Dag Mountains, Kazakhstan to the north by Uzbekistan, and it is almost entirely desert. But other than those scraps of geography all we had really heard was a steady stream of rumours and urban myths about the eccentricities of the former president, Saparmurat Niyazov Turkmenbashi.

Turkmenbashi was the sort of priceless lunatic that only extremist ideologies seem able to turn up. A true Soviet relic, the man made David Ike look like a Cartesian realist and creationism seem the result of rational enquiry. He existed on an entirely different plain of consciousness.

Turkmenistan was the only Soviet satellite that didn't want independence when the Union collapsed in 1991. Moscow gave the country no choice so Turkmenbashi, then just the humble communist party leader Saparmurat Atayevich Niyazov, waited until a load of Aeroflot planes were refuelling at Ashgabat airport and then declared Turkmenistan a free nation, gaining independence, ultimate power and the country's first and only airline.

After winning 98 per cent of the vote in the country's first "democratic elections" he managed to keep Turkmenistan from collapsing into civil war and lawlessness while its Central Asian neighbours did just that. He declared international neutrality, billing the country as the Switzerland of Asia, and set about harvesting the nation's vast gas deposits.

Alongside these laudable achievements he ruthlessly clamped down on political opposition and fostered one of the more bizarre personality cults in the modern world, setting himself up as a semi-deity and taking the title Turkmenbashi, "Father of All Turkmen". He renamed some of the days and months after friends and family, he made his book *Ruhnama* (The Book of the Soul) part of the curriculum, and forced learner drivers and students to pass exams on it. He banned beards and gold teeth, pop stars from lip-synching and newsreaders from wearing make-up. But not everyone's perfect.

The old mentalist died a year before we arrived, and some of his more eccentric decisions had been reversed, but his legend and the deliberate veil of secrecy around the country added to the intrigue and expectancy.

In order to gain permission to cross Turkmenistan with nine people and four cars, we had agreed to be escorted by a properly licensed guide. He was expected to ride with us, so for a while we'd be up to ten, our maximum capacity, and I was interested to see how he would cope with the rigours of trekking: the breakdowns, the late nights, the wrong turns, the backtracking, the committee meetings, the farcical sense of organisation—and Tony's feet.

In fact, he had a pretty good introduction to life on the Trek. We'd arranged to meet him straight off the boat at the Caspian Sea port of Turkmenbashi (the former-President even took to naming cities after his self-appointed title). We were fully one week late, and the poor chap had been waiting there the whole time. At least he now knew what to expect.

The guards at the border wore thick safari suits despite the heat and looked Chinese—broad Mongol faces, thick black hair, slanted eyes and a chestnut complexion. But our guide, Ilya, looked like a Belgian professor, with mousy blonde hair, milky skin and light blue eyes.

"Do you like camels?" a young looking border guard asked me.

"Um… not really."

I'd spent three uncomfortable days on the back of one in the Sahara a few years back. They bite, they sneeze, their ungainly gait and ridiculous shape make them a terrible ride.

"They have good milk. You must try it."

It hadn't occurred to me to taste their milk.

Processing us at customs took hours, our first introduction to the Turkmen bureaucratic machine that we would get to know well, but it was a relief just to be off the damn boat. We were charged $60 per car as a tax on petrol, something that we argued vehemently against. But we were placated the second we got to the pumps. The government-subsidised petrol in Turkmenistan was cheap. To fill up all three Trabbis, a total of 75 litres, cost $1.50. The attendant also demanded $1.50 to work the pump, but no one argued.

ASHGABAT

From Turkmenbashi we drove through the night to reach the capital, Ashgabat, City of Love. The famously barren Karakoum Desert makes up about eighty per cent of Turkmenistan, and the roads through it are long, straight and sleep inducing. The wind had swept the sand into tidy, rippling piles that stretched to the horizon and swathes of salt lay crystallised in the troughs like pockets of snow. We drove through a village of one-storey buildings, where cows and camels strolled vacantly down the streets or stretched out in the shade and scratched their backs on fencing.

"The Great Silk Road", a sign announced somewhat hopefully from among the peeling, crumbling low rises and dusty, wooden shops. Nearby, women squatted by huge pans over open fires along the road.

I knew that Turkmenistan was considered a police state, and although I had a rough idea of what that meant, I'd never been to one and couldn't be sure exactly how it worked. I soon learned that there is little clever about the name, but that it's pretty self-explanatory: it means there are police everywhere. Every hour on that long drive to the capital we would pass another checkpoint. It was a lottery whether they stopped us or not, but if they did, Ilya would jump out and show our papers.

"Thanks for not asking for money," Megan shouted at one group as we left, still smarting from the constant "taxes" we had been paying in Azerbaijan. As the early hours floated by I fell asleep in the back of Fez, and when I woke we were at a large, grand hotel in the city. Everyone was raving about the drive into Ashgabat and I was gutted to miss it, but my room had a bathtub, probably my favourite place to unwind. There were no plugs, something I have learned is a feature of former Soviet states, so I blocked up the hole with tissue wrapped in plastic from a bin liner and relaxed in the hot water. A welcome introduction to the capital—this place isn't so bad after all.

"So what do you think of Turkmenbashi?"

I was breakfasting at the hotel, which we were sharing with a group of forty cyclists who were riding from Istanbul to Beijing.

The waitress smiled sweetly, "He was a great leader."

"There are those who say he was a deranged megalomaniac."

Anger flickered across her face: "He was a great leader."

She cleared my breakfast and hurried off.

"Careful there, mate," came an Australian voice from the next table. He was leathered, tattooed and drinking vodka. It can't have been later than 10am. "You don't want to get anyone into trouble. The whole place is bugged. All the hotel rooms, the restaurants, anywhere foreigners go."

It could be true. Turkmenbashi was famously suspicious, so much so that we were warned not to film or photograph except at certain tourist sites. I shared a vodka with the Aussie while someone did a cash run, and suddenly we were all millionaires—I got a thick wad of 1.13 million manat for my $50 bill.

"It reminds me of Vegas," Megan said as we drove through the Legoland streets of central Ashgabat, "everything here looks like it was meant to."

I could see her point. It was all well manicured, perfectly polished, neat and tidy. But nothing in Vegas struck me as pretty and I felt the same sanitised sickness in Ashgabat. It didn't appear real, not grown organically as the city had developed, but built very deliberately by a man with a strange marble vision. The stunning high-rise office blocks and apartments stood in complete contrast to the rest of the country. It looked as if a demented utopian with a curious lust for marble was left in charge of city planning and accidentally blew the national budget. Which is almost exactly what happened. On close inspection I saw many of the buildings were virtually empty—sterile phallic monuments to one man's industrial delusions. The giant architecture was out of place and preposterous, deliberate ostentation in a country that looked like it had bigger problems to deal with.

Walking through an Ashgabat bazaar, it was easy to forget where I was. There was such variation in the people it was like strolling through Turkmenistan's history. Alexander the Great offered me Half the Known World by the Age of 32; there was Genghis Khan in Rape 'n' Pillage, first left after Timurlane's Mass Murder Emporium; Catherine the Great was on the vodka stand and security provided by one Joseph Stalin.

With predecessors like that, it's no wonder old Turkmenbashi was a little extreme.

I asked Ilya why everyone looked so different and he gave me an answer tinged with Soviet schooling: "During Soviet times there were fifteen republics and you could travel freely between any of them, so people from the whole of the Union came here. My grandparents came from Russia after the earthquake."

The earthquake happened in 1948. A nine or ten on the Richter scale, it flattened Ashgabat in a second, killing 110,000. In typical Soviet fashion Stalin claimed just 5,000 had died and sealed off the area for five years so the city could be rebuilt.

"After that seventy per cent of people in Ashgabat were Russian. Now it is two per cent. Most of them went back to Russia in the '90s," Ilya added, looking wistful, "I would like to go to Russia too one day."

The young Turkmenbashi survived the earthquake, though his whole family didn't, and sixty years later I could see his image all over the rebuilt city. There were gold statues and busts of him along main roads, he was on factory buildings, bank notes and vodka bottles, in hotel lobbies and police stations, even in people's homes. The country's slogan, *Halk, Watan Turkmenbashi*—people, nation Turkmenbashi—was painted all over the place.

I saw his *Ruhnama* on shelves in most official buildings. I hadn't read it myself, but I understood the book was an attempt to invent a history for Turkmenistan. That was the biggest challenge facing Turkmenbashi, trying to create a culture and heritage for his people. To forge a nation, you need a sense of a shared past, some heroes to celebrate, some victories to unite, a sense of commonality. In that respect Turkmenbashi did a good job of holding the country together and keeping it away from the Iranian extremism just over the border. Admittedly he set himself up as a semi-deity, but most leaders tend to have a bit of ego.

Drinking to the personality cult in Turkmenistan

I asked Ilya what he thought: "Niyazov? We loved him. The people here were hungry so they needed a leader. Someone to help them. He did a lot for us. You can enjoy yourself, you can have fun, you can pick up women. But if you have politics, then it's a problem. Otherwise—no problem."

I wondered how the people would remember him. Would there be a Khrushchev-style denunciation of the cult of personality? Looking around the place I doubted it. Already I could see the posters of his successor, the neatly named Gurbanguly Berdimuhammedov, hanging on public buildings. Out with one cult, in with another.

BATTLE LINES

Initially we hadn't really divided up the cars, thinking anyone could drive any car they fancied. But at a petrol station in Ashgabat I had a row with Lovey that would cement divisions.

The issue was Fez. There was a bit of stigma attached to the little car. It was clearly breaking down the most, the problems had been there since Budapest, but as Megan and Marlena were driving it they were attracting some blame. Someone branded them "The Muppets", which they found offensive and it created a bit of an us and them mentality. Previously I had flitted between Fez and Ziggy. But since Brady arrived in Baku he had been in Ziggy and I had been riding in Fez and now I was getting some of the flak.

So I asked Lovey if I could drive Ziggy. He said no I couldn't because I was "careless". I asked what he meant, and he said I'd slept on the handle that lowers the passenger seat and bent it. He also mentioned an occasion when I had scraped the gears, then claimed the problems with Fez were due to such carelessness.

I disagreed and pointed out that Fez had been driven the most—from Budapest to Germany and back twice—while the other cars were stationary, and Carlos drove it around Budapest for a month before we even set off. As Tony had agreed, it was natural that there was more wear and tear. But Lovey made it clear it was the fault of Megan, Marlena and me: "It's carelessness. You're just careless with it."

I should have pointed out that carelessness is losing your wallet, credit card, camera and $300 of group money in the first few weeks of the trip. But of course I didn't think of it at the time, and only dwelt on what would surely have been the most stunning and witty riposte in the history of disagreement while stewing for some hours after the incident.

I asked Lovey if he would drive Fez and he made it very clear he was going to drive Ziggy from then on. And there it was: battle lines.

Megan and I couldn't help but feel smug when, two days later, he wrecked the oil pan on the Mercedes by ploughing over some loose stones. Careless, careless.

J Love was good company half the time, but sometimes he could be very difficult. "He's spent all day storming around like a four-year-old toddler," admitted Brady, exhausted from spending a day in the car with him.

The two had been riding together since Brady arrived, and I called them the Brady Bunch. One night I found them wrapped up watching *Brokeback Mountain* in the car, it was quite romantic and I was very jealous.

So now it was mostly Megan, Marlena and me in Fez, Lovey and Brady in Ziggy, Tony and Zsofi in Dante, and Carlos and OJ in Gunther. The fixed divisions were a little weird, but they certainly made me more protective of my car as I became keen to look after old Fez better and check him out more regularly.

Megan and Marlena were good company, always laughing about something, and the three of us got on well, and I felt protective of them. It was nice to feel like someone had your back.

THE DARVAZA GAS CRATER

I was keen to explore Ashgabat, but there wasn't much time, and Tony told me there was something much better to see. He said there was a crater in the desert filled with fire, which he said burned constantly, day and night. Our guide had never been, but we knew it was near the town of Darvaza out in the middle of the desert.

So again we headed into the vast, barren emptiness—yellow, black and grey sands, bearded with dry brown shrubs that spiked bare feet. The road began as an artery but gradually became a vein before squeezing into a capillary and fizzling out into the dunes. It was a long, hot drive but as the sky darkened, a dim and distant halo developed like a Polaroid in the dusk. It was far from the road, the Trabbis would never make it, but we stumbled upon some tents and the semi-nomads there agreed to take us. We piled into the back of an old Soviet truck, and even that thing struggled in the dunes, but the guy kept letting air out of the tyres to increase the traction, and eventually we cleared the steeper mounds.

In the waving sands I lost all sense of perspective, and despite seeing the glow on the horizon, I couldn't work out how big the crater would be. It had been quite a journey out into the nothingness, but when we arrived there was a collective sigh of relief, then whoops of amazement when the scale of the crater became clear.

A huge oval hole brimming with fire, it must have been 100m across and 50m deep. Buttresses of sharp rock ribbed up the sides of the pit, awash with yellow and orange flames. Plumes of bright fire shot from jets in the centre of the crater, dampening down momentarily, then erupting high into the air. The whole thing glowed like amber melting in a campfire.

Dante's inferno, the fires of hell, Mordor—I half expected Frodo to turn up and hurl the ring in—a truly magnificent sight. I stood at the crater's edge and felt the bright warmth on my skin, then a gust of wind threw the full force of the heat at me, making my eyelids prickle and forcing me to leap away, shielding my face. It was impossibly hot.

I asked the truck driver who had dropped us off where the fire had come from. He didn't know, but said it had been there for the 21 years of his life. Maybe forever. Was it some natural phenomena? If it had existed for centuries, here in of all places the land of Zoroaster, then surely temples would be all around. Fire worshippers would have had a field day. I could imagine the offerings being thrown into the flaming crater. It would be a wonder with a global reputation.

No, it must be a modern creation. Ilya agreed. "I think maybe there was an explosion here and many people died," he told me cryptically, digging deep in his vodka-sodden mind, but he couldn't expand or follow the thought any further.

I wandered around the crater looking for signs and found a bundle of twisted and broken metal pipes leading from the ground out into the crater, where they had snapped off and burned. It looked like a gas pipe, which made sense. Perhaps the Soviets or Russians were drilling, maybe there was an accident, an explosion. The crater caught fire and rather than explain what had happened they simply closed off the area and left it to burn out. But the fire didn't burn out, and it will burn on, until it has sucked all the gas from its reserves below the surface.

The flames threw yellowish light onto a tall dune next to the crater. At the top someone had piled rocks in a sort of monument, the ghostly column flickering like a strobe above us as we laid out mats and slept in the fire's warm breeze. It was Marlena's birthday and she stayed up late drinking a merry amount with Megan and Tony. Zsofi, Lovey and Brady stayed up too, experimenting with filming the flames, but I was exhausted and drifted easily into a comfortable doze in the blinking light.

Our guide had met us in a smart shirt, with suit trousers and shiny shoes. But his dress had slowly disintegrated and as we broke camp the next morning I noticed that he was a bit of a wreck. His shirt was unbuttoned and hanging open, his chest exposed, trousers replaced with cargo pants, his hair scuffed up, eyes wild and nails dirty.

The Trabant Trek effect.

A Country You Cannot Leave

The oil pan on the Mercedes smashed again while we were heading from the fire crater to the border. It was terrible timing. Our visas had just a day left on them, and Turkmenistan is not a good place to overstay your welcome. Luckily I had struck up a conversation with a man at a nearby bazaar. He randomly gave me a tape of local music, and later happened to pass us sitting on the side of the road. He invited us back to his house for dinner and a place to stay, at considerable risk to himself. Foreigners are supposed to be registered every night in Turkmenistan. We ate in the Turkmen style, sharing a few big bowls between everyone, and drank in Russian style, knocking back shot after shot of vodka with fizzy pop chasers.

"I like you, Dan, I think you might be Russian," Ilya told me the next morning. A curious assessment based, as far as I could tell, on my ability to drink silly amounts of vodka, go to sleep at the table, wear a skirt and fall over in the shower, gashing my back to the extent that I needed medical attention and three injections.

Megan: "Oh god, you're still bleeding."

A new word entered my dictionary. Subcutaneous—as in "it's a subcutaneous injection"—an injection under the skin, but not into the muscle. I had one of those and two intramuscular (they do go into the muscle). I'm not sure what they were, tetanus maybe, but the next day I developed a fever, cold sweats and diarrhoea. I was lucky that Marlena is a trained nurse, and she and Megan regularly cleaned the wound and changed the bandage. An infection in that environment could have been nasty.

The lads managed to get the Mercedes repaired and we got to the border just before it closed, only to be told that it wasn't the correct point of departure. We were meant to be at a crossing 100km away. Despite our protestations, they wouldn't let us out of the country.

When foreigners overstay their visa in Turkmenistan a committee is formed to discuss what to do with them and reissue the paperwork. This hideous bureaucracy was a parting gift from the Soviets, along with a fierce drinking culture and a penchant for ruthless dictators. We would have to wait for the committee's decision.

Because our papers had all expired Ilya warned us that it was dangerous to head into the nearby town, which, like the rest of the country, was swarming with police.

So we had no choice but to wait it out there on the Turkmen-Uzbek border, a strip of dusty soil crowded with queuing trans-nationals and hawkers flogging knock-off electronics. Not the best place to recover from a gouge in your back and the shits.

Marlena, who had already been with us a few weeks longer than expected, decided she wasn't going to get drawn into our border saga, and opted to head back to Ashgabat and try to get a flight home. Even that wasn't simple, and the poor girl ended up stranded in Tashkent, Uzbekistan, for two days waiting for her embassy to rescue her. It was sad to see her go, especially for Megan as the pair shared a real rapport. But she needed to get home to her studies and she'd pushed it long enough. We weren't really in the right place for any kind of leaving bash, she just gave us a wave, jumped in a taxi, and that was that.

The rest of us sat in that checkpoint sandstorm for three days while a constant stream of Uzbeks and Turkmen examined the cars, tapped at the chassis, demanded to see the engines and tried to buy things from us. Every day we thought we'd get out of there, but always Ilya would turn up to tell us there had been another delay. The incessant attention became wearing and I stopped responding when the thousandth person asked what my name was.

Despite Ilya's warnings about going into town, no one could stand the border crossing any longer. Three days of sitting in sand was too much, so we headed out to find a café to relax, eat and contact our embassies about the problems we were having getting out of Turkmenistan and the exorbitant fees the travel agency and the government were demanding to process our paperwork.

Anyway the traffic cops who lined the streets didn't have cars or radios, just whistles, and we soon learned to speed up and look the other way when we heard them—how could they catch us? It became a cat and mouse game around the city, avoiding eye contact with the police when they attempted to flag us down.

Maybe the game antagonised them. We can't be sure.

Things seemed to be going fine; people were unwinding, we had a beer and some good food. Then the police turned up, called us out of the restaurant and said they were arresting us for having dirty cars. The Trabbis had gone 6,000km through dense forests, high mountains, choking cities and dusty deserts without a wash and they'd picked up a little muck. It appeared that this was a serious offence in Turkmenistan where automobile care was clearly more important than running water or an ATM.

The cops wanted us to go to an expensive carwash, but OJ negotiated and we managed to get a local to wash our cars with a bucket for a dollar each. We had so little money left that Ilya paid.

We pulled up in an empty car park overlooked by a block of flats. Within minutes there were Turkmen swarming over us. All ages of them, kids on their way home from school, teenage girls, giggly and practising English, old men wanting to know the cost of the Trabbis, young men wanting to see our mobile phones. Two police cars watched over it all. Things got so crazy that a man with a wheelbarrow turned up to sell watermelons to the crowd.

"Do these people have nothing better to do?" TP asked. Perhaps not. But I guess we were quite a sight for the locals. The attention really seemed to rile the police. The poor chaps wanted to throw the book at us for having dirty cars and ended up policing a mass public demonstration. They became enraged and demanded we form a column and follow them. Some kind of police chief turned up and Ilya, who I think had been threatened, started to get angry and nervous.

There was a lot of discussion and then they led us out of the town and told us never to return. We were banished.

The KGB Are Here

The police took us to a closed, out-of-town bazaar, the nearest Turkmenistan has come to a mall. It was a couple of acres of empty stands and trucks swarming with mosquitoes and conditioned by a dusty breeze. The police were determined to lock us in. This caused some consternation, particularly among the Americans who refused at first to even enter the place. Carlos and I weren't as bothered—it seemed a good spot for a kick about.

"They want to help you—you cannot stay on the street, it is not safe. They think it is better for you to stay here," Ilya explained, but no one really believed him as we'd been living on the streets for days now. No, it was clear that we'd been locked up.

Thankfully there was a bar full of truckers on site. Ilya was straight in there buying the vodka, so Megan, Carlos and I joined him. It gave me an opportunity to chat to a few people about life in Turkmenistan.

"A few years ago there were people who wanted a revolution," a truck driver told me, "and there were a lot of important people who said a lot of stupid things on TV. But we knew they were not stupid, we knew these people so we believe what they say.

"But about two years ago they all die. They don't just get killed in one day—it is many things, injections and things over a long time. But they all go.

"I should not be talking to you, it may be dangerous for me," the man said, reproaching himself for letting the vodka loosen his tongue. "Many people disappear, yes, many people."

I asked him whether he knew anyone who had disappeared.

"Yes, a friend of a girl I used to work with. He was a political activist who wanted revolution. One day he was just disappeared. Yes, many people disappear. But this is the way it is. It is like this since Stalin, it has always been the way. I hope I am still alive in the morning.

"People have many thoughts of revolution. But with so many police everywhere, always watching, there is no chance of revolution. People think of it but there is no way."

Carlos and I stayed in the café for a few hours to learn Russian swearwords from farmers. When I wobbled out of the place after one too many toasts I found Ilya walking through the darkness.

"Two men from the KGB are here."

Words to send a chill down anyone's spine. Why?

"It's complicated, things are very strange. It is a long story. Over there are many drug makers," he gestured towards the far wall of the compound, "so the KGB are here to protect you."

I said that I wanted to meet them, so he took me over. The officers were typical Turkmen opposites. One was a tall, dark haired man in his thirties with an intelligent face. His assistant was squat and plump with a broad hazelnut head, wearing what looked like a GAP outfit—fitted stripy jumper, dark jeans and loafers. They seemed friendly enough. But it was an odd feeling being watched. I couldn't get used to it. I asked Ilya whether they were there every night. "No, they are only here now to look after you. If anything strange happens you must find them."

I wondered what he meant by anything strange, but he waved me away and talked with them in Russian.

Later we wandered back up to the café and Ilya opened up a little. The KGB is now known as the KMB—the Committee of National Defence. Different name, same job. Are they here to protect us or watch us?

"Yes they protect you, but it is also desirable for them to watch you."

Are we in trouble?

"Not you. But maybe me. This could be a problem for me. Maybe I disappear now," he smirked. "Until a few months ago this whole province was closed off. You needed a special permit to go here, it took two weeks to get one even for me. It is because it is on the border with Uzbekistan. But the new president he makes it free to go anywhere."

I asked one of the KGB why the area was closed off when Turkmenistan had good relations with Uzbekistan and had declared neutrality. "It is the border," he explained, "you must be careful."

"Yes, we keep a pretty close eye on the Welsh," I told him, and he laughed.

Half an hour later I heard shouting from near the gate to the compound. I faked taking a pee and went to investigate. I saw Ilya getting dragged away by an official. He returned ten minutes later with a thick set Turkmen.

"We have to move," he told me, seeming shaken and avoiding eye contact, "you are honoured guests. It is not right for you to stay here in this bazaar."

I couldn't help but laugh—honoured guests who'd been banished from the city and imprisoned in a mosquito-infested sandpit with the KGB for company.

"These people are from immigration," he gestured at a dark car, "they say it is not right that foreigners are camped here, just five kilometres from the border."

We had spent the previous three nights camping literally on the Uzbek border.

"You must stay in a hotel."

It was ridiculous. The street cops had put us there, the KGB had decided just to watch us, and now the border police wanted to haul us back into the city.

"It is illegal for foreigners to stay outside. They must be registered at a hotel. This is the law," Ilya added with a shrug.

We had no choice. We drove back in a surreal convoy with police, immigration and KGB vehicles to a hotel that was actually a worse place to sleep than the bazaar. We crammed in, four to a room, and I spent the whole night knocking mosquitoes and bed bugs away, and trying to avoid lying on the gash in my back. I rose early just to get out of the filthy pit and again waited for the Turkmen to let me leave their country.

But more delays, more paperwork, more problems with our guide. When I met Ilya in the morning he already had a beer in his hand and was talking about being robbed by the police. He said they had beaten him.

In a different country our guide may have been tempted to abandon us in the face of this fierce stream of misfortune. But we were Ilya's problem and his responsibility, and he knew he would be punished if he did not keep us out of trouble and get us out of the country. But he seemed resigned to punishment.

By the time we got our new visas the border had closed, so we spent yet another night camping on a sandy crossroads.

"I'm sick of this shit. I promise you now I am never coming back to this country," was OJ's analysis. Turkmenistan had divided opinions. Certainly OJ and Lovey hated the place, and even the normally unflappable Tony had let his exasperation show. But I felt a little more reserved. We were the ones who overstayed our visas, and although it wasn't our fault that the Mercedes broke, we had to deal with the consequences—five days of bureaucracy. We knew when we entered the country that we weren't meant to go anywhere without a guide and the correct papers, and that we should be registered at a hotel in every city. We were told that not cleaning our cars would attract unwanted attention. But we just ploughed on, convinced of our inalienable right to freedoms that in Turkmenistan have yet to be won. Turkmenistan operated a different system, and I was pleased to get an understanding of it, if only to more greatly respect the liberties I took for granted back home.

I got up full of hope that we'd make it out of the country, five days later than we'd planned. But within minutes of breaking camp and pulling away, the gearbox broke on Fez. It was embarrassing being towed up to the border, but Tony put a positive spin on it: "People have crossed borders by foot, on planes, by boat and on trains. But how many people can say they've been dragged across a border?"

Thanks, TP.

We got there at lunchtime, so of course the border was closed. We were sitting there in a totalitarian, isolationist, pariah state, hidden away in Central Asia, impervious to all Western influences but one—the all-pervading power of euro-cheese. Even there, on the Turkmen-Uzbek border, they played Steps. Could the agony get any worse?

We were all hot, thirsty and frustrated, so Tony and Zsofi headed up the road in Dante to find water. But the hours ticked by and they didn't return. They had been arrested in town for not having any papers. It's quite easy to get arrested in Turkmenistan. There was plenty of groaning, but Ilya went to negotiate and we got them back just as the border was closing. We were fined $150 for something as we left the country. But we had literally nothing, so Ilya had to pay.

It felt like escaping from a prisoner of war camp—Carlos and I whooped and high-fived when we saw the "Welcome to Uzbekistan" sign. Through some strange quirk of fate I entered the country shoeless and topless, walking behind the rest of the cars. I genuinely felt like I was in a prisoner exchange, crossing the 500m of no-man's-land between the countries.

The Uzbek guards kindly stayed open late to process us, and then let us out into the night. We were still towing Fez.

UZBEKISTAN

With Marlena gone it was just Megan and me in Fez, and we got on well. She was no girly girl, very hands on with the car, push starting it, filling the oil, defiantly driving around despite the jeers of men who found it hilarious that there was a woman behind the wheel. She was a great communicator, always expressing what was on her mind through a combination of word, song and charades. Often I heard her singing strange ditties to stray animals.

Trapped in a five-foot by six-foot plastic lunch box for three months, you get to know someone. Not that I could tell you too much about her history, her family, her past. Her parents were teachers with the military, she had lived on military bases in Turkey, Korea and Europe. She had a brother and a sister, both older. She was freeloading at her sister's and did a mundane office job before hitting the Trek.

But once you're Trekking these details seem pretty irrelevant. More importantly, I could tell you that she was always keen to fix a flat, get dirty filling up the car and insisted on carrying her own stuff. She hid food in restaurants to take out to stray dogs. The sight of a camel, yak or bison would make her laugh out loud. She sang to animals. She didn't like sleeping in tents, could drive long into the night and rose before most. She wasn't squeamish and knew how to dress a wound. She could be confrontational.

She could be pessimistic, and tended to fear the worst. If something went wrong, which was roughly every other hour, she could quickly freak out—"aagh, it's the end of the world"—and rather than try and deal with the issue, she tended to rip holes in everyone else's suggestions. She really wanted to be taken seriously by the boys, but her nay saying approach meant she often got ignored—which pissed her off ("I suggested that, like, twenty minutes ago"). But generally she was good, easy company, we laughed a lot and looked out for each other. She changed the bandage on my back and kindly told me when I smelt. I provided her with countless hours of wit and diversion, which she seemed to enjoy the most while listening to her headphones on full volume.

Of course, we could wind each other up, but there was a refreshing spirit of camaraderie in Fez as we escaped the terrors of Turkmenistan.

KHIVA: SANITISING THE SLAVE TRADE

Whenever we entered a new city it was Trabant Trek custom to drive around in laps, hopelessly lost, rapidly stressing out as various wants failed to be sated. Some of us needed internet, others food, for some the priority was a bed, others were gagging for a bar. This city centre dance did serve to help orientate us, but also ensured we arrived in frustrated mood, having spent an hour pissing about in headless chicken mode.

Having already passed one Khivan junior school three times to the sound of loud shouting, we should have known that parking outside would attract a lot of attention. As a sortie headed out to find accommodation, those who remained with the cars were swamped by kids in uniform. Initially they circled us guardedly, but soon the braver souls piped up with Asia's favourite question: "Where you from?"

This question must have been ingrained in the locals from an early age, and it was the only English that older folk seemed to know. For some of us it took on an almost shamanistic quality, having an instant irritating effect. I could be sitting, working, reading, writing, talking, even sleeping, and someone would approach, tap me on the shoulder and insist, "Where you from?"

"England."

"Oh."

Then just stares. No follow up. For me the silence used to be vaguely awkward, although the locals always seemed happy enough to stare, but by Khiva I had begun to enjoy the empty pause, imagining my would-be interrogator might feel some discomfort. I hoped that every second that ticked by they were realising the futility of their question. What were they hoping to get from that single use of dodgy English? Did they really need to wake me up?

Now I know why all those beer-bellied builders get a British Bulldog tattooed on their arm. It is so, when they are on holiday in the Costa del Sol, drinking Stella with their shirt off, the answer to the question on everyone's lips is emblazoned garishly across their upper arm.

I considered my first tattoo: Britannia, riding a bulldog, draped in a Union Jack, underlined with the words "English, so sod off."

As I said, arriving in a new city could be frustrating.

After the advance party had found a place to stay, we pulled the cars inside the ancient city walls and found a welcomingly clean guesthouse. I shared a room with Megan and in the morning we were served an eclectic breakfast— honeyed figs, sweet oat biscuits, a fried egg, strips of tomato wrapped in baked eggplant, cheese, sausage and sweet, watery tea.

Having spent so long in enforced company, I was keen to do some exploring on my own. But for some reason I felt unable to explain this to Megan and so resorted to giving her the slip, a cowardly manoeuvre I felt bad about. And Megan, not being the type to shy away from confrontation, brought it up later that day.

"You ditched me."

"Uuh… yeah… sorry, I just sort of wandered off…"

"You ditched me."

Khiva is a strange place. There has been a city there for millennia, but its golden age was that of the Silk Road and the slave trade. When, in turn, the road and the trade dried up, the city fell off the map—a Russian protectorate, slowly dying in the desert. But the Soviets decided to make the best of the place and embarked on a huge programme of restoration. This meant forcing out many of the inhabitants of the old walled city, sending them to live in new Soviet concrete apartments, and rebuilding their former homes. The result is a sort of living outdoor museum. Everywhere is the sound of workmen scrubbing the place up, plastering, tiling and hammering exposed beams protruding, petrified and ancient, from the sides of narrow, cool alleys. Gaggles of old

French tourists, the first we'd seen in a long time, added to the exhibition ambience.

People do live there, but it felt like a mock up. The town didn't seem like a home, there was none of the detritus of thousands of years of existence. Most signs of the past had been lost in the restored buildings. And such empty streets—Khiva was a ghost town. I wanted to feel the vibrations of its history, but instead felt the sun dazzling off the newly buffed city walls.

There were some signs of life. Baked clay ovens stood outside a few homes, looking like giant termite nests, with gaping sooty holes in the top. But only the riveted cart tracks in the stone paving betrayed centuries of use.

As a prototype for future restoration projects, I wasn't convinced. Would Stonehenge bear the same ethereal magic if it was scrubbed up and polished, its fallen stones righted, its altar restored? I doubt it. Part of the beauty of visiting these places is seeing what hand time has dealt them. Their decrepitude tells its own story.

Just like cities in the West, Khiva has its own financial district. Not quite a Wall Street or Canary Wharf, actually it's a bunch of men sitting around the bazaar looking bored and fanning themselves with huge stacks of cash. Currency is an issue in Uzbekistan. With the highest denomination of bill being worth about 40p, you have little choice but to wheel around barrows of the stuff, and when I asked to change a $50 bill a local had to run out back and chop down a small forest to make the notes.

Strolling among the stands of walnuts, raisins, almonds, mink hats, wolfskin waistcoats and surprisingly large amounts of toiletries, it was difficult to imagine the place filled with the slaves who made the city rich. The entrance to the bazaar is the East Gate, or Executioners Gate, a long dark passage with grated alcoves on each side where the Persian, Turcoman and Russian slaves would sit and starve until they were bought. A Russian would cost you four good camels, a Persian just a donkey. The rare visitors who made it to Khiva and back described seeing thousands of slaves manacled together in the market. Those who tried to escape would be nailed to the East Gate by their ears and left to bake in the extreme Uzbek sun. Lovejoy?

A Frightening Example of the Trabant Trek Approach in the Qizilqum Desert

TP, OJ and Carlos spent much of the second day in Khiva working on Fez. The car still had a problem with the front right wheel, what would become known to all of us as "the bearing issue", and, as we prepared to leave, TP didn't seem too convinced that the situation had been resolved.

"There is a chance that the wheel will come off while you're driving, so watch out for that," he said, which is possibly some of the least reassuring advice a mechanic has ever given. I pressed him on what I should be looking out for and he shrugged: "Strange noises… if it comes off you'll know."

I'm not too good at identifying "strange noises" in cars, particularly in rattling old Trabbis on terrible roads, and I wasn't entirely comfortable with the thought of the wheel falling off. Wouldn't this have some influence on my control of the vehicle? Was that dangerous? TP seemed happy enough, he was always my yardstick on mechanical matters, and so I put the thought out of my mind.

We left Khiva in similar fashion to our arrival, with two hours of driving around in circles trying to find the right road. You'd have thought the road to the capital, Bukhara, would be well signposted. Maybe it was, but I'm not sure we found it. The road we took was vaguely well paved but entirely unlit as we followed it into the night. Somewhere along the way the decision was made to stop and sleep.

I woke up in the desert. As far as the eye could see it was rolling dunes and tufts of dense weed. Definitely the desert. We had approached this leg as we did most, making a rough stab at the distance by looking at the sketchy diagram in the guidebook, then going for it. We estimated it was about 400km, maybe a seven-hour drive? But we didn't realise we would be crossing a desert, and the feeble Trabbi headlamps hadn't illuminated this important fact during our rough night time excursion. So I was a little surprised to be out among the dunes, but in good spirits as we slowly pulled ourselves together and headed off.

We drove for hours in that vast, lifeless emptiness without seeing much, and then around noon, someone ran out of petrol. This was a bad sign. Once one car had run out you could be sure the others weren't far behind. But no one had thought to fill the spare tanks, assuming there would be somewhere to buy gas along the way. There wasn't. And so we were stranded about 250km into a 400km-wide stretch of the blazingly hot, frighteningly empty and practically uninhabited Qizilqum Desert.

This sort of situation is beyond the realms of naivety and far into the now well-trodden frontiers of our stupidity. Who goes into the desert without enough petrol to get out again? And without any food or more than a few gulps of water between eight people? It is genuinely mind-boggling, and the pull-quotes write themselves:

"They didn't respect the desert."

"They were under-prepared."

"They were thick as pig shit."

All true.

Fez had the most fuel left, so Megan and I volunteered to take all the spare petrol cans and head off in search of fuel. To add to the fun we only had a handful of Uzbek money, and a few dollars. To increase our range some excess petrol was decanted from Dante into Fez and we set off, leaving the rest of the group standing around in the middle of nowhere.

It was quite a relief to be on the road with just Fez and making our own decisions without the committee meetings. Not that there were too many decisions: just follow this long, straight road until you find fuel. But the sensation slowly turned to trepidation as we watched the kilometres tick by on the odometer, our own feeble fuel supply running down with few signs of life.

We passed a petrol station that looked like it had been abandoned for some time, then found a man at a truck stop who waved us a long way down the road when we asked for benzene. We banged on the window of another abandoned petrol station, to no avail, but this time I noticed a man nearby riding a donkey. Now I know donkeys don't need petrol to run, but things were getting desperate.

"Shall I ask him?"

Megan laughed, "Why not?"

He was a scruffy little man, so small his donkey looked like a stallion. It wore a saddle made of blankets, with no stirrups, and the man guided it by poking it in the rump with a sharp stick. We got chatting with the wee chap, who seemed as surprised to see us as we were to see him, and he even let me have a ride on his donkey, who we learned was called Pedro. We raised the benzene situation and were pretty stunned when he gestured that he could help, saddled up and trotted off into the desert. He disappeared behind some dunes, and Megan and I looked at each other.

"Is he coming back?"

After a while the huddled little shape reappeared, this time carrying a couple of Coke bottles. They were full of petrol. Amazing. Out there in the Uzbek desert, Pedro the Donkey and Petrol Man. What a double act.

We bought both bottles at an extortionate price, exchanged a lot of back slapping, hugging and posing for photos, then headed off, with another 20km added to our range.

This pattern continued for the next two hours. We would get worryingly close to running out of fuel, eventually stumble across someone who could sell us a Coke bottle full, then limp on into the desert until we found another stop. It was edge of the seat stuff, as running out of fuel out there would not have been pretty.

Gradually the desert gave way to irrigation and foliage, then low-rise homes and shops—a great relief. When we finally reached Bukhara we spent the last of our money on a well deserved plate of food, then Megan got a cab into the city to find a cash point and fill the tanks. I slept in the sun for an hour, then we made the two-and-a-half-hour drive back into the desert. The round trip was a little like running out of fuel in London and sending someone to Manchester to get some. Other than having to smuggle the illegal plastic petrol containers through a police checkpoint outside the city, and a scary moment when the guard lent into the car to light a cigarette literally inches from our fuming gas cans, all went well.

Shortly before nightfall, and seven hours after leaving them, we found the group, limping along the highway towing the Mercedes. Tony ran out of Dante cheering and hugged us. It felt good. The Muppets had become the cavalry. The others had found twenty litres between them and begun to slowly crawl towards the city, but they wouldn't have made it without us.

Tony: "We thought we'd lost you. We thought you must have broken down somewhere and were just sitting it out. Aaah, man, it's good to see you guys."

We'd come bearing significant luxuries—hard bread, stale biscuits and warm water, and we all sat around eating, drinking and celebrating. Another scrape with catastrophe under our belts.

BUKHARA

We arrived late in Bukhara and managed to find a place to stay, but pretty much everything else was closed and OJ was hungry. You wouldn't like OJ when he's hungry.

As I have mentioned, OJ is a big man with a big appetite. The sort of man who snacks on a king-size Snickers with a 1.5 litre bottle of Coke, burps and is hungry again. I would go so far as to say that OJ's food fetish began to wear me down. I like to eat—my belly is testament to that—but I'm not especially into food or cooking. OJ could spend an entire evening meal talking about the stuff: the best paella he ever had, the traditional method for making chapattis in India, the various pros and cons of long grained rice versus its short grained cousin. Lovey and Tony loved these conversations too, sometimes comparing burrito places in DC or launching into long diatribes about mayonnaise. This used to bore me senseless.

That night OJ charged around the city looking for food, frightening anyone who witnessed him. After finding nothing but frustration, and slightly scared that OJ might start eating small children, we ended up cooking noodles in the kitchen of the guesthouse.

Since the vehicular segregation in Turkmenistan, partnerships had formed across the group—Tony and Zsofi, Lovey and Brady, OJ and Carlos, and now Megan and me.

The confirmation of our new alliance came in Bukhara. She found the guesthouse that could take us all in, and so got first dibs on the best room. It had a double bed, air con, *en suite*, TV, fresh, clean sheets, and I was invited to share in the luxury.

It was probably the nicest place we had stayed in months. I enjoyed it so much I even did my washing in the shower, a rare occurrence. In that situation I guess there was a chance of romance blossoming. It didn't, though that didn't stop the rumours. Why let the truth hinder the gossip? Instead we were accomplices, sharing each other's grievances and the inevitable bitching. It was a good friendship.

I had a brief look around Bukhara, but wasn't especially impressed. In fact, I remember it best for the guesthouse. Time was still against us, so we only lingered a couple of nights before continuing east, towards one of the highlights of Central Asia—to Samarkand.

MAPS? WHERE WE'RE GOING WE DON'T NEED MAPS

Did I mention that we didn't have any maps? We didn't have any maps. It's true. We bought maps for all of the 21 countries we were planning to cross. But OJ left them on the shelf of his apartment in Washington DC. So, for six weeks and 8,000km we had been asking directions.

"Samarkand," I'd shout out of the window at terrified pedestrians.

We'd pull over in Uzbek towns and ask for directions to the Tajik capital of Dushanbe, which is a little like pulling over in Surbiton and asking a passer-by if he knows the way to Aberdeen.

Initially the locals would gaff off in their local tongue, but when they realised our incomprehension they would join us in pointing and gesticulating. In Europe people tend to point in short sharp motions, angular juts and thrusts. In Central Asia the movements are more curved, a right hand turn becoming one half of a breaststroke. We were often lost, especially in cities, and adopted a pragmatic approach to traffic laws, performing U-turns, illegal lefts and pulling over in terribly unsafe places.

I wasn't entirely truthful; we did have some maps: the little diagrams in our guidebooks. But they were clearly not designed for road travel, bearing few road names, a strange sense of distance and marking junctions haphazardly.

I don't know how many hours our lack of maps cost us, probably in the hundreds. But in a strange way it was liberating—blundering from one place to the next relying on our own initiative and the courtesy of strangers.

"Excuse me. Can you point me in the direction of Cambodia?"

To Samarkand

London is big on stone, but in Samarkand the thing is tiles—clay baked aquatic colours pieced together in delicate mosaics that shimmer across the buildings in the yellow wash Uzbek sun. If ever you need someone to retile your bathroom, I would recommend an Uzbek.

People have lived and traded around Samarkand since before Christ, and even Alexander the Great was struck with wonder at the ancient city. But Ghengis Khan sacked and levelled the place, leaving it a shell until another famous Mongol leader made it his capital.

Fourteenth-century Samarkand was the centre of an empire that sent hordes pillaging their way across India, the Caucasus, the Middle East, and deep into Eastern Europe, destroying what they couldn't steal. The man in charge was Timur the Lame, Timurlane, a petty chief from a small Mongol settlement 50km from Samarkand. His reputation is as hero to his people and villain to his enemies, and history has struggled to judge him. He marked the cities he sacked with huge pyramids of human skulls—80,000 counted in a heap in Baghdad alone—and historians estimate the numbers he slaughtered in the tens of millions. But he was a lover and collector of fine art, and a keen

Brady, Lovey Carlos and OJ arrive in Samarkand

chess player who invented his own more complex version of the game, with twice as many pieces and a larger board.

His victories stretched from Poland to Delhi, and although he sacked much of what he conquered, he took artists, scholars, philosophers and craftsmen back to Samarkand, which became a glorious hub of creativity, propped up by Timur's ruthlessness.

The travellers and traders who returned from the empire's capital spoke of a vast and beautiful city and it became romanticised in Western imaginations. To Poe, Marlowe and Keats this was a city that encapsulated the majesty and mystery of the East.

Even now the city's skyline is dominated by the imposing turquoise dome of the Bibi Khanum Mosque, built using the riches looted from India in the winter of 1398 when Timur sacked Delhi and beheaded 100,000 prisoners. Ninety elephants were needed to bring the haul back to Samarkand.

The mosque's dome towers over the modern buildings that surround it, as if it were built by a race of giants or aliens. Arriving at its gargantuan arch it is easy to imagine how dumbstruck a foreign traveller would have been in the fourteenth century. There would have been few other monuments of such height and scale in the known world, apart perhaps from the Aya Sophia in Istanbul.

Yet the building's ambition was also its undoing. The great dome of the mosque was too big, and within years of completion great cracks had appeared in it and the building quickly became unsafe. The dome is a nice analogy for the end of the great empire—it reached its zenith, and the fulfilment of its own opulent glory was also its death sentence. Timurlane's empire, like his architecture, became too big, too overstretched and ultimately crumbled from within.

The best story is every guide's favourite. An inscription on Timurlane's mausoleum warned that anyone who disturbed the great Khan's grave would unleash war on the land. In 1941 Soviet archaeologists opened up the cracked jade tomb that had sat in the Samarkand necropolis for five hundred and fifty years. Inside they found the perfectly preserved body of a short man, with Mongol features, who was lame on his right side. Flecks of muscle still clung to his body, and a dark moustache still whisped across his lips. Within a few days Hitler launched Operation Barbarossa, the invasion of Russia. True story.

It is a credit to the Soviets that the buildings have been so meticulously restored. By the end of the nineteenth century they were little more than crumbling ruins. Many of the domes had collapsed, the minarets fallen in on themselves, tiles and mosaics carried away. But the Soviets went about the renovation with vigour and their work is magnificent. Once again the buildings gleam with the reflection of bright mosaics, particularly the necropolis, which has stood for millennia, stretching back to before Timur's time. Even Genghis Khan's troops refused to touch it.

The restoration of Samarkand was so stunning it forced me to reassess my thoughts on Khiva. If Khiva had looked as ruined as pre-restoration Samarkand, would I have gone there at all?

I wish I had stayed longer. But as ever we were at the whim of immigration officials, who seemed determined not to issue us with decent length visas. So after just one night we left for the short trip to the Tajik border.

Chaos Theory

Chaos Theory: A water vole farts in the Thames, and tsunamis strike the coast of Fiji. Or something like that. A small opportunity missed or a detail overlooked had consequences stretching far into our trip.

Our water vole was the Baku-Turkmenbashi ferry. If that had taken the twelve hours it was meant to, rather than the four days it did, we would have got to Turkmenistan earlier and had time to make repairs and get out of the country without overstaying our visas. That would have saved us five days and a few hundred dollars. The delay impacted on our Uzbek visas, leaving us just six days in the country. You could spend six days in Samarkand alone. In the end we probably stayed a night too long in Bukhara, maybe even Khiva—we should have pushed on to the wonders of Samarkand earlier. Tashkent, Central Asia's main city, got missed out all together.

Perhaps if we'd not bargained so hard at the Baku port we would have got onto the earlier ferry. It left twelve hours before ours and may have ended up saving us a week. But I guess there is no planning for these circumstances.

We arrived in Turkmenistan on 31 August. By 15 September we had covered just a couple of thousand kilometres. Constantly, whenever we hit the road, something went wrong. A car would break down, mostly Gunther, but Fez had trouble too. It seemed that we could only drive for an hour before a major stoppage and I don't remember doing a decent ten-hour journey in the right direction. We ran out of gas, we ran out of water, we took a wrong turn, we broke down, we found a spot for a swim.

We left Uzbekistan on the last day of our visas, having barely spent any time in the country, and were now probably running about a week behind our loose schedule, despite all our efforts to catch up.

There were certain personal restraints on time. OJ and Tony P had promised loved ones that they would be home by the end of November and Zsofi needed to get back to Budapest around the same time so she could study for exams. Time is also money, and Megan was running out. For these reasons it was important not to get too bogged down.

But there were also official factors. We had our visas for Russia, which would be expensive and time consuming to replace. And we were well into the two-month process of applying for our China visas. So we had pretty set windows to get through Russia and China, and we were falling behind. We needed to make some time up, get some miles under our belt and claw back at our schedule.

In front of us stood the greatest physical barrier we had yet faced—the great jagged wall of mountains that is home to the Tajiks, rough, mountain tribes living in the least developed country in the region. For most of the 1970s and 1980s the country was a staging-post for Russia's activity in Afghanistan, and just ten years before it was gripped in a bloody civil war. The long, porous boundary with Afghanistan was home to rebels, smugglers and warlords, the infrastructure in the mountains was harshly underdeveloped and opportunities for help, mechanical or medical, would be few and far between.

The route we hoped to take through the country was over one of the world's great mountain ranges, one that no Trabant had ever tackled—the Pamirs. Nobody had any idea how the Trabbis would cope with the steep gradients we expected to encounter, or the extreme elevations, with some passes over 4,000m high.

Despite the challenges that loomed in the mountains on our horizon, spirits were high. It had been refreshing to do some genuine sightseeing in Uzbekistan, and there was a welcome lack of paperwork at border control as we entered Tajikistan.

Our new visas gave us a fortnight in the country, but we hoped to be through it in nine or ten days. Our optimism couldn't have been more misplaced.

4

THE PAMIR MOUNTAINS
Tajikistan
13 September – 26 September 2007

Q) Why do all Trabant drivers go to heaven?

A) Because they've already experienced hell on earth.

GUNTHER'S REPRIEVE

We waited for ten minutes then turned back to see what had happened to the others. Gunther was pulled onto the side of the road, a dark puddle spreading into the dust beneath him. OJ and Carlos were emptying out the boot.

OJ was angry: "We're ditching the Mercedes. The oil pan's gone again."

The road we were following into the mountains was rough, unpaved, and littered with loose stones and pebbles. One of the bigger chunks of rock had struck the underside of the overloaded, low-riding Mercedes, tearing a gash in the exposed oil pan and leaving a dark trail along the track.

"I'm fed up with it. We're getting rid of this piece of shit," OJ said through gritted teeth as he flung something out of the boot.

My first thought was agreement. This was the third time the oil pan had cracked in a month, and the repair normally cost us at least a day. It always happened on the same sort of road, the boulder-strewn, cratered paths through sandy deserts or rocky mountains. We probably should have driven slower on them.

But it wasn't just the oil pan that was giving us trouble. The windshield smashed in Romania, although that was entirely our fault, and we'd had to remove the remains of the LPG tank that Gabor, our Budapest mechanic, forgot to take out. More time, more money. The hydraulic suspension was a nightmare, often refusing to go up, which limited the Merkin to about 10kph. Sometimes we had to jack up the rear and rev the engine for a while to get it to lift. And the Red Baron, which handled like a large boat, had had more punctures than all the Trabbis put together. Whatever we called it, Gunther, the Red Baron, the Merkin, the Great Gherkin, it was a disaster magnet.

But old Gunther cost us just $3,000 and was hopelessly overloaded. We had filled it with enough spare parts to start our own junkyard, all manner of

The Mercedes, characteristically broken down

odds and ends that I would never fully understand. Huge arced chunks of metal riveted to rusty plates on springs. Small, loose bolts in plastic dishes with light bulbs and bent washers. Greasy rods wrapped in plastic bags, tangled with dusty sheets and frayed rope. It was Tony's domain and in those early days we mostly left it to him to organise. He used a thoroughly personalised filing system indecipherable to even the most sideways thinking cryptologist. Carrying a junkyard across the world in a 1979 Mercedes estate was almost as stupid as trying to get three Trabants across.

"Maybe we should have called this Merkin Mission," suggested Megan.

Lovey was a bit more realistic about ditching it. The Merc is meant to be our workhorse, he explained. If the Trabbis were carrying all the extra weight they would probably be breaking down regularly too. This was a typical Trabant Trek meeting, on the side of the road, in the middle of nowhere and with no warning or time for extended contemplation we were going to make a decision that would affect the whole project.

Although disagreements could get quite heated over small details, what to eat or where to stay, when it came to the big calls a dispassionate logic tended to settle on the group. There was generally a mature and reasoned discussion, one of the few things we got right, and I think people felt pretty comfortable putting their point across.

Factored into our Merkin decision was the Pamir Highway, the next great test for our motorcade. And, of course, the Pamir Mountains. As the Indian subcontinent pushes at the belly of Asia, the ripple and shock forces up the land right into the heart of the continent. The tectonic plates crack, split and push skyward, creating epic mountains. Some of the world's highest ranges collide in the Pamir region, the Tian Shan to the north-east, the Hindu Kush to the west and the Himalayas to the south-east. It was the roof of the world according to locals, and it felt like it. Even through gaps in the low foothills we were struggling to pass, you could see mile upon mile of peaks.

The highway itself is a feat of Soviet engineering, the second highest highway on the planet, built to link a remote outpost of their empire. It scales passes 4,600m high, rising and dipping through freezing deserts and snowy plateaus in the sky. The valley kingdoms are so isolated, so remote, that they have entirely different languages.

We had been told that the highway was not in terrible condition, but warned that parts were incredibly steep, perhaps too steep for our overloaded Trabbis. The East Germans never imagined people would be taking the cars far above Europe's highest roads, almost higher than Mont Blanc, and we couldn't be sure how the engines would respond to the atmosphere's thinning oxygen supply. Tony thought he could adjust the carburettors to let more air in, but no one really knew. We did know that a serious breakdown in the Pamirs could be disastrous, and without the Mercedes we would have even fewer spare parts for repairs.

In the end we compromised—we would keep the Mercedes but ditch a load of weight to try and reduce the amount of breakdowns. There was no doubt we didn't need all the spares, something we blamed Gabor for. But I just knew we'd need something that we threw away, probably just when we got to the other side of the next mountain.

I tried to find some shade near Fez while Tony and OJ worked on patching up Gunther. Tony was still very much chief mechanic, but OJ had been his willing apprentice for a while and could do a lot of the work. Plus he had The Strength of a Thousand Men special ability, always useful when working on cars. Lovey was very proficient, too, but I rarely got my hands dirty. I could change the tyres or check the filters, but I hadn't really got too involved with the mechanics. I wanted to learn, but there always seemed to be three people working on a problem, and any more was too many. And my lack of knowledge meant it was sometimes quicker just for Tony or OJ to do it. Did you know that Americans call spanners "wrenches"?

We stopped there for four hours while Tony improvised a patch for the oil pan out of steel putty, but by now everyone was quite used to these unplanned breaks, and books came out, music went on, someone got the gas burner going and set about cooking the salty noodle soup that formed a large part of our roadside diet.

Sweet Home Alabama came on, and I overheard OJ announcing: "You know, this old song still makes me proud to be American."

Johnny America sitting in a camping chair with his bulging muscles, wearing his Yankee hat; Zsofi cleaning her face with wet wipes in her daily battle against the grime; Megan sitting on the bonnet of Fez reading; Carlos pottering incessantly. I was stripped down to my pants due to the extreme heat and squinting into my battered laptop. What a strange and motley crew we were.

THE ANZOB PASS

Our caravan was going ridiculously slowly as we crawled the Mercedes delicately along the rugged trail. We were following a winding river valley, cut deep into the mountainside and flanked with shingle cliffs. Everywhere the rock face was coming away, and hundreds of Chinese labourers used diggers to clear the path and dynamite the more threatening boulders. On a few occasions we had to wait while a man in a JCB shifted tons of rubble from the road.

The pace was becoming frustrating and I was annoyed. I kept getting ahead of the group, then waiting on the side of the road. When they caught up I'd race off again. Finally Lovey lent out of his window and shouted, "Dan, just go ahead. We'll meet you in Dushanbe."

Thank god for that. Megan and I would go on to the capital, scout the place and find a hotel—maybe put a brew on. It was only about 140 kilometres, a few hours, no big deal. Easy.

We made it through the crumbling rock formations into a fertile river valley where the once wide waters had deposited beaches of rounded, grey pebbles, threaded with streams and canals. The water was heavy with minerals, looking chalky blue, and when we dipped our feet in at a ford we found it icy cold—straight off the glaciers. We splashed about a bit, burying our water bottles under boulders in the stream, hoping to chill them.

A jeep from the Red Crescent pulled up. There was a German inside who looked shocked to see a Trabant out in the Central Asian mountains. He didn't seem pleased. I would have been delighted to find a Morris Minor out there, but he had a stern demeanour and kept shaking his head.

"What are you doing here with a Trabbi?" he asked in strict English, "this is not safe." I explained our mission and his brow furrowed.

"This is not a good idea."

By now I'd heard that from so many people, the Red Crescent would just have to join the list of doubters. We asked about the Pamir Highway.

"The Pamir is very high. This could be a big problem for your cars. The road is ok, but very steep. You are going to Dushanbe? The next pass is very high, very difficult, maybe the worst in all Tajikistan," he told us, "It will be a good test for you. You should approach it during daylight. It is not safe at night."

With his warning fresh in our ears we stocked up on water, petrol and Snickers bars at a town made entirely of mud and rocks. The Anzob Pass peaks at 3,372m, and although it was late in the day, we began the ascent.

Fez didn't sound good. The engine was throaty, guttural. We needed high revs in first just to make it up the steep path. He began to lose power, so I got out and popped the bonnet thinking maybe the exhaust had come loose and was making that god awful coughing sound. I couldn't see anything so cleaned out the air filter, let the engine cool for a bit, and we carried on, spiralling up the craggy grey-brown slopes.

But the revs got higher with even less traction, I felt the steering shift. Suddenly turning right became incredibly light but turning left was stiff and awkward. Then Fez just stopped. The engine continued to rev, but to no avail. The wheels weren't turning. It was the same symptoms as in Turkmenistan and I guessed that the transaxle had gone again. The last time it happened it was not a quick repair job.

I went to the front and looked under the bonnet. Then Megan and I stood on one side of the car and wondered what had happened. She circled around and then I heard her laughing with a strange mixture of shock and despair. She was standing on the opposite side of the car, hiding her face, afraid to look.

"I think I've found the problem," came her voice, muffled by her hands, "the wheel has come off."

It was true. The front right wheel was no longer attached to the vehicle. That could be the problem. This was the same wheel that Tony had removed back in Khiva last week. I remember him saying to me: "Just tell me if it sounds like it's gonna fall off."

Well it did.

It was perfect timing. We were high up the mountains, the sun was setting and within a few minutes we were smothered in darkness and the temperature began to drop. We had to laugh. No tools, no torch, not even a box of matches. Awesome. We were 3,000m up the worst pass in Tajikistan without two sticks to rub together. We ravaged our backpacks for warm clothes and resolved to hitch down to a cabin we had seen and wait for the others.

The shack was the home of two young boys. I couldn't quite work out what they were doing there. They seemed to share similar thoughts about us, but they served us a delightful selection of fat and chewy mutton. Fat is a delicacy in Central Asia and every time I picked at the plate in the hope of finding a piece of nicely barbecued meat I seemed to come up with a huge lump of lard. Decorum insisted I ate it. The boys didn't seem like they had too much to offer, and we were grateful for what we got.

They set up a bed for us out in the cold mountain night. The cabin was built around a stream that had been funnelled into a hose. The spot must have been well known because throughout the night truckers stopped to fill their bottles and dowse their overheating engines or brakes.

Every time someone approached I woke up, protective of my bag of highly valuable but completely useless electronics. I remember coming to in a daze, being shaken by a dirty man in a greasy jacket demanding that I open up the cabin.

"It's not open," I muttered, but he continued to hammer at the door until it began to give. I saw one of the boys open up and reason with him, then he left. The same thing happened again a few hours later and the disturbances fractured what little sleep I found.

At some point in the night the other Trabbis arrived. We had left them a note attached to Fez and they came back down the mountain to find us. They said they almost missed the car in the darkness. That would have been bad—us stuck on the mountain thinking they were on the west slopes, them on the east side, thinking we'd gone ahead to the capital. The diagnosis was just as bad.

"Fez is fucked." Thanks Lovejoy. "Do you have the piece?"

"Err… piece?"

"The bolt."

Oh dear. And of course, the job would be a lot easier with one of the A-frames we had thrown away earlier that day. Nothing could be done that night, so the rest of the team decided to head back down the mountain to find food and shelter, while we'd try and do repairs and attempt the pass again in the morning. I opted to stay up in the hills for an uncomfortable night of dozing and half dreams. It was freezing up there; I only had a thin cover and shivered uncontrollably. I curled my back up against Megan's in the vain hope of getting some shelter from her snug arctic sleeping bag.

As a place to kip it was one of the stranger ones, but we managed, and in the morning, as the sun broke over the peaks to warm my bones and lift my chill, I was treated to some of the best views yet. I watched a huge bird of prey fly low overhead, grazing the trail and circling the thermals, gradually ascending as the warm air lifted its wings. We were in the Anzob Mountains according to my hosts, though the guidebook called them the Fan Mountains. Truly it felt like the roof of the world, and I told Megan that I could stay up there—maybe open my own café, I joked, pointing at an old ruined stone shack along the track.

Around eleven o'clock a passing family told us they had seen the Mercedes on the side of the road four kilometres away, leaking oil. So we hitched down and met the others. The Mercedes had broken again on the previous night's descent. It was now patched up, but all the cars had really struggled with the incline. I went up in Dante with Tony to check out Fez, and it was so steep at points that I had to jump out and push the car to help it up there. As Dante's passenger door was sealed shut to counter its tendency to swing open at random, I had to contort myself through the window as the car was moving. I managed this extraordinary feat with grace, agility and only minor bruising.

A new plan was formed. A group of us would get a lift with some truckers all the way to Dushanbe. That would help reduce the weight in the cars and the forward party could sort out a hotel. There was no point in eight of us staying up there on the side of the mountain. So Megan, Zsofi, Brady and I went on with all the bags we could carry.

Even the big Russian Kamaz lorries were struggling on the steep slopes, and one of our chosen carriages could only take one passenger, so I jumped in alone.

It may have only been a hundred or so kilometres, but it took seven hours. I shared the cabin with two local men who were alternating the driving. One was everything I'd expected of a Tajik—thin, aquiline, Iranian features and a long, slender nose, with wide, close-set eyes. The other looked whiter, more European.

They shared chewing tobacco between them the whole trip. I was told it was also mixed with heroin or opium from the mountains, but it seemed to keep them going. On their recommendation I tried a small amount and it made me feel happy but quite sick. To my alarm I was asked to move over for three hours of the descent while one of them put all his weight into holding the gear stick in second. He explained to me in charades that if he let go the transmission would pop out of second and into neutral. Then we would go straight down the mountain, he added, with some dramatic flourishes.

They were an interesting double act. One of them would ask me questions in Russian, I would answer as best I could, and the Iranian-type would transfer my garbled Russian message to his partner, no doubt convoluting it as much as I had done to the original question.

At one point I was presented with a glove-box-hot apple that worms had at the very least tasted. Bollocks, I thought, as I bit in—that means I have to share my Snickers.

ON CRAP

When on the road you crap in a lot of strange places, particularly in the mountains, where there seem to be unique rules on the etiquette of excretion. Where in England you might nip for a piss if you were caught short, in Tajikistan you will find human faeces. There was shit everywhere. I'd heard that some Afghans used sand to wipe, and it may have been the same in Tajikistan, for rarely were these human stools topped with toilet paper, nor were there pans of water easily to hand.

This blasé approach to bathroom functions did have its positives. Often it was nicer to drop off out in the open, rather than squatting over one of the festering, stinking shit pits. But other than the pungent aroma of the pits of doom, I never found the squat too much of an issue. For Carlos it was a different story. The Spaniard was normally pretty light on his feet, but for some reason he found it impossible to squat down on his haunches. It was some kind of physical irregularity. Many times I heard the sound of Pedro stumbling about nearby, trying to stay upright with his trousers round his ankles and his arse dripping.

I had often thought of the valve type flush toilet as one of Britain's greatest gifts to the world. But the light relief provided by Carlos' attempts to squat forced me to reconsider. Why miss out on all that comedy?

WILL WE, WON'T WE IN DUSHANBE?

In Dushanbe chewing gum was money. Through some quirk of deflation, there were few low denomination coins in circulation. So you received Wrigley's Orbit in lieu of change at most shops—in the supermarket the cashier had a tray full of it. I was disappointed to learn the currency could only be exchanged one way when they refused to let me use a packet of faded Juicy Fruit to pay for a beer.

To nineteenth-century Russians, the mountainous Pamir region of khanates and tribes was a piece in the Great Game, another step towards India. In the 1930s the Soviets kindly created a full republic, inventing Tajikistan, and for the next sixty years propped the new nation up and used it as a staging post for their war in Afghanistan.

The rugged land was the Central Asian country worst affected by the collapse of the Soviet Union—high unemployment and infant mortality, a reliance on imported food, no real exports—and within a few years civil war raged, pitting Islamist rebels against pro-government forces from the northern city of Khojend, Tajikistan's richest city and long the power base of the ruling elite.

The war ended in 1997, with compromise and the promise of political representation for the rebels. Since then the UN and the Aga Khan Foundation had supported the isolated mountain towns, which were slowly becoming more self-sufficient.

Dushanbe, the capital, was the most Westernised city we had visited since Baku, with a fried chicken place, bowling alley, discotheque and, strangely, an Ecuadorian restaurant. (I think it had something to do with the UN presence.)

A fountain-filled square opposite the opera house served as the city's centrepiece, and during the warm evenings it would fill with locals sitting out to relax with a drink. Among a strange-looking mix of Persian and Russian I saw two fearsome old babushkas wrapped in layers of scarves and throws knocking back Russian lager together, while nearby a dark, thin-featured man with a beard drank brown tea and smoked incessantly.

One afternoon a dancing bear was in the square and it was a pretty disturbing sight. The bear wasn't dancing so much as rocking in the way you expect of mental patients in straight jackets—side to side its muzzled snout swung while it beat its paws in a dark rhythm. Its owner, a tall, bony man wrapped in traditional robes, prodded the bear with a stick to manoeuvre it. I tried to take a surreptitious photo, but the owner was wily. He saw me and started shouting for money as I turned and pretended not to hear.

Later that day I again crossed the square, and, on its owner's command, the huge bear reared up on its hind legs and ran at me. I was sure the old man was getting his own back and I discovered that being charged by a seven-foot mountain bear is one of life's scarier experiences, but I did the best I could: let out a high-pitched scream and legged it.

We based ourselves at a hotel nearby. The Trabbis arrived about six hours behind us, and the next day we began preparing for the Pamir Highway.

"No. It is not possible for you to get across the mountains so quickly. I think five days in a good car. In yours…" The tour guide's Teutonic voice tailed off. "Last month we had a group of Italians stuck in the mountains for a week when they broke down. They had to get a part shipped from Europe. But they had all the right equipment and they had a satellite phone… Do you have a satellite phone?"

Carlos and I looked at each other. We had a battered Nokia, which had yet to find any signal in Tajikistan.

"No."

The guide shrugged as if the argument was won. We were sitting in his two-room office, the walls pinned with maps of the Pamirs. He looked European, spoke with an almost German accent and claimed to know the Pamirs as well as anyone. Carlos and I were responsible for finding the best way to the Pamir Highway and getting the necessary permission to travel through the autonomous region of Gorno-Badakhshan, through which the highway cut.

We asked about an alternative route, a quick, straight path through the centre of the country, which seemed the most direct way into Kyrgyzstan, our next stop.

The guide laughed. "No, no, you don't go over there, that's rebel territory— the area is full of the militants who lost the war. They wouldn't hurt you, but they would take dollars off you all the time. They will dress up in police uniforms and demand money. Anyway the border is closed to foreigners."

He frowned and flattened out some papers on his desk, "I don't think you have planned your stay in Tajikistan very well."

Carlos caught my eye and grinned. We hadn't really planned it at all.

The guide stood up and pointed at a map on the wall. "If you do not do the Pamirs then you must go north, there is a route out of the country," he said, tracing a line with his finger. "It will take three days. You will have to go back over the Anzob Pass. But the borders between Uzbekistan, Tajikistan and Kyrgyzstan are disputed. It is a mess. The Uzbeks have claimed strips of land, some of them only a few kilometres across. But you still need a visa to pass these areas. So maybe you need a new Uzbek visa—or maybe you can drive around the Uzbek land, I don't know. I can offer no guarantees about this route. But with your schedule, the Pamirs are not possible."

Carlos and I headed back with the options heavy on our minds. Heading north would take three days, but would mean missing one of the highlights of the trip, and tackling Anzob again—not something we fancied. But taking on the Pamirs would probably take six days if all went well. Far longer if we had problems. We had thirteen days until our Kazakh visas expired, so we needed to get out of Tajikistan, cross Kyrgyzstan, then bomb through the Kazakh steppe and into Russia. Maybe 2,500 kilometres of mostly bad roads, many through the mountains, in thirteen days. In a normal car, no problem. But it had taken us two months to get 10,000km by Trabant and much of that was on good European roads.

Overstaying our Kazakh visa would certainly have financial consequences, but it would also leave us even less time to cross Russia, an already challenging 1,000km of unknown and rarely used Siberian roads—in a week.

After working through the scenarios, Carlos and I reluctantly agreed that we couldn't attempt the Pamirs. With our schedule it was just about possible to cross them, but everything would have to run like clockwork. And to date things had hardly run like clockwork. Maybe more like a maladjusted sundial. During a solar eclipse.

We put the decision making process to the rest of the group, who were disappointed but understood our argument. "The question is," concluded OJ, "do we want to do the Pamir Highway, or do we want to get to Cambodia? I want to get to Cambodia."

And we all agreed.

Later that evening the weariness I had been carrying in my bones for the past few days turned into a fever, so I threw on all the clothes in my backpack and wrapped myself up in bed to sweat it out.

I was woken by Lovejoy. He was excitable.

"We can do the Pamirs. I've been speaking with these Swiss people, they've just come off the mountains—they said it was easy. It's only two days to Khorog, and then two more to the border. It'll take four days."

I felt terrible, delirious, sweaty, aching, shivering.

"What car were they driving?"

"They were in a big 4x4."

"Right."

"But they said the roads were fine."

I was exhausted and in no mood to argue.

"Dude," I offered in resignation, "I really want to do the Pamirs. If it's possible then I'm up for it," I said, not realising the consequences of the words.

I had cast my vote.

That night Lovey went round lobbying and the next day I lay in bed feeling bad while the rest of the group sorted out passes for the Highway and worked on the cars. We were ready to go by seven, but Lovey still needed to work on some footage that he wanted Brady to take home with him to LA.

Brady had decided not to attempt the mountains and was flying out from Dushanbe. So, in typical Trabant Trek fashion, we didn't even leave till midnight. We had eleven days to get to Russia.

GOODBYE, GUNTHER

If we were going to make it across the Pamirs in six days we needed everything to run smoothly. So within a few hours of leaving Dushanbe, Dante broke—the clutch plate ground to pieces.

We parked up by the road and slept. TP, OJ, Lovey and Carlos dealt with it the next day. I incurred the unspoken anger of the group by lying around in Fez and dozing. I still felt rough, and there were plenty of hands helping out, but in these situations I guess you have to at least make a gesture. And I didn't. At 4pm we set off again, already two-thirds of a day behind.

I led in Fez, asking the bemused locals for directions. A bearded man on a horse with a long stick guided us some of the way, our progress so slow that he kept overtaking. In one hamlet I pulled up beside a hunched old man wearing long robes. He had been staring at us intensely.

"Khorog?" I asked.

"Khorog?" he spat back, then his craggy face broke into a mad toothless cackle. "Khorog? Khahahahkahahakahaha," and he waved us down a dirt track.

Our route took us along the Pyanj River, the border between Afghanistan and Tajikistan, and as we made our stop-start progress the Afghanis gazed at us over the water. Just a hundred meters of milky blue rapids divided us, but it could have been a hundred years. On the Afghan bank, laden donkeys plodded along rough paths cut into the mountainside, the trail propped up in places by piles of uncut shingle. Many of the men wore traditional robes and had cloths wrapped around their heads. They supported their weight with crooked shanks and returned to homes made from piles of boulders loosely wattled together.

On our side we drove along patches of semi-paved road, passing 4x4s, people carriers and Russian Kamaz lorries. Many of the kids wore football shirts, mostly Real Madrid, and went to school in whitewashed buildings with corrugated roofs courtesy of the Aga Khan Foundation.

The Pyanj flows fast, coming quickly down from the high peaks, and the riverbed forms impressive and noisy rapids, swarming with battling eddies and

Tony, Zsofi, OJ and Lovey on the Pyanj River

counter currents. During a quest for engine oil I asked a local if it was possible to swim across. He held an imaginary rifle up to his shoulder and let off a few phantom rounds into my chest. It would be great to touch Afghanistan. I wasn't sure why, but we all had a strong urge to go to the place. I settled for throwing rocks onto the Afghan side of the stream and sharing cheers and waves with the Afghans I could attract.

The roads were in a shocking condition and just 20km into the second day's drive Ziggy started having battery problems. We made ragged progress and ended up towing him to the nearby town of Cigar. Tony, OJ and Lovey spent a long time looking at the car, but they decided we needed a new battery, and it was getting too dark to tow the thing on the rough, cliff-hugging roads. So again we bedded down to sleep on the trail, having covered just 30km all day.

Cigar had a surreal stretch of perfect paving running through it—a stark contrast to the narrow, winding tracks we had been following through the mountains, and we hoped the road might stay like that for a few hundred kilometres.

The next morning we found a new battery for Ziggy, breakfasted, filled up on petrol and got back into the cars with a sense of hope that we could really push on for Khorog. It was going to be a great day.

But within a few minutes of leaving we were back on the potholed paths, ripe for breakdowns, and ten kilometres later the clutch went on the Mercedes. We got a tow back into town and spent another day and night with a mechanic getting it fixed.

The work cost us $40, but we ate well, slept out under the bright stars, and most of us were in good spirits when we headed off early the next morning. We joked that our new target wasn't Khorog, but to get more than 30km in one sitting—something we'd yet to achieve in the three days we'd been trying for the Pamirs.

An hour later, and just 20km on, the oil pan went again on the Mercedes. Maybe it was the beauty of the scenery, or the decent night's sleep, or the fresh mountain air and cool streams, but we took it well and Tony spent the afternoon patching the thing up while we sat about.

We set off again that afternoon, four days into what should have been a twenty-hour drive, wondering if we would ever make it out of the mountains.

A white 4x4 from the UN passed us as we were push-starting Ziggy, which was still struggling with battery problems. The UN personnel were in the area as part of the World Food Programme and were checking that local schools were handing out the amount of food they claimed. Their car's exhaust had been redirected through a chimney that towered high above the engine—an ominous warning of how high the rivers could get. I asked one of the UN guys for some guidance with our route. "All good" was the verdict, the river fords were passable. What about the proximity to Afghanistan?

"It's safe. There used to be fighters coming over until '97, but after that none."

In 1997 Tajikistan's civil war ended. The rebels, who lost, had been supported by the Mujahadeen in Afghanistan. The Afghans had flooded across the porous national divide to provide men and arms. Now they do the same to smuggle heroin and opium and Tajikistan is one of the world's biggest confiscators of narcotics.

"There are still mines, though. Don't go off the roads between here and here," he gestured at a large section of the map, "there were a lot laid during the war."

As we wound our way through the valleys we saw the detritus of conflict. The odd burned out armoured personnel carrier, tank tracks and abandoned military installations. Every few miles we would pass another pair of soldiers; ridiculously young lads, fresh faced without hints of stubble, carrying machine guns and patrolling the border.

We managed just ten painful kilometres before another setback. The Mercedes' clutch went again and during the inspection Tony noticed the oil pan was still leaking. This time it was too much. Tony started hitting the car with a branch. He had hated the thing ever since we got it, but had resolutely nursed it across half of Eurasia. But those last few days had been its final chance; Tajikistan proved the better of it. This time we were all in agreement—we had to abandon Gunther.

In retrospect old Gunther probably wasn't the best car in which to attempt the Pamir Highway. As Lovey said, "This thing was built for German families to drive along the Autobahn."

So not ideal for attempting some of the highest, most rugged roads on the planet. But still, we felt let down. We'd tried so hard to get the Red Baron across and it had cost us so many days and so much money. But we couldn't keep going; it was slowing us down too much. So we decided to strip it of anything useful and leave it by the road.

It was a strange situation, parked precariously at a passing point in a road that looked chiselled into the huge cliff face. The river gushed noisily fifteen metres below us, and every hour another Kamaz would squeeze past.

Night fell quickly, making the job of unloading and repacking all the cars on a precipice that little bit more exciting. To take the spare Trabbi parts we needed from Gunther we had to throw out everything else that wasn't strictly necessary as we reckoned that overloaded Trabbis were more likely to break down and less likely to make it over the mountains.

We had a mass clear-out, dumping a huge pile of stuff: camping gear, books, spare parts, odd tools, cooking equipment and anything else that had survived the previous ditching sessions. Zsofi's giant rucksack was lucky to make it. Then we stripped Gunther—battery, alternator, fuses, seat belts for towing, petrol, rear view mirror—we salvaged all we could.

After hours of organising, repacking, discarding and debating, we were ready. We said our goodbyes to Gunther, held a mock wake, closed the doors, removed the number plates and left the keys in the ignition. It would be of use to someone round there.

We pulled the cars into formation—Dante, Fez, then Ziggy—finally it was just the three brothers, a new era for the Trek. We revved up and pulled away.

But Ziggy didn't move. He started, stalled, then died. The new battery was kaput. We weren't going anywhere.

What can you do? Grin, bear it. Half of us went to sleep, half of us worked on installing a new alternator. I was in the sleeping half.

We woke early the next morning, did final checks, and set off minus one Mercedes. It was strange looking behind and not seeing the lumbering beast following us. I'd love to know where Gunther is now. Whenever we went to get it repaired someone would offer to buy it from us for a pittance, so I'm sure it ended up being put to use.

Mornings in the mountains were always cold, but as the sun stretched out and the shadows retreated I began removing jumpers and settling into the view from the back of Fez. Megan was driving, we were leading and the ride was terrible. We hit some almighty bumps, two in particular that flung the car up in the air, probably the worst bumps we'd ever hit. At one point I heard a loud, twanging snap from beneath me. I assumed it was the springs in the seat going and didn't mention it.

We kept getting ahead of the convoy, and Megan would throw a mini hissy fit. She'd stop the car, look angrily behind her and snarl, "Where the fuck are they? Why can't they keep up today? Why are they driving like grandmas?"

She wasn't in the best of moods. Her lack of composure when things weren't going right was probably the thing that wound me up the most. I suggested she was driving a little fast and we should try to keep together.

"I'm not even driving that fast," she snapped, "and you can talk."

I had had my own moments of impatience. All that time stuck in the mountains had begun to get to people. We'd been living off green tea, stale bread and soup. No one had washed in days and we were covered in grease and muck from working on the cars, and dust and sand from sleeping on the road. Tony and OJ, who had done the bulk of the maintenance, were caked in a thick coat of grime—they looked like street urchins.

Tony: "I'm not even going to try and wash this shit off. I'll only get dirty again in like two minutes."

During one particularly vicious bump the tail end of Fez's exhaust became detached and for a few hundred metres we used it as an impromptu plough. A couple of minutes later we realised something was up and when TP had a look he saw that Fez's left side had slumped. After a record-breaking 100km stint, the rear left control arm had snapped. Completely sheered in half.

I was pissed off with Megan. I felt she'd been driving recklessly because she was in a mood and, maybe unfairly, decided she'd broken Fez.

We found a welder, but it was a huge break, and Tony was convinced that unless we replaced the entire piece the break would keep reappearing—the sort of niggling injury that really slows you down. Of course, there was no chance of finding a new Trabant piece out there in the mountains. I was angry.

I wandered into a nearby field to try and draw out my frustration, and watched a cow tied to a stick eating a neat circle into the grass. OJ found me, filmed me having a moan, and then we sat beneath the shade of a pear tree. A woman from the farm came over and offered us some freshly washed tomatoes. A few minutes later her toddling son came out with a tray of walnuts and then a loaf of tasty, thick bread. Tony turned up and we sat and ate using greasy, oily hands. The woman's husband came home and insisted we step inside for tea. She put on a wonderful spread of dried berries, almonds, biscuits and toffees, with more bread, tomatoes, walnuts and tea.

They wanted nothing, they didn't even join us to eat, just saw dirty, unkempt foreigners and did what they could to ease our burden and show their hospitality. The gesture filled me with warmth, lifting my spirits and again I wondered at the kindness we'd been graced with for so long. How would I have reacted if I'd found three filthy Tajiks sitting under a tree in my garden?

The weld was done quickly and we made it to Khorog. It had taken five days to get 400km. A demoralising nightmare and without a doubt the hardest leg of the trip to that point. We had to ditch a car and a load of equipment to make it, and we hadn't even reached the Pamir Highway. How would we handle that, especially with even fewer parts and even more weight, in the unforgiving, isolated Pamir Mountains, where the passes reach three miles high and the temperature drops well below freezing?

We booked into a guesthouse and took it in turns to use the washroom. There was hot water in a bucket which you used a pan to scoop onto you, but

The fleet crosses Tajikistan

after so long covered in filth it was very welcome. Later we ate mountain food, made plans and got some rest. In the morning we would head for the Pamir Highway.

THE BREAK UP

The next morning we stocked up on supplies at the bazaar. Murghab, the highest town in Tajikistan at 3,650m, was 300km away and there was very little in between. Marco Polo had complained bitterly about the cold when he crossed the mountains 750 years before us, so I bought a heavy blanket for warmth along with water, thick bread and cured sausage in case we got stuck some-where. Someone came up with the bright idea of sending our bags ahead in a van to lighten the load in the Trabbis, then we headed off in caravan, one Mercedes short of a full trek.

The Pamirs had loomed large in our consciousness for so long and my head was full of questions. Would our cars be able to make the inclines? Did we really have the time to tackle the mountains? What if we broke down up there? How would the carburettors cope with the reduced oxygen in the air?

The unknowns added to the excitement as we drove through a warm sunny

107

lunchtime, beginning on the low foothills leading to the first pass, a gentle warm-up on the nursery slopes. The road was wide, well-paved and undulating gradually when, thirty kilometres out of Khorog and with no warning, there was a loud bang from under Fez. The car listed to the left and the sound of tyre on chassis filled the cabin as we ground to a halt.

Thirty kilometres. Thirty kilometres. The distance hung on our horizon like an angry dust storm—the near unbreakable limit of a day's travel by Trabant in Tajikistan.

Megan and I jumped out to take a look. The rear left wheel was jutting strangely into the wheel arch. Megan was on her hands and knees, muttering profanities as she investigated under the car and waited for the others to realise we were missing and turn back. When the formation had assembled we got the car up on a jack and removed the wheel. The reinforced metal bar that held the control arm in place was sheered in half, a recurrence of the injury we had welded the day before.

"The guy did an ok job," Tony said of the welder, "but it's a bad break. I still think we might need a new piece. We can go back into town and get it welded properly, maybe try and get it reinforced, but this is probably going to keep happening."

We had ditched the replacement part back on the Turkmen border three weeks ago. "It is almost impossible to break one of these," Tony had confidently asserted at the time, "they have been reinforced."

"Maybe we should go back to Turkmenistan and get the piece?" Carlos suggested with a smile, to widespread derision. We discussed getting a new part. There were a few people in Hungary who would ship it to us, but where to? Bishkek in Kyrgyzstan? That meant getting over the mountains. Dushanbe? That meant going back on ourselves. And how long would it take?

Either way, our Tajik visas had just four days to run and we had learned in Turkmenistan that the former Soviet republics of Central Asia are pretty per-nickety about visas. Lovey confirmed our suspicions: "The Swiss people I spoke to in Dushanbe had overstayed their visas when they were in Murghab and they had to go all the way back to Dushanbe to sort it out. It was going to take them two weeks to do."

Back to Dushanbe for a two week wait was a nightmare scenario that would jeopardise our China visa's fixed entry date and possibly the whole trip.

"So maybe we should dump Fez and carry on," OJ suggested.

Adding to his line of argument was the dodgy bearing on Fez's front right wheel. It hadn't been properly fixed since the wheel fell off on the Anzob Pass, and despite multiple attempts Tony had been unable to find a new bearing to fit. He freely admitted that we were driving Fez until the wheel fell off again, but he couldn't give us a decent approximation of when that would happen. From our previous experiences I thought it destined to occur as far from civilisation as physically possible, when we were low on food and petrol, at night, in subzero temperatures, with no cash left in a country that thinks Mastercard is a cotton derivative and we'd found a rare stretch of road that you could actually hit 70kph on.

The problem with dumping Fez was that, without the Mercedes, we would be down to two cars. Dante could take two people, Ziggy three, but there were seven of us. Megan knew she was running out of money and probably wouldn't be with us much longer. But we would still be one space short.

OJ: "So someone either goes home or follows by public transport."

So we draw straws to see who drops out? To me that was a horrifying scenario. It was unrealistic to think anyone could follow the Trek by public transport—the Trek operated in its own little time zone and it would be nigh on impossible to keep track of.

"Unless anyone here is seriously considering dropping out anyway, I don't think we should consider that an option," I ventured. I would rather ride in the boot of Ziggy for the next two months than have to fly home. I would prefer to spend a month in the mountains working on Fez than face the short straw.

But even if we got the car welded that night and set off the second it was done, making it to the border before our visas expired would be a massive gamble. Judging from our previous progress a two-day trip could take us a week.

Eventually we agreed that trying to reach the border was too risky, and we would have to get new visas. Luckily there was a tiny airport in Khorog, so someone could fly back to Dushanbe and get the extensions. There was no point in the remaining six people all sitting it out in Khorog, so we decided that three trekkers and Megan should go ahead by taxi to Kyrgyzstan, taking all the gear they could carry. That would help reduce the weight in the Trabbis, increasing the chance of them making it over the mountains, and also limit the number of people with visa issues.

Two people would stay in Khorog and work on the Trabbis and one person would fly to Dushanbe. Various combinations were experimented with, but eventually we decided the Europeans (Carlos, Zsofi and I) would go ahead with Megan. As chief mechanic, Tony had to stay with the cars, and he chose OJ to stick with him. Lovey would fly to Dushanbe to extend the visas and try to get a new passport for himself, as he was running out of pages.

The decision was made there, on a dusty stretch of road somewhere outside Khorog. We were dividing into Team Europe and Team USA.

There was a strange symmetry to it. We were almost exactly two months into what we hoped would be a four-month trip. We were almost geographically half way, about 12,000km into a 24,000km journey. We'd shed the support vehicle that we felt was holding us back, and after Megan's departure we'd be down to the elite six who planned to go the whole way to Cambodia.

And after two months of trekking, and for most of us two and a half months away from home, we'd enjoy a break from the road, even if it was an enforced lay-off. Team Europe would be spending a week in the Russified Kyrgyz city of Bishkek, while Team USA would have a week in the stunning mountain town of Khorog.

We bought lots of beer and went back to our hostel to discuss the divide and work through a number of potential scenarios for the next few weeks. It was entirely possible that we wouldn't meet up again for a fortnight, even three weeks.

We got drunk and, knowing we were parting, laughed easily and let the pressure of the past few months ebb away. It was a nice reminder of the camaraderie that had developed among us all. I felt happy and sucked away on the grainy, green tobacco-opium powder a trucker had given me near Anzob. You put a pinch of it under your tongue for five minutes, then spit the dregs out. It tasted bitter, nasty and caused the under tongue to throb. It made me feel light-headed, grin inanely, grind my teeth and concentrate on not being sick. Then I dressed up as an explorer using a lamp stand and outdoor rug, complete with walking stick and compass and collapsed in bed.

Driving Ziggy into town the following day to find a bus to Murghab, I was struck by a feeling of loss. There was a chance that I would never drive a Trabant again. I kept thinking that this could be the end of Trabant Trek for Team Europe. The cars may not make it over the mountains. They may break irreparably, or have to turn and head back through the north of the country—both options had been raised the previous night.

But I was also excited to get away from the cars and the mountains; the last week had been a nightmare for everyone. A couple of weeks in Bishkek would be fun, I thought. Maybe we could go on a few trips out of the city and meet some new people. And I was pleased Carlos was with me, I liked the little Spaniard.

We took a last group photo with the cars, said our goodbyes and I gave OJ a hug. I'd always found the giant Slav comforting and knew I'd miss him.

"See you in ten days," he said.

"Maybe three weeks?" I replied.

"Don't even say that."

As I climbed into our hired taxi with Carlos, Megan and Zsofi, I felt pleased to be heading off without the limitations of Trabant travel. But it felt like the end of a story, or the closing of a book, and I just hoped that Trabant Trek would reopen for Part 2.

5

THE HIATUS
Tajikistan and Kyrgyzstan
26 September – 29 October 2007

Q) What do you call a Trabant that's been driven to the top of
a steep hill?
A) A bloody miracle.

THE PAMIR HIGHWAY

Retracing the steps we had taken the day before by Trabant, I was immediately
struck by how different it was riding in a normal car. For the first time in two
and a half months people weren't staring at us.

Hey, it's us.

But nothing.

No waving, no screaming, no kids running alongside our cars, no old men
tapping on the chassis and raising querying brows. Even the police weren't interested in stopping us. Our star had truly fallen. But we used to be famous.
Whatever, get to the back of the line. We were just like any other backpackers,
except there really weren't too many other backpackers around.

But as I pushed myself back into the comfortable seats of our shared taxi
I was secretly looking forward to being a casual tourist for a few weeks. I could
revel in the anonymity. I wouldn't have to get up at seven. There would be no
worrying about the cars, the group, the plan, the money, the breakdowns and the
myriad other daily concerns.

I guess Team Europe had the plum deal; we just had to get to Bishkek and
sit tight. I didn't know anything about the city, but it was the Kyrgyz capital and
would surely have some welcome diversions. But Team USA would have to
deal with the visa issues, and then wrestle the cars over the mountains. In retrospect I would like to have done it, but at that moment, in that comfortable,
quiet interior, I was pleased to leave the Trek behind.

The Pamir Highway between Khorog and Murghab reminded me of the

Carlos in our first snow storm

Turkmen desert, except freezing cold and two miles high. Millions of years ago it would have been a desert at a reasonable level—another chunk of rolling Central Asian plains—but the steady shove of the Indian subcontinent had raised it year by year until that bleak plain sat 4,500m high, incongruous in the mountains.

We stopped at thermal springs and dipped in boiling hot, greenish water that smelled of eggs. The flow had been funnelled into a small rest stop with a café and a TV. I imagined the other trekkers would be delighted to find that little oasis in the desert, and maybe spend some time there. But we had just half an hour as our shared taxi was keen to plough on. As was customary in the region, there were seven of us in the five-seater, with two crammed into the boot. Luckily we had sent our bags ahead.

We arrived after dark in Murghab and stayed at the Murghab Hotel, where there was only enough electricity to power two light bulbs. As there was one on in the kitchen, our group could only light one of our two rooms at a time. There was no heating and it was genuinely freezing. Washing my hands under the rusty tap outside felt like thrusting them into a furnace.

At dinner we sat on mats on the floor with an old man and his old son. The father was white haired and Chinese-looking, his eyes seemed almost closed, and he rocked back and forth when he laughed like an old bear. His son was deferential, filling up his father's cup at every opportunity, and pausing to allow him to speak. The old man dipped hard Chinese bread into his tea. We shared two cups between us—one person would drain their ration then hand it back to the younger old man, who would pour the dregs into a dish, then refill the cup and pass it to the next person. It felt primitive and natural to share the simplest of commodities, hot water and a few tea leaves.

The next morning we went to hunt down the bags we had sent ahead and I got to see Murghab in the light. The town was a jagged mix of one-storey buildings connected by dirt tracks with one wide paved road running through it—the Pamir Highway itself. Deceptively large, there were 400 pupils at the local school. The following morning I walked in with one of them and, despite living in one of the most remote and isolated towns in the world, he had the same attitudes you'd expect of any fifteen-year-old. He hated learning the periodic table for chemistry, and didn't know why he was studying Arabic, English, Russian,

Chinese and Tajik.

We hired a 4x4 to take us and all our excess baggage to Osh in Kyrgyzstan, a twelve-hour drive. The scenery was far more spectacular then the previous day, a geologist's dream. Out of endless desert sprung a huge icy lake of deep aquamarine formed by a meteor in another time. Peaty bogs turned to hard brown tundra and frozen streams irrigated the bleak permafrost. Thick yellow grass met jet-black sands and dense shrubs clung to orange earth. A swarm of sand floated like a heat haze on the horizon and, rising from the opaque mist, the hills escalated in tiered colours. Ochre sands and a kaleidoscope of stones flanked the arrow straight path.

Man had made little impression on that landscape. Just three signs of human existence: the long road, lined by electricity poles and flanked by the fiercely barbed-wire Chinese border. We hugged that border for hours, with its menacing lines of razors. I was surprised to find a lone gate in the fence, near to nothing, with no path leading up to it, but invitingly open.

We stopped at a mountain village for tea and were served by a strikingly good-looking family, high cheek-boned with broad honest faces, the epitome of mountain health. They served deer with hard bread and a sour yoghurt made of yak's milk. To much amusement Zsofi dropped her purse into the toilet pit just as we were about to leave, and the husband had to fish it out with a pole.

The border was spectacularly located on a high pass, and it must be one of the world's longest crossings—more than twenty kilometres of no-man's-land between Tajikistan and Kyrgyzstan. At Kyrgyz customs Zsofi noticed the guards were tearing pages from the register to use as toilet paper.

The final border post was closed by the time we reached it, but after some negotiation we bribed the guard $10 to let us through. It was such a relief to leave Tajikistan behind; we'd been stuck there too long. None of us knew how long it would take Team USA to escape.

IMPRESSIONS OF OSH AND BISHKEK

Osh is Kyrgyzstan's second city, and famous for its bazaar. Though I'm not a big fan of markets, Carlos loved them, so we had to investigate. My favourite stall sold a single roller blade, four wind-dial telephones, a selection of second-hand electrical sockets, various ratchets, one faucet, two plates, a cashier's tray, a wing mirror, one large cooking pot and assorted nuts, bolts and screws. This was the man's entire business.

Cobblers lined a rusting bridge repairing tatty shoes over a dirty river.

From the thick crowd an old man held my hand tight. "Manchester United?" he asked.

"Yes."

"Aha," he celebrated this victory of communication long and hard before expanding, "Anglia Ruski tree nil"

"Yes, we beat the Russians."

"Aha," another victory cry, but he still wouldn't release my hand, "Chelsea?"

"No, Chelsea are boring, Chelsea *eta skoochnaya*."

"Aha," he loved that one and squeezed my hand tightly. The conversation was typical of my travels. Pretty much everywhere I have been in the world, except the United States, people speak the international language of football.

"Beckham, America?"

Even there, in that strange outpost of civilisation, Beckham's move to the States was big news.

Many of the city's buildings still bore communist murals depicting strong-boned, clean-shaven men in factory overalls and bright-eyed, independent women in jeans in front of ploughed field and assembly lines. At least Sovietism was a victory for women's rights.

A fantastic variety of hats topped the streets. Little skull caps, clinging to the back of the head, sharp cut fedoras in pale blue with embroidered ribbons, the sweeping Pamir hat looking impossibly balanced and ready to topple.

In Kyrgyzstan one of our main sponsors, the pharmaceutical giant Richter, had a base. We met some of their representatives in Osh and they helped us out with new visas, and found us a car to Bishkek.

We arrived in the capital after a long and cold crossing over the mountains, where we were snowed in overnight. After so long sleeping rough in Tajikistan we were all looking forward to the accommodation Richter had promised to provide. We had dreams of hot showers, clean sheets and central heating. But when we started pulling into a downtrodden, ill-paved courtyard my heart sank. We got out of the car, and a thick breeze scooped up heaps of dust, sand and litter and swung them into the shawled faces of poor old ladies. This was not what we were hoping for.

Our apartment had the demoralising ambiance of a prison block—even the cockroaches looked embarrassed to be seen there. Then the cherry: no showers. It is hard to overstate my disappointment. It was the simplest of pleasures, but to be clean would have made a world of difference. After speaking to the housekeeper we were told there were public washrooms across the street.

NOTES ON SHOWERING ETIQUETTE IN CENTRAL ASIA

The showering situation was quite an adventure. The facilities were very much communal, shared between three large apartment blocks. Inside what I shall politely call the gentlemen's washroom, but may be better termed a small, filthy cesspit, there were three showers, which in my experience were shared between six or seven people.

The routine was this: you jump in the shower for a quick rinse, wait for the naked men surrounding you to start staring, then step out and begin to lather yourself. You will have to wait near a shower for at least five minutes, dripping and soapy like some fluffy yeti, for a gap to appear beneath the crowded nozzles. When you see a space it is imperative to jump in quickly and wash off the suds, before the other nudies get annoyed.

You may then retreat to the relative safety of the dressing area, pleasantly decorated with live moss, where people perpetually leave the door open to the wider world, leaving you horribly at risk of a terrible exposure.

Of course, I always seemed to arrive in the washroom when there was a deep queue for each shower. So I would have to hover, in full naked glory, waiting for my go and wondering where to look. I normally stared at my miniature aeroplane bottle of shampoo, which was about the size of a teabag, its instructions written entirely in Russian, a language so foreign it uses a different alphabet and utterly, utterly indecipherable to me. I knew this ruse was wearing thin, but I had yet to work out the correct posture to adopt when standing in a room full of naked Kyrgyz.

But I tell you this: I saw more cock in those ten days than the preceding ten years. And the Asian penis has been hugely underestimated.

CROSSROADS: AN UPDATE

We were scattered. The team spread across two countries and three cities in and around Central Asia's craggy, imposing mountain ranges.

Lovey's trip to Dushanbe to sort out visas for our American contingent turned into a lengthy mission. The Tajik capital happened to be hosting an international conference and every hotel in the city was booked, forcing Lovey to prostitute himself to find a place to stay. The poor chap spent most of his days queuing and arguing at embassies, walking the same streets between the internet café, consulate and his accommodation.

OJ and Tony P, the other members of Team USA, were in Khorog, high in the Pamir Mountains. By email we had received the disturbing news that both of them were under house arrest, closely monitored by the Tajik police. In Tajikistan it was illegal for foreigners to be out without their passports, which Lovey had in Dushanbe, and the pair were repeatedly arrested during their first few days without documents.

You would think a six-foot-three goliath of a Yank and a moustachioed Mexican with a Mohawk would be able to escape attention in a small Tajik mountain village. Maybe the brightly coloured German cars blew their cover?

All I had to go on were a few emails, but I knew they had been subjected to constant police harassment and were bound to their home-stay, where, thankfully, the owners had taken pity and begun to feed them for free each night. I wasn't sure what curious cabin fever their enforced proximity had created, but during a Gmail chat both complained to me, quite separately, that the other smelled.

Team Europe—Carlos, Zsofi and I—were settling into our accommodation, which may have been the inspiration for *Prisoner Cell Block H*, but without the lesbians. Actually we were probably Prisoner Cell Block Q or R, nothing as luxurious as H, where I heard they had their own shower.

Our continuing mission, to get to Cambodia, had taken some violent twists in the preceding weeks and now we were stalled, scattered and in limbo. Between us we needed new visas for the next four countries along our route: Tajikistan, Kyrgyzstan, Kazakhstan and Russia. It being ex-Soviet territory, any brush with authority exposed you to the delightful whimsy of former Soviet bureaucracy, and the visas were a handful, taking a week to secure.

And all the delays added to a new and potentially much greater hurdle. Looming large in the distance was China, an undoubted highlight of the trip, a booming country and culture we were all desperate to taste. But also a system of paperwork and officialdom that made Turkmenistan look like a Parisian hippy community of liberal utopians.

To get the car papers for our expedition in China had taken three months and was costing us $8,000. Our points of entry and exit were fixed, as were the dates, and the Chinese insisted we pay to have a guide with us for the whole month. Hence the ridiculous costs involved.

We were supposed to be entering China from southern Mongolia, thousands of kilometres away, but it was pretty unfeasible that we would get there when our visa started in a fortnight. Infuriating we were already on China's western frontier—both Kyrgyzstan and Tajikistan had open borders with the country. But the Chinese were refusing to let us change our point of entry. This meant we would have to circumnavigate the whole of north-west China, a trip of thousands of kilometres up the length of Kazakhstan, across miles of Siberian wilderness and down through Mongolia, a country with more horses than cars.

Of course, this was our original route, but judging from previous form it would probably take three weeks to a month, and Team USA still had to make it over the Pamirs.

So we had to face up to the very real possibility that we might miss our visa dates and not be allowed into China. What could we do? Apply for a new visa? It would take at least two months to do and no one had the time or money to wait it out.

We therefore began to seriously contemplate an alternative to China. We had only put down a $2,000 deposit on our visas, there was another $6,000 owing, so the way we figured it we had $6,000 to play with to find a way of avoiding the country.

There was a lot of debate, with our three separate groups throwing ideas across the mountains by email. Our "best idea" (and I use that term loosely) was to ship the cars through or around the country. We had to get our atlases out, but one option was to drive to Vladivostok, Russia's icy eastern port, and get a ferry from there to the northern part of South Korea. We could then drive down the Korean peninsula to the southern port of Pusan where we would get a cargo ship to take us around China—possibly to Singapore. From there we could drive north through Malaysia and Thailand, and east into Cambodia.

Crazy.

The other option was to drive to Ulaanbaatar, the Mongolian capital, and try to get the cars onto a freight train to take them through China, possibly to Bangkok, Thailand, or Ho Chi Minh City, Vietnam.

Mental.

Both options meant taking on the challenging drive to the north-east of Asia a month later than originally planned. The weather was closing in, it was already freezing in Bishkek, and it would mean tackling snow and ice, which we hadn't anticipated. The area was also the most isolated part of the trip, a terrible place to break down, and if we went through Mongolia there would be few roads. We could also end up spending a couple of weeks at sea.

A third option was to try and get the cars shipped straight from Bishkek to Bangkok.

With these hazy, half-formed plans we began to get in touch with shipping companies. Everything was in flux and it was odd thinking that our route and our trek could be changing dramatically. Personally, I was excited. I love change, and I loved the idea that we could tackle the Chinese challenge by doing something completely ridiculous like taking to the sea with the Trabbis.

I wonder what Korea is like in November?

MEGAN HAS LEFT THE BUILDING

After a week in Bishkek, Megan left us. We knew she was going, so it was no surprise, just a disappointment. We were horribly into the red, and she didn't even have the original budget, so we always knew she wasn't going to make it to Cambodia. She had hoped to leave from China, then Mongolia, then maybe Russia or Kazakhstan. But, as our delays increased, her point of departure shifted gradually further west until it settled gently, but uncomfortably, like an unwanted aunt on a sitting room sofa. She flew out of Bishkek early on the morning of 9 October, three months after I first met her.

Carlos, Zsofi and I stayed up late to show her to a taxi. It was a sad farewell, deep into a cold Kyrgyz night, with a few damp eyes. We tried to film the occasion, but the tape ran out at the point of departure. We waved goodbye to the cab, Zsofi continuing a forlorn flapping until the car was well out of view.

The three of us walked back arm in arm, and I felt a keen sense of loss. We hadn't really spoken much about her going, so despite the forewarning, it still seemed a shock to see her empty bed. Zsofi must have felt the same; she took to sleeping on a mattress on the floor of the room I shared with Carlos.

Megan had been with me since my first day of Trabant Trek, 9 July, when she and Carlos greeted me at Budapest airport. We'd spent a lot of time together. While driving Fez on some endless sandy road I remember hearing her cackle and looking up to see she had taken a picture of my reflection in the rear view mirror. The photograph showed me sitting in the back, topless, in just my pants, wearing sand-smudged glasses and a hat, unconsciously pulling a face as I pored over the words on my laptop. She said it was her abiding image of me because she had seen it so often.

My image of her isn't a still one, and couldn't be captured by a camera. She is moving, dancing; performing a jig to conclude a short story or illustrate an episode. Thrusting her hips to a rhythm only she hears, pulling a pout and shifting her head to an imagined beat. Her feet twist, crabbing her sideways, knees bouncing off each other comically before she finishes with a flourish, hand on hip, arms and legs cocked, pulling a ridiculous mockery of a model's stare.

It makes me laugh every time. Megan Calvert dances her own dance, and made my Trek all the brighter while she did.

RELIGION, VODKA AND GAYS

Central Asia is nominally an Islamic region. But despite extremist neighbours like the Iranians and Afghans, rarely did I notice manifestations of the faith. I don't remember hearing the call to prayer, nor was the veil much in evidence. Perhaps the tall mountains had sheltered the region from the extremism lapping at its borders. Maybe the Soviet approach to Islam, attempting to fuse it with communist ideology, helped water down the religion's illiberal edges. I don't know, but although a lot of the people of Bishkek claimed to be Muslim, no rule had been abandoned more whole-heartedly than abstinence. Judging from the huge proliferation of vodka, bandied about like nuclear secrets at an Axis of Evil conference, the culprits for that imported and un-Islamic hedonism were likely to be the Russians.

In newsagents and grocery stores across the region it was quite usual to knock back a shot of vodka when picking up your morning paper. On the counter you might find a stack of grubby shot glasses, next to an open bottle of the local brew, and a plate of some sort of chaser: sliced cucumber, salted tomato, diced apple or whatever was to hand.

These "shop shots" were generally pretty huge, often seventy or eighty millilitres, cost just a few pence, and were indulged in at regular intervals by working men of all persuasions. Religion really was no boundary. I got chatting to a serious, staid-looking man with a long Muslim beard ("We Muslims do not think it right to cut your beard") and a little Islamic cap on the back of his head—"For Allah".

"My religion is very important to me," he said, offering the local blessing by rubbing his hands down his face as if he were washing before going to the mosque. Then he walked into a shop for a shot of vodka.

"Isn't it Ramadan?" I asked as I followed. I had met a man the other day who turned down water because it was daylight.

"Huh? Bah," he washed the thought away with the fiery potion.

The effect of regularly quaffing terribly strong booze was tangible. I'm English and even I had noticed the amount of pissed shopkeepers and bus drivers. One morning I went down from our apartment to the little store to buy some eggs for an omelette. It was shortly before 10am and two men in their thirties were in the shop for a quick nip before they headed off to work. A quick nip was a giant glass of vodka, downed in one, followed by a chunk of salted tomato.

Of course, as an intrepid field agent keen to discover all I can about foreign routines, I joined the men for a drink. They laughed a lot, but I knocked back the burning paint stripper without grimacing, shook hands and left.

The result was a merry morning of high-spirited banter and easy laughter. The men seemed to be on to something so I stuck to the drink for the day and ended up in our regular nightclub, Golden Bull, where I happened upon Kyrgyzstan's number one teen pop star, the nationally renowned singer, model and TV personality, Mikayel.

He was the club's head of house, working the stage and occasionally showing off some rather impressive dance moves to the delight of the screaming ladies. On our first meeting he had appeared very vain, showing Carlos and me a succession of videos on his mobile phone and offering a running commentary of each: "Oh and this is the one where I do a spin. And this is the one where the girls are screaming. And this is me singing. And this is me on stage…"

It went on and on: "And this is me, and this is me, and this is me…"

I asked if we might take a picture: "Oh yes, but not here, come with me."

He escorted us to the lobby where there was a giant poster of him, looking sultry, emblazoned with his name.

"We take it here, it is better," Mikayel said, ushering the bouncers out of the shot.

We took a few snaps and then he insisted on looking through them.

"Oh no, not that one, that one is terrible. No delete it. No not that one. No delete it."

"Um, ok," I hesitated, but he watched intently to see that I did as I was told.

"Oh no and not that one. Delete it."

"Ok."

"And no delete. Delete… ah, there that one, good. Look at my smile. This one is the best. You may keep this one."

"Oh, well thank you."

It turned out that young Mikayel, who was 22, owned a stake in Golden Bull, and took me into his own private VIP suite within the club for a one-on-

Kyrgyzstan's favourite pop star, Mikayel, with the author

one interview. But his opening question caught me a little off guard: "So what is your orientation?"

As far as I could tell we were facing north.

"No, no. Oh…" he flicked a limp hand at me, "tut, it doesn't matter."

Um… do you mean sexual orientation?

"Yes," he crossed one leg tightly over the other and lent an elbow on his knee.

"Well I'm straight," and as an afterthought, in case I had not properly bridged the language barrier, I added, "I like girls… I'm not gay."

"Ok, ok." Bishkek's biggest celebrity paused to light a cigarette and eyed me. "It is just that you held my hand for so long when we met."

"Oh, sorry. I am quite friendly…"

"What does that mean?" his eyebrow lifted.

"No, not like that. I mean I'm tactile… I'm just a friendly person."

I was back-pedalling pathetically. There was a pause and I watched him measure me: "But you have had gay experiences?"

"Excuse me?" I tried to regain the initiative, "are you gay?"

"Oh no," I saw him try to drop the camp inflections of his accent, "it took me a long time to persuade the media that I am not gay."

A young boy came in, bowed in deference and carefully presented two vodka shots from a tray. My host did not acknowledge him, the lad was clearly just a serf, but Mikayel lifted his glass and looked me in the eye.

"Come, we drink. To friendship," then quickly he added, "we only drink half," he gestured at the midway point of the shot, raised the glass then took a quick sip. I did the same.

"Are you religious?" I asked.

"Oh yes, I am a Muslim. Islam is very important to me."

We finished the rest of the vodka.

After my homosexual denial he seemed to lose a little interest in our interview. He kept being called out to the bar to fulfil minor obligations, while I stayed in the VIP area steadily drinking the free vodka until it was time to leave.

We met again in the club a few days later and he blanked me. Heartbreaking.

EVICTED

We were told our accommodation was student digs, but I saw few students there. The residents seemed to be the down on their luck, fallen-on-hard-times types: old men with crumpled fedoras and un-ironed shirts, a woman in her thirties with a perpetual scowl and a middle-aged lady who refused to meet my eyes and ignored my daily greeting.

The courtyard was a menacing mix of old industrial waste, concrete slabs, metal pipes, bald tyres, threatening drunks and playful children. One night the beggars who lived under a curve in a pair of thick-set pipes set light to a few tyres and sat around the toxic smoke swigging vodka and shivering in their rags.

The next morning I was kicking a football about with a few kids when a man in his early thirties approached and tried to head butt me. I wasn't sure what he was shouting and hoped he was being playful, but a kid behind him drew his finger across his throat and gestured that I should scarper.

So the following day I was a little relieved to be told by our Richter contacts that we had outstayed our welcome in their free accommodation. They explained that there was a conference taking place for nurses from all over Kyrgyzstan and our rooms had been booked up. We had been there two weeks, it seemed fair enough.

The Richter girls showed us to a pleasant, family-run hostel, full of back-packers, where there were showering facilities and a breakfast option, all for $6 a night.

I was pleased to get away from the seedy side of town, but four days later I returned to pick up some contact lenses that I had forgotten, and our rooms, the ones booked up by the nurses, stood glaringly empty.

YURT LIFE

Our move to new accommodation provided a pleasing respite from the perils of over-familiarity. For the first time in months we were surrounded by new, English-speaking faces: Kiwis, Brits, French, Israelis, Hungarians, Spanish, Americans. We'd found the backpacker trail, alive with travellers' tales: where to go, what to see, who to avoid. A wealth of facts, half-truths, misinformation, opinion and downright exaggeration channelled through the men and women who followed those strangely narrow corridors, as defined by the guidebooks that united us.

The vodka-soaked stories that accompanied our evenings were probably as close to a recreation of the old Silk Road as we would get. Israelis and French coming from China warned of pickpockets on the Xinjiang bus. Kiwis heading south to Pakistan informed us that the Khunjerab Pass would be closing in a few weeks, sealing the border for the winter. We came from the west with dark warnings of Turkmen bureaucracy and the importance of avoiding the Baku-Turkmenbashi ferry.

It must have been that way throughout Marco Polo's time, but instead of carrying grubby backpacks the men had laden camels. Instead of gossiping into the night at hostels and guesthouses, the traders would have rested up at *cara-vanserai*, posted at intervals a day's walk apart along many of the routes. I imagine the same spirit of banter and adventure, nurtured by the local bever-age, with a few delicacies from home.

After an evening's exuberance during the Rugby World Cup semi-final, when I made enemies of a room full of Frenchman, alienated my companions with terrifying football chants, fell in a concrete flood ditch, inexplicably broke a bathroom mirror and then accidentally left the only pub in Bishkek that shows English sport without paying the bill, I awoke with a hangover.

The Israelis made me a hot concoction of ginger, honey and lemon as a cure, a Kiwi offered me Berrocca and the Hawaiian insisted I could drink it off. With such meetings of minds does the world's knowledge spread. Or maybe it's the internet. Either way, the relief of new conversation helped us through our third week in Bishkek.

Initially I was sceptical about our new home. It was a *yurt*: a circular tent, with curved wooden props and a skin made of hides. In the top was a round hole that acted as a skylight during the day and a chimney during the evening. The hole also released any stored warmth and encouraged a stiff chill that developed as the night progressed until the small hours felt like a recurrence of the Karoo Ice Age.

Perhaps I had a romanticised notion of *yurt* life. Something involving nomads wandering the steppe, and pitching camp where the prey died, cooking tough mutton over the fire inside a hide covered shelter. In the morning they would wrap up and stroll down to an icy stream to fill a skin with water, then stoke the fire for a brew.

But our *yurt* had been set up in a back garden in one of Bishkek's less desirable neighbourhoods. It was not a large garden, it was very obvious we were in an enclosed space, and there was a dormitory next to us where the less adventurous or more wise were staying. The nights were accompanied by the steady chorus of hounds, who only gave up at about the time that the cockerels kicked off.

I took to sleeping in a thick Russian military jacket that I'd bought in the bazaar so I could overcome the *yurt*'s chill, but enjoyed our new friends and the joys of access to a kitchen with a kettle.

After three months of early starts on the Trek, I fell into a strange, dreamy pattern in the unformed malaise of Bishkek. We were killing time, treading water, and for the first time since the long, lazy summer of my first year at university I had nothing to do. I was dossing. With nothing to get up for there was little to go to bed for, and I slept badly in our thin shelter, then lay in late. My day involved going into town to find a bite to eat and browse the web for news from home. Then I would find somewhere else to eat.

"Hey, I think I lost weight," Carlos told me, plucking at the sagging waistline of his jeans.

"I think I found it," I replied looking at my own taught paunch. Must do some exercise, I thought, for the millionth time in Bishkek.

In the evenings I might visit Metro. The bar was a tiny microcosm of the West, almost like the set of *Cheers* had been displaced to the heart of Asia. You could order a burger or a burrito with your Bud. Sports channels churned out American football and baseball. I couldn't help but overhear snippets of con-

Our *yurt*, home for two weeks

versation. A burly-looking American with a crew cut: "I can't imagine anything worse than being sent to an Afghan prison. I've seen Afghan jails and they are frightening. Must be the worst place on earth…"

A nerdy-looking NGO type: "…you know they're looking for a new macro consultant at DPNG. They need someone to work in their democratisation department…"

It was a strange group of contractors, the military and charity workers, eating pizza in their little oasis.

Although not entirely frustrated by that general torpor, I was affected. I had less energy, spontaneity was dying out, a numbness had taken hold.

I managed to find a shipping company who could take the Trabants from Bishkek straight to Bangkok. They said it would take just a couple of weeks, and cost a little over $6,000. To Carlos and me, the option held a lot of appeal. It had begun to get seriously cold in Bishkek, and heading north into Siberia seemed foolhardy, if not dangerous. But no decisions could be made until Team USA had arrived. So we sat tight and waited

THE REUNION

BANGKOK. It hovered in my mind like a giant, flashing out-card. We ship the Trabbis from Bishkek, straight to the Thai capital. It would take two to three weeks. While the Trabbis are en route, we meander through China, taking in a few sights, then collect the cars and continue the short trip to Cambodia.

Nice and easy, and within a month we could be on a Cambodian beach, sitting on the bonnets of our cars, warmed by the thick orange sun, sipping Buckets of Joy and telling tales of far away places. We'd be local celebrities, and could relax, knowing we had accomplished our mission, raised a few thousand dollars, and were the first people to get three old Trabants across half the world to Cambodia.

A blissful time, running through old stories with the boys and laughing at the days when we were stuck in bleak, miserable Bishkek. Maybe spend a fortnight on the beach? I'd be home for Christmas. $6,300. That was the price of the shipping, a little more than the money we would save by skipping China and that country's exorbitant car visas. Such a pleasant daydream.

The other option? The long northern route through Siberia, fraught with risk and danger. We drive up the length of Kazakhstan, then veer east for a thousand miles into the Siberian wilderness, before dropping south into Mongolia and Ulaanbaatar, the world's coldest capital city.

It was the route we always planned to take, but we were six weeks late. We had imagined Siberia in autumn. We would get Siberia in winter. A time when the temperature dips below - 20c, when snow covers the half-paved roads and icy winds slash across the land.

Then the solace of Mongolia? To quote the guidebook's advice: "We would not recommend driving in Mongolia. What appear on maps as roads are often little more than goat paths and the country has virtually no road signs."

Perfect.

And the icing on the cake. From Ulaanbaatar we would have to ship the cars to Bangkok anyway. We just get there a month later, a month colder and a month poorer.

So there was no contest right? Right?

On Thursday 18 October, Team USA arrived in Bishkek. Carlos, Zsofi and I waited at a junction to greet them and guide them in. We caught sight of Dante first, with OJ at the wheel, trying to drive and change gears with one hand and operate a video camera with the other. Dante's passenger door was still sealed shut, so I jumped in through the window and gave the big Slav a hug.

It was great to see the Yanks. It had taken them more than three weeks to cross the mountains, and now we were all together we could work out what was going on. We went straight to dinner, but it was immediately obvious that there were differences of opinion over what to do next. The boys looked knackered, Lovey seemed sullen and wasn't eating—never a good sign.

"If we ship to Bangkok from here then that is the end of Trabant Trek," he said.

The End of Trabant Trek.

I wonder how many times I heard that phrase. How many more times would it be uttered? "I think about fifty," Carlos predicted.

But Lovey had a point. It was just a few days' drive from Bangkok to Phnom Penh. Maybe give it a week to get down to the coast. Just one more week of driving.

"We're only half way," Lovey followed up, "so we drove half way to Cambodia and then shipped the cars the rest? That defeats the point."

OJ chipped in: "But we're going to ship anyway. Even if we go north to Ulaanbaatar we're still shipping through China, so what's the difference?"

OJ was not a big fan of going north.

Lovey: "Yes but if we ship from Mongolia then at least we have driven as far as we possibly can along the route. Then we ship because we have no choice."

The discussion continued in this fashion as we headed back to our homestay, and a few more people revealed their positions. Tony P said he would not be shipping south no matter what and declared that he would head north on his own, without the cars if necessary.

OJ expressed concerns over the timescale. He had promised his girlfriend he would be home by the end of November and was determined not to let her down. The end of November seemed a pretty ridiculous promise to me, but I didn't want to say. Surely she would understand? But OJ was adamant. Would it be possible to head north, ship the cars, and drive from Bangkok to Cambodia in six weeks? We worked through the route and the timing, went over the calculations, and guessed we would get to Bangkok by 5 December if we were optimistic, 15 December if we were realistic.

"So I can't go north," OJ said.

If we went south we would lose Tony. If we went north we would lose OJ.

Then a phone call and another bombshell. Zsofi's father, who had lent her the money for the Trek, had heard about our situation and was withdrawing her funding. He thought Siberia would be too cold and dangerous, and shipping the cars was just ridiculous. She had about a month's money left.

"For me this is the end of Trabant Trek," she told us.

The End of Trabant Trek. Forty-nine to go.

Lovey said that if we were to ship the cars south he would probably go north; maybe take one Trabbi with Tony. He wasn't definite, he wanted to be diplomatic, but he was very much in the northern camp.

Carlos was more drawn to the southern option: "Siberia is cold," he said, "I don't really see the point. I told my friend about all this and he said, 'Hey, if you ship from Bishkek, you are not failures. You will have driven to Kyrgyzstan in Trabants man. And raised ten thousand dollars. That's amazing.'"

These discussions went back and forth all night, and I fell asleep to the sound of a drunken Tony and Lovey going over the same points again and again.

Bangkok. In a month we could be sipping piña coladas on the beach. But it did seem too easy. Maybe it was a cop out. Surely we should drive as far as the cars, the governments, our tempers and our budgets would allow before resorting to shipping.

The more I thought about it, the more I thought I would regret not pushing on. This was an adventure and I wasn't ready to give up. If we could find a way around China, then I would head north.

Birthday Boy

19 October was my birthday. Twenty-five. I woke up early, ate a healthy breakfast of fresh grapefruit and muesli, drank decaffeinated coffee without sugar, flossed, went for a jog, showered, removed hair from the plug hole, got a smart, respectable new look, put on clean, ironed clothes, applied for a mortgage, got a small business starter loan, and began the quest for a wife.

None of that is true, but I suppose some people think it should be. I imagine my grandfather would tell me that he had already founded and sold two newspapers by the time he was my age. My mother was raising her first child.

But times change, and my fellow trekkers, who were mostly older, seemed to have just as few tangible links to responsible society as I did. Once I entered the cycle of job, home, family and bills it seemed there would be little opportunity for gallivanting across the world until I retired from it all, in what forty years? I didn't see the need to rush into the rat race, and I was strangely happy to celebrate my birthday in Bishkek, a city I hadn't even heard of a few months before.

We spent the afternoon doing a clear out of the cars—stripping them and cleaning them up, redistributing the weight more evenly and trying to get organised.

They were in a pretty sorry state. Few of the doors locked or even closed, most of the tyres were old, bubbled and bald. Fez's brakes were dodgy, we were still waiting for the front right wheel bearing to come apart irreparably, and we weren't sure how good the new weld on the rear left control arm was. Somewhere on the drive in Kyrgyzstan, OJ drove Dante into a cow. The bovine was alright, but the cow was a little shaken up, and the front of Dante was cracked.

A new issue had reared its head. Tony called it the "sticky throttle", and explained that the accelerator had a tendency to get stuck down. "It's fine on the highways," he added, "not so good in the cities."

We drank beer and I was presented with a card and cake, which was rather touching. Then we went to a restaurant for dinner, the six trekkers plus a bunch of new friends from the hostel, before heading to Metro and on to Golden Bull, via a tense standoff with some taxi drivers following an incident related to the etiquette of urinating in bushes. When I got back I heard that OJ was locked in the toilet, asleep in his own sick. Carlos rescued him.

Being away from the cars for so long had given me a chance to walk. It sounds strange, but I hadn't really walked anywhere in months. A few nights after my birthday I did the stroll from the centre of town back to the hostel. It was about three in the morning, and Bishkek was quiet. I felt calm in the ghostly silence of a sleeping city and the simple stroll gave my mind the chance to relax and wander.

Man was born to walk. As the only mammal to spend its days on two feet, it is something that defines us, that makes us human. It was the great evolutionary leap from the trees and onto our hind legs, freeing up our hands and allowing us to use tools, to build, to stroll about the savannah with a spear.

It was a mild night and I paced out a steady rhythm that my heart and lungs soon fell into time with, sending me into a meditation.

I must walk more, I thought.

I'll file that one with "learn to dance" and "take more exercise".

I'm only 25. Plenty of time.

THE PLAN: A CONCLUSION

The next day we got an email from the Chinese saying that they had managed to push back our visa dates by a fortnight. We stared long and hard at the route and eventually decided that we might just be able to make it to the agreed border point in time. It would be close, but it was possible.

So all the plans for shipping were abandoned, all those weeks of uncertainty brought to an abrupt halt. Living in such shifting sands, I suspect someone of a more structured persuasion would go slowly mental. But we Trekkers were used to it.

OJ agreed to come north with us; he still hoped to get home in a month, but had been persuaded to stick with us and see how it went.

Zsofi decided to go against her father's warning and stick with us too. She had enough money to get to China, but she said she would no longer be contributing towards the $6,000 for car permits in the country. This caused a little consternation, as it meant more costs for the rest of us, but we didn't argue.

A guy called Horst Meinecke had been following the blogs, and he'd lived in Mongolia for three years, so he sent me an email full of advice including this promising snippet: "… there will be hardly anyone to render assistance. No tow trucks, mechanics, spare parts, or people around. People die that way in Mongolia. We always had an emergency bottle of vodka in the glove compartment of our Mitsubishi Pajero, but in a serious situation, that would tide you over only for a few hours, but at least you fall asleep for the last time happy."

How reassuring.

We got prepared for the freezing conditions ahead by stocking up on jackets, thermals and blankets at the market. We bought gloves and quilts and thick socks, even some wool to insulate the cars with. We managed to barter some new tools and a power pack from a Swiss couple in exchange for some old guidebooks. On a rare warm day in Bishkek we completely stripped and cleaned out the cars, then repacked them with the new insulation.

A month behind schedule, and down to three cars and six trekkers, we were getting on the road again. We were heading north, onto the vast, icy Siberian plateau. We were taking the Northern Route.

6

THE NORTHERN ROUTE
Kazakhstan, Russia and Mongolia
29 October – 23 November 2007

Q) Why do Trabants have heated rear windows?
A) To keep your hands warm while you're pushing them.

Bye Bye, Bishkek

There was a little trouble trying to get out of Kyrgyzstan. We had forgotten to collect customs papers for the cars when we entered the country. No one at the border had said we needed any, and there was no obvious place to get them, but apparently we should have asked for them and of course they were needed on exit.

The problem was far from trivial—the first solution a friendly but unyielding official suggested was returning to our point of entry to get the papers. Unfortunately that was 500km away across the mountains. Out of the question.

After some negotiation we found we could get new papers in Bishkek, but would have to pay a fine based on engine size. Seeing as we were driving 600cc lawnmowers across the world, this wouldn't have been a big financial penalty. But it would have cost us another precious few days in the race to China.

We ended up playing the charity card, explaining our mission and showing the officials some photos of us with kids at a Bishkek charity, the Centre for the Protection of Children. A local, who was acting as translator, was eventually won over by the cause and negotiated our release. At the Kazakh border we remembered to ask for customs papers.

It was great to be back behind the wheel of Fez. After a month in Bishkek it felt like a new beginning, a new adventure, the drive north through Kazakhstan, east across Siberia before the long road south through Mongolia, China and South East Asia, all the way to the Gulf of Thailand. The weather was intensely different; it would be a while until the T-shirts could come out, and after Russia we would be out of the old Soviet sphere and into the realm of the Chinese.

Dante in the Siberian forest

Fez, too, felt different. Maybe it was a month away from the wheel, more likely it was the running repairs he had received over the Pamirs. The exhaust pipe, which had become detached in Tajikistan, was now welded firmly to the underside of the car, making the whole cabin rattle. The noise, combined with the unique seating arrangement in Fez, limited conversation between driver and passenger. And I'm not sure exactly what the welder did, but some of the exhaust was now funnelled into the cabin. It was a bearable amount—a light headache and a bit of dizziness—but when we switched on the heating the full force of the fumes was redirected into the car. This was unbearable, as in throat stinging, eyes watering, lung burning, carcinogenic unbearable. At least we weren't heading to the coldest reaches of the continent. No, wait…

Carlos was my new driving buddy, replacing Megan. We had driven together for a few weeks at the beginning of the trip, then, as the two male members of Team Europe, we had spent the best part of a month exploring Bishkek. We got on well, I considered him my closest ally, we had shared stories and jokes and I had ignited in him a passion for *The Mighty Boosh*. The only downside to this new partnership was Carlos' taste in music. He seemed to listen almost exclusively to Spanish love ballads. Thankfully the stereo in Fez was long gone, but many times I woke in the back of the car to overhear Carlos driving with his headphones on singing the female vocal lead to a frightening Catalan romantic anthem at the top of his voice. Believe me, this is disturbing.

Despite his musical leaning Carlos Gey was great company. A friend once called for him on the mobile number we occasionally shared.

"Can I speak to Carlos, please?"

"What's the password?" I asked.

Without a pause he just said, "GAY".

We laughed about that for a long time.

Carlos' English was good, and he picked up new words, phrases and insults quickly. But he was also good at making it appear that he understood when really he didn't. So a typical conversation in Fez might go like this:

Me (lying in passenger bed): "I've checked the tank, we've got about four litres left."

Carlos (returning from stall with water): "Okay."

Me: "There's not much life around here so we should probably stop at the next place we see and fill up."

Carlos nods. Then a pause. Then he gets out of the car: "I'm just going to see how much gas we have left."

Me: "No, mate, wait. I've done it, Carlos…"

But he's already out of the car, hood popped and checking the tank. Because when Carlos decides to do something he goes ahead and does it.

A new driving buddy, a new team, a new feel to the car: new conditions on the road and steadily deteriorating weather. This was Trabant Trek Part Two.

KAZAKHSTAN

Despite the backwards portrayal of Sacha Baron Cohen's pseudo-Kazakh, Borat, Kazakhstan was actually the largest, richest, and most developed of the Central Asian countries.

Abundant oil and gas deposits meant there was plenty of money floating about in the cities, although there was also some pretty extreme poverty, particularly in the countryside.

Under the Soviets the vast, empty country was something of a dumping ground. Huge swathes of land had been left uninhabitable by nuclear testing, and it had served as a remote home for gulags and forced labour camps. Dissidents like the author Dostoevsky were banished there, and Stalin sent whole peoples to the barren steppe.

The nation's president, Nursultan Nazarbayev, had been in charge since the Soviet collapse in 1991, when Kazakhstan suddenly gained independence and a nuclear arsenal, and the progressive, reformist leader never seemed likely to voluntarily relinquish control. The president had overseen the overhaul and expansion of the country's economy and built a new capital, Astana, to mark his nation's emergence as a regional economic power.

Although we wouldn't be visiting any of the cities to see these changes, we had become pretty adept at gauging a country's development from the snacks available at its petrol stations and the quality of its roads. In Kazakhstan we could buy fizzy drinks, crisps and chocolate when we filled up, and the roads were wide, straight and newly tarmaced. After the trials of the mountains, we couldn't ask for much more.

As ever it was late when we crossed the border and, over dinner at a roadside café, we decided that we should make the most of the good roads and rush through Kazakhstan as quickly as possible. Time wasn't on our side and we hadn't heard too many great things about the cities on our route. So we resolved to try and drive in shifts, non-stop. That plan was messed up when, shortly after 4am, Dante's front left wheel inexplicably unattached itself and shot off on a solo mission into the night. I was asleep at the time so I asked Carlos what had happened.

"It was a cold and dark night and the moon was shining," he told me (I think he knew I was taking notes), "you could hear the whisper of the cold telling you that you were going to die." He paused for dramatic effect, and stifled a laugh.

"Suddenly I saw all these sparks coming from Dante. They pulled over and I saw the wheel was missing. So I pulled up to them. Tony just looked at me out the window, he didn't say anything, just stared out. The look on his face was priceless."

We drove around a bit looking for the renegade wheel, but it was too dark in the cratered steppe. Tony said he had seen it roll off into the night. "It went that way," he pointed in a vague arc.

"How fast were you going?" I asked.

"About seventy."

"So the wheel went that way," I swept my arm over the dark horizon, "at 70kph?"

"Yeah."

We decided to camp for the night and have another look in the morning.

At night Carlos and I turned our little Trabbi into The Fez Hilton. There was no passenger seat and the driver's seat was removable, so with a little re-arrangement we had two fully reclined beds. We had heaps of warm weather gear, and the blankets, duvets, sleeping bags and cushions aided the most comfortable car sleep possible.

My sleeping pattern was all screwed up by the random routines of Bishkek, so it made sense for me to do the late driving shift. I regret it because it meant that I really saw little of Kazakhstan other than the dimly lit arc of Fez's headlights on tarmac, and the rear end of Ziggy.

We didn't find the wheel the next morning, but I got my only really decent look at the famous Kazak steppe—the huge, arid plain that dominates that latitude of Asia. The soil was sandy, but spotted by wiry grass. It stretched out for hundreds of miles, undulating but not rolling, with little that could be called a hill, and no trees.

As we drove into a cloudless blue sky, the distance was slowly filled by a low gathering of pinkish cotton candy. It rested low on the horizon, as if we were high in the mountains, flirting with the clouds, not driving through the low plains. When we got close enough I realised the thick smog was coming from an industrial city with chimneys spewing a tower of smoke high into the air that then cooled and settled over the area like a toxic halo. As the sun dipped low behind us, its rays slowed in our atmosphere and the reds of the solar spectrum picked out the cloud in a frightening pink. As we left the scarlet aura we followed a line of enormous piles of burning rubbish, dumped in the fields and set alight.

On and on we raced, our Trabbis lapping up the good conditions and behaving themselves. I did a shift from 5pm to 5am, pretty terrible driving hours, but I had slept all day so fatigue wasn't a problem. For a few hours the steppe was swathed in a thick mist. Doing 80kph in misty darkness in a rattling, vibrating Trabbi felt like driving a rocket. In the fog it felt like flying a MIG through a turbulent cloud—we could have been doing over 300kph, not 80.

We crossed Central Asia's largest country, the ninth biggest in the world, in 44 hours—more than 1,500km. A Trabant Trek record. Very proud of that one. On 31 October, after thirty hours of straight driving, we left the country, and the "stans", behind for good.

Central Asia was bad for us. We lost a car, three people, two roof racks, thousands of dollars, vast quantities of spare parts and roughly a month. We gained an intricate knowledge of the region's customs and visa systems, particularly the Americans, who now had two sets of Turkmen, Tajik, Kyrgyz, Kazak and Russian visas. I could take you on an intimate tour of Bishkek's bars and eateries, and I had gained the street equivalent of a PhD in Traffic Cop Psychology.

As we sat around at the Kazakh-Russian border, I struggled to sum up my thoughts on the region. We had such varied experiences: a month in urban, Russified Bishkek versus a fortnight stuck in the remote Tajik mountains; staying in renovated, historic Khiva versus camping on the dusty Turkmen-Uzbek border; the long straight roads of Kazakhstan versus the rock strewn mud track of the Anzob Pass.

It was hard to weigh it all up. In Turkmenistan, Uzbekistan and Tajikistan the police interference was regular, and we were stopped constantly and unnecessarily although we were rarely bribed. In Bishkek I wished there were more police, I didn't feel safe at night.

A combination of the poor roads causing breakdowns and delays, the slow pace in the mountains, and the bureaucracy involved in getting new visas made the whole experience a testing time. But once we dumped the Merc the roads were less of a problem, and the visa issues had followed on from the breakdowns. There was no doubt that it was the most difficult part of the Trek to that point, though the end of each region had seen it declared the toughest. That slow ratcheting up of difficulty was one of the inadvertent successes of the route planning.

Most of us agreed that we would go back to Central Asia. I would like to see more of Uzbekistan's Silk Road cities, I would recommend the Darvaza gas crater in Turkmenistan to anyone, and Tajikistan's Pamir Mountains were probably the most stunning drive yet.

But, we concluded after some debate, we probably wouldn't take Trabants.

Entering Russia

Driving through Siberia was exactly how I imagined. Thick forests of skinny, densely packed, skeletal trees, topped with a dusting of snow, and rooted in a bed of ice. For thousands of miles the road ploughed through the bright white landscape.

We camped our first night on packed snow, deep in a scary looking forest, but the next day the surroundings developed into rolling golden plains, the afternoon sun picking out a yellow haze across the horizon. We went through one strange looking wood, where only the very tops of the tall trees bore leaves, the trunks, hidden in perpetual shade, hadn't bothered with foliage. The forest looked like it had a crew cut.

It was cold, cold enough to freeze our windscreens and leave icicles on our wing mirrors, but nothing like the dire predictions we had been given. It touched – 8C at night, very manageable with all our bedding. Everywhere we went locals told us it was unusually warm for that time of year. Some good luck at last. It snowed a few times, but nothing heavy enough to slow us down.

I had an image in my mind of the stereotypical Russian: gruff, shouting, impatient and quick to anger. But that cliché was thoroughly dispelled by the people we met during our first few days in Siberia. At the very first café we entered, a man enquired about our route, told us there was a quicker way and insisted on leading us to the road. Once there he reached into the back of his car and pulled out six beers for us as a parting gift. A few hours later a bunch of lads led us around a town to find an ATM, then took us 20km up the road to a petrol station. The police pulled us over nearby, but only to take our picture.

When we arrived at our first big city, Novosibirsk, I immediately hated it. A sprawling, industrial traffic jam covered in mud and ice gridlocked beneath a dirty grey sky. But Fez obviously took a shine to the place. He chose to give up right in the city centre, causing chaos as we pushed him across a six-lane highway to park outside the city's library. The night shift, comprising Tony, Lovey and me, stayed up to fix Fez, while the day shift got some sleep. Throughout the night a bunch of local lads, including two off-duty policemen, stayed with us and brought us beer. They said they had to go to bed at about 3am, but returned twenty minutes later with hot sandwiches and coffees. The Russians were winning me over.

Twice that night, in the ice and the snow, we removed the engine, adjusted it and replaced it, only to find it still wasn't working. There are few things more demoralising, but Tony and Lovey were in good spirits and conversation was good. As day broke and the rest of the gang began to stir, we still hadn't got the car going. Luckily OJ got chatting to a couple of girls who had been studying in the library, and one of them insisted we go back to her grandparents' apartment to wash, do laundry and stay the night.

How could we refuse?

Kataya looked East Asian, but Asya was thoroughly European, a buxom blonde. Kataya's grandparents properly took us in, giving Zsofi some much needed pampering and a whole load of clothes, and Carlos a very fetching stripy sweater.

The next day, random strangers from the housing estate worked on the cars and a wonderful family nearby fed Carlos and me a huge lunch and dinner with lashings of vodka and gave me a scarf. It was hard to refuse an invitation to Kataya's friend's 21st birthday party, and despite reservations about our schedule, we decided to go.

I presented the birthday girl with a bottle of red wine. "We're Russian girls, we drink vodka," she replied, to the cheers of her friends. Later, Carlos chose to remove his shirt, an inexplicable manoeuvre that only served to frighten the women folk. They were a fun bunch, dancing to terrible R'n'B and cheesy pop. It could have been a 21st birthday party anywhere in Europe. How weird is the formation of the world's culture that there, two months after staying on the

Afghan border, and a thousand kilometres further east, we seemed to be back in Europe.

I was tasked with getting up at 8am to go to the car market and find a new bearing for Fez, so I resisted drunken antics, but I did have a clear-the-air chat with Lovey. In Bishkek he had read a blog I'd written which criticised him for threatening to go home back in Armenia. He said he hadn't meant to bring it up the way he did, at a dinner with a load of old friends, but he'd been backed into a corner. In the blog I wrote that he had gone down in my estimation, something he said he hoped wasn't for good. The chat helped to bridge the gap that had opened in our friendship.

THE ATM

The next day we got back on the 24-hour driving thing. The road quality deteriorated, making it hard for the drivers to drive and hard for the sleepers to sleep, slowing the whole process down. Luckily the route was well used by truckers, and so had rest stops every few hours where the drivers could grab a coffee or instigate a change over. We continued in this manner, without stopping, for three days.

As we neared Irkutsk, Fez was kind enough to break down near a mechanics' workshop and although it was closed, when they saw us jacking up the car in the cold and the snow they invited us in to use their lifting equipment. It made the job ten times easier and again we were left praising thoughtful Russians.

As we set about the car, some friends of the mechanic turned up with some weed. I hadn't smoked since Budapest and I was keen to see what they had. The bifta was rolled strangely, a backflip with a long, wide roach that must have been half the joint. It was soap and it was pleasant. Later they embarrassed me when, as I was undoing a bolt under the Trabbi and surrounded by the Americans, one of the Russian dope-fiends came up to the car and bent down:

"Hey, Daniel, come," he waved the joint towards me. I looked at the Yanks. I knew they weren't into it but I didn't know how much they disapproved.

"You want?" the stoner waved the bifta at the Americans.

"No, no, no, no," they all shook their heads and looked at the ground.

Well bollocks to them, I thought, I'm not getting peer pressured into NOT smoking a joint. I shuffled towards him, awkwardly squatting under the raised car, and then he insisted on giving me a blowback. For those who never had a smoke when they were fifteen, that is where he reverses the spliff in his mouth, puckers his lips and pouts them close to mine, as if we are about to kiss, then blows smoke into my gob. A sensual manoeuvre when performed with an attractive, new female acquaintance at a party—but wholly inappropriate when attempted with a gold-toothed, slack-jawed Russian man in front of disapproving colleagues under a broken Trabant.

Of course, immediately after the incident I spent five minutes loosening a bolt I should have been tightening (I was coming at it from reverse, honest guv). Embarrassing.

We made it out of the garage in the early hours, got something to eat, then found an ATM, which promptly ate OJ's card. The big Slav cracked in a terrible way, shouting, ranting and hitting stuff—I would have hated to be the plastic bin in the bank-o-mat booth. I actually had to walk away; I thought he might lash out at me, for I had led him to the machine.

In moments like those my reaction was normally the complete opposite—calm, rational: "How do we sort this one out then?" kind of thing. When I was a teenager my grandmother gave me *Letters from a Stoic* by Seneca, and I'd always respected the old Roman's attitude to misfortune. But then he ended up tutoring Nero; hardly got across the virtues of restraint and self-discipline there, did he?

But it wasn't really the time to explain Stoicism to OJ, who kept repeating his own mantra: "I'm gonna smash that fucking machine up."

After getting a local to phone the emergency number in the booth we decided to camp outside the bank until it opened.

ZSOFI

Siberia was taking its toll. A combination of the non-stop driving, the lack of sleep and the bleak environment started to get to people.

Zsofi wasn't in a good way. I wasn't sure what it was, there seemed to have been a constant train of things for a while, but I guessed she was just run down. It had been tough on her those last few weeks—the threats hanging over her from her father, knowing she probably couldn't finish the trip, lying to her family about going north. She was also suffering from being the only girl left, and had been left out by the rest of us a bit. We didn't pay her as much attention as we should have, but more importantly her relationship with Tony had soured.

The two of them had spent a lot of time together, they'd shared pretty much every journey in Dante, and right from the start they had been very cosy.

But, as far as I could tell, they hadn't been getting along since they had been re-united in Bishkek. I'm not really sure whether there was an incident, or just the gradual build up of resentment that can come with enforced proximity, but they were finding it hard to even look at each other, and that was pretty tough considering we were spending so much time in the cars. It was easier for Tony, who could chat with old friends like Lovey and OJ. But for Zsofi, feeling unwell and upset and with no female company, there wasn't really anywhere to turn.

Throughout the "OJ's card being eaten by the ATM" incident, Zsofi wasn't asleep in Dante, as I had expected, but instead pacing around a grubby housing estate in the cold.

"Why don't you sit in the car in the warm?" I asked.

"If I sit down I will fall asleep, and I need to drive," she said, sounding desperately unhappy, "I'm not very well."

Once we'd decided to sit it out until the bank opened, I went to break the news to Zsofi, who was still pacing.

"Hey, Zsofi," I held her arm—she was wrapped in a big ski jacket which had that cold plastic feel on the outside—"we're gonna stay here tonight."

As she turned, her face caught the light of a street lamp and I could see a bright tear trail down her cheek and I heard a little sniffle.

"Oh, sweetness, hey, hey, come here," I drew her into me, held her, and gave her a kiss on the cheek. She had no shape under all her layers—it was like hugging a bin bag of clothes earmarked for Oxfam.

"I'm so tired," she whimpered, "I really need to sleep."

I kissed her again on the cheek, wiped at her tear, rocked her a little and made soothing noises. We hung there for a minute.

"I really don't think I can keep driving like this. These twelve-hour shifts are too much. I need, like, ten hours sleep for the next two nights. I might stay in the next city and you guys can go on."

I wasn't sure what to offer her other than understanding. We hung there again.

"Shall we set the tent up?" I asked.

"Yes."

"Can I stay in there with you?" I asked—I knew she hated sleeping alone.

"Yes please."

We found a terrible spot to camp—in the central square of the housing estate—but she didn't want to pitch on concrete because it was so cold, and I wasn't going to argue.

145

The next day she told me that she hadn't been given her November allowance by her parents. She was nearly out of cash and definitely wouldn't be able to finish the trip.

OJ got his card back from the bank and after a full day's driving we hit Irkutsk that evening. We'd made an abysmal 1,100km in 72 hours.

BACKPACKER

I was alone. The Mongolian embassy had put the wrong date on my visa and so I needed to get a new one in Irkutsk. But I wasn't sure how long that would take, and there wasn't much time to play with, so we decided that I should stay behind to sort it out while the Trek raced ahead to try for Mongolia before the border closed for the weekend. I hoped to follow by airplane, if I could find one.

After a few weeks of constant driving, and months staying in tents, *yurts*, cars and the open, I was looking forward to a hotel room. A horribly drunk but very friendly policeman led us through the city in a convoy. He took us down pedestrian-only roads, over pavements and used his police car to block off traffic for us, clearly revelling in escorting our strange Trabbi circus. The Hotel Irkutsk was an international affair, not a young person in sight, and cost three days' budget a night. But it had a bathtub and I enjoyed lying in hot water properly for the first time in months.

I'm here now, I thought, I should probably make the most of it. Wake-up call at 8.30am, head down to breakfast, on the way skip past reception and book a flight to Ulaanbaatar, along with a cab to the Mongolian embassy, hand my laundry in for collection on my return. Act like I am just another one of the businessman tugging cigars at the bar.

The embassy went smoothly and I got my visa the next afternoon. But at the airport I was disappointed; there was no flight, not one till the next week. So I resigned myself to a weekend in Irkutsk.

Heading back into the city by bus instead of driving a brightly coloured lunchbox, I thought that people would have stopped staring. But they couldn't get enough of it and they didn't let up for a moment. Waiting to cross the road, the driver of the car at the lights stopped to gawp for so long that motorists behind him began hooting. People were transfixed. I hadn't seen many other tourists, it was the low season, but I didn't expect Russians to be too interested in a lone backpacker. And that was what I had been reduced to. Squinting under a streetlamp at the map I tore out of our guidebook, carrying all my belongings on my shoulders, longhaired and stubbly, wearing a dirty green Russian military jacket, faded blue flat cap and chocolate scarf. The girls in Novosibirsk had said I looked like a *bumsh*, which is the Russian word for a bum. So maybe people thought I was a touring hobo? Saved up enough from begging to head out east on my hols? I guess that would be worth staring at.

GENTRIFYING THE BADLANDS

I had expected a Siberian city to be rugged and basic, based around necessity and survival. But Irkutsk couldn't be further from that.

The city was once the rough Siberian hub of Russia's expansion east, an expansion fuelled by convicts and undesirables serving sentences of forced labour. But the dynamics of the city changed in1826 when Tsar Nicholas I banished to Siberia the so called "Decembrists", leaders of a failed uprising in St Petersburg. They brought with them more refined ideas and turned the place from a remote badland to a cultural centre. Dubbed the Paris of Siberia by Chekhov when he visited at the turn of the last century, the pretty, tree-lined avenues were flanked by ornate and impressive mansions and museums.

In a square by the junction of Lenin Street and Karl Mark Street stood the seemingly compulsory Lenin statue, arm pointing the way forward. I'd lost count of how many Lenins I had seen since we entered the Russian-speaking world, and it really was a world—a huge swathe of the map. Had any man of modern times made more of an impact on the globe? From the Caucasus to eastern Siberia we saw his statues dominating central squares, his mantras adorning factory walls and his vision idealised in freezes and paintings.

I guess the only people with a comparable modern influence are Jesus and Mohammed, though I doubt Lenin's legend will last a fraction as long. Already in cities like Bishkek, Lenin had been relegated from his central position in the main square and replaced with a local hero, part of the long process of nation building. Lenin had been moved round the back, tucked among the evergreens, and I suppose one day he'll be moved from there.

Further down Lenin Street I was surprised to find a Stalin bust in a small, modest square. He wasn't named and there was no plaque, but I'm pretty sure it was him, with the glowering eyes and thick moustache. The first Stalin I had seen.

The decision to leave Irkutsk came suddenly. I woke up late on Friday having spent the day catching up on sleep, ate, then wandered around looking for a bar. There was a place called Liverpool tucked down a side alley. I had to have a look. Inside it was covered in Beatles memorabilia, Russian dolls of John, Paul, George and Ringo on the mantelpiece, live music playing in one room, and a Roy Orbison gig on the TV. With the help of a Russian acting as interpreter I tried to quiz the waitress on how the pub got its name. Is the owner English?

"No, Russian."

So why the name?

"Because it is the only pub in Irkutsk."

She refused to expand. I heard a northern voice, and found a couple of lads from Leeds sitting at the bar. They were taking the Trans-Siberian Railway across the country, but seemed to be having a completely different trip from me.

"The Russians are great, aren't they?" I said.

"Well, they're alright once you get beneath the icy exterior. But most of them are moody bastards."

I was surprised. "Well there are a lot of lovely ladies about."

"They're alright. Nice bodies. Don't make much of their faces though."

We were surely on a different trip. The Russians had been great to us, and we boys had constantly been turning our heads at another well-dressed, good-looking lady. Maybe the Trabants were our golden ticket, the source of our powers?

We kept drinking and chatting, as they were pleased to talk to a Brit after going three weeks pretty much only speaking to each other due to their lack of Russian and the absence of tourists in low season Siberia. It turned out that one of them lived in Chertsey for a couple of years, just a couple of miles from me.

We had been chatting for a few hours and it was early in the morning, but I knew I had the luxury of a hotel room the next day, so was in no rush. But then disaster. I idly flicked through their guidebook and saw that there was a train to the Mongolian capital of Ulaanbaatar leaving at 6am—in about three and a half hours. Fantastic news. I could actually get to Ulaanbaatar in time to get my China visa with the rest of the gang. But terrible news. I was in no state to take on an hour's sleep followed by a 36-hour train ride. But what choice did I have? I drank up, returned to the hotel, packed my bags, had an hour's kip, and headed to the train station. No one spoke English and I got sent around the houses, but finally determined there was no early train at all—the next one was at 8.30pm. What a waste of a perfectly good hotel room and a decent night's sleep. I cursed the guidebook and headed into town to find a café to sit, write and wait for the train.

Standing outside a café, waiting for it to open, I counted how much cash was left in my wallet—about $12. A man in his thirties came up to me and asked for money. I said no, but accidentally dropped a 100-rouble bill, about $4.

He stepped on it.

I asked him to move, and he stepped back, very deliberately and obviously scraping the note with him under his foot. I laughed and bent down to pick it up, but he wouldn't get off it. Then he dragged it away a bit and grabbed the note. I grabbed the other half and we engaged in a tug of war based around the four-inch long strip of paper.

I was shouting at him to let go, our faces inches apart. He didn't look tough, he was vaguely handsome, and looked clean, but when he gritted his teeth I could see they were in a terrible state—the classic sign of the desperate (and the English, according to our American Trekkers). This impasse went on for a stupidly long time—and long enough for me to consider what to do. I thought about head butting him. But once you've had time to think about these things the moment tends to pass. And anyway what then? What if he head butted me back? I didn't fancy an early morning head butting competition with a desperate Russian mugger.

He eventually wrestled control of the note, jumped in the air and ran off, looking behind once to see if I was following. I just stood and stared. What a pathetic mugging, on both our parts. Him too cowardly to mug me properly, me too cowardly to defend myself.

That night I caught the train, and it had a bed. That's all you need to know.

THE WORLD'S COLDEST CAPITAL

When I got on the train I was in Europe. When I got off I was in Asia. It's not true, but that's how it felt. I'd only really headed south, hardly east at all, but the people looked entirely different. Asian. Well, Mongolian actually.

The train pulled in around 6:30am, an hour early. Typical that I get the only train to arrive early in the whole of East Asia at the very time I'm in a comatose sleep in a decent bed. The Trek had clearly already hit Ulaanbaatar because the assembled touts claimed to know where the guys were.

"They are at our place," a kind looking lady told me. I trusted her but didn't

Ulaanbaatar

want to be complacent, so asked a few questions about the gang. She had all the answers so I went with her.

The hostel the boys found had a TV in the front room. No one was up yet and I hated to wake them, so I flicked on BBC World. *Asian Business Review* came on and normally I would have lapped it up, as I love the news, it has a meditative affect on me, but that morning I realised how much I'd changed.

News Anchor: "So the rise in interest rates could have an effect on the equities sector?"

Expert: "I believe so and that means firms like..."

Absolutely no interest. Dealing so intently with life's little problems—eating, sleeping, moving—had made the issue of Asian economics seem a little removed. The Northern Ireland Secretary flashed up on screen, Shaun Woodward MP. It was the classic shot, standing outside parliament, interviewer off camera. I hadn't heard a politician talk for months, but it was so depressing. I don't remember what he was talking about—in fact he wasn't talking, he was regurgitating some message in slow deliberant dullness, so devoid of charisma he may well have been a government autobot, constructed in the depths of Downing Street from faded manifestos.

Chinese visas were done pretty smoothly. I wrote that I was a journalist on my form and it caused a bit of a stir. They demanded my press card, photocopied it and asked a few extra questions, but I got the visa fine.

I had raced to Ulaanbaatar from Russia because we planned to leave straight after getting our visas done. But it was Trabant Trek, and of course we didn't leave. There was work to be done on the cars. It turned out I could have had a weekend in Irkutsk and then taken the two-hour plane, rather than the 35-hour train, but there we go, it was Trabant Trek.

The neighbourhood we were staying in was full of pretty well-dressed folk. The kids were hip-hoppy, a little skatery, then you'd see the odd traditional orange sash and gown. There was a young indie vibe, plenty of independent retailers like the Homestay Hip Hop Shop. They loved their hip- hop. Despite the appearance of the locals, who looked entirely Mongolian, in many ways that place felt more European than Irkutsk. It could have been Eastern Europe. Everything was anglicised—or maybe that should be Americanised—and there were far more English speakers than in Siberia.

We passed King Pizza, California Restaurant, the Detroit Bar (slogan: "Shut up and Drink"). Americans didn't even need a visa to get into Mongolia and, like most of the places we'd visited, English-speaking locals found my accent more difficult to understand than the Americans'.

I strolled around Sukhbaatar Square in the centre of the city. City squares. Across the world people have the same idea: clear a big space in the middle of the city and whack a great statue or column up there with a national hero on the top, in this case Sukhbaatar, who liberated the country in the 1920s. Try and flank the square with a few good buildings, maybe an opera house or a museum and *voilà*, a centre for civic pride, national identity and a focal point for protest *à la* Trafalgar, Tiananmen, Catalunya, Mayo.

My fleeting affair with the Russian language was over. It is amazing how much of the world speaks Russian. Before the trip I hadn't really thought about it, but we'd been using Russian since early August, when we arrived in Georgia. Three months of it and we'd all picked up a fair amount—OJ in particular was very hot at it, and we could all read the Cyrillic alphabet. But Mongolia had its own language, and then we'd be dealing with Chinese. That would be a problem.

Some nights it dropped to - 20C. There was no wind chill, but it was still crazily cold. Exposed fingers ached and burned within minutes, cold feet began to hurt. One evening we bought a few beers to keep us warm while we worked on Fez's brakes. But every time we cracked one open it froze before we could finish it, and they were only little 330ml cans. I watched steam rising from an open manhole like effluent ghosts escaping from the sewers. Water bottles left in the car overnight turned to solid blocks of ice.

In the mornings the cars rarely started. On day three we spent an age trying to get Ziggy going, pushing the Trabbi around the circle of the courtyard we were parked in, gathering quite a crowd of onlookers. An unhealthy Trabant resonates at a specific frequency that sets off every car alarm it passes, as if the other vehicles are shrieking a warning or crying out in agony. The morning was spent stopping and gasping after another failed attempt at push starting the car, surrounding by flashing lights and ringing alarms in the freezing cold.

Finally Ziggy was going and we thought we'd pull start Dante. But that didn't work so Tony popped the hood and found some cheeky tykes had nicked the battery. Who steals a car battery? It had cost us $8. And they tore the font of the bonnet up to get at it.

We had been warned to park near the guard's hut, and we didn't, so we probably deserved it. Carlos had heeded the advice when parking Fez and enjoyed a little game of "I told you so". There was a bit of rivalry between the cars.

A Note on Genghis Khan

When I think of Mongolia I think of Genghis Khan, and the country certainly isn't shy of its heritage. Genghis' face appears all over the place, from restaurants and bars to chocolate and beer. In one bar I was able to order a double Genghis with Genghis. I did some research into the all-conquering Khan and found that pretty much our entire route to that point would once have been in Mongol hands.

I had never fully grasped the size of this empire before—when Genghis died it stretched from the Caspian to the Pacific, four times the size of Alexander the Great's and twice that of the Roman Empire. By 1300, seventy-three years after his death, that area had doubled to include all of China, Korea, Tibet, Pakistan, Iran, most of Turkey, Georgia, Armenia, Azerbaijan, habitable Russia, Ukraine, Hungary and half of Poland. One-fifth of the world's land area.

From the gates of Vienna in the west to the jungle of South East Asia and all in between was either controlled by, or a vassal to, the Mongol Emperor. As the Americas had been forgotten by Eurasians, and sub-Saharan Africa was mostly unknown, this must have seemed like pretty much the whole world.

At their peak the Mongols were taking on Saracens in the Middle East, Hungarian knights in Europe and invading the island of Japan on the opposite side of the world. Mind-boggling in its enormity, it makes a mockery of Hitler, Napoleon, Catherine, Attila, Victoria and Xerxes.

Since the seventeenth century, when the current version of the Mongolian nation was established, its capital was always a tent city. The highly mobile settlement could migrate to seek new grazing and had a variety of uninspiring names like Camp and Capital Camp.

The Mongols weren't natural city dwellers, and large parts of Ulaanbaatar were still made of tents, albeit with electricity. Driving around town to find spare parts for Fez, I saw a bit more of this behind-the-scenes UB. The outskirts of the city were made of one-storey wooden shacks surrounded by the impeccable *gers* or *yurts*, their chimney puffs joining in the low atmosphere to create a thick, opaque haze across the city. The *ger* was still very much a part of life.

Inside the mechanics' *ger* that we visited it was warm, spacious and well-kept, the central stove heating the place up nicely, the walls decorated with blankets showing horses playing on an idyllic steppe. Most front yards seemed to have a *ger* and I asked the owner of the workshop, Chinzo, who lived in them.

"Families. Sometimes the family of the people in the house, sometimes just another family. It is our way of life."

The whole suburbs of neat, round felt tents were quite a sight and I hope it stays that way.

One Week Later

Although the original plan was to stay in Ulaanbaatar for a few hours to get our visas and go, it turned into a week. And not the "let's spend a week in the world's coldest capital" sort of a week, but a Trabant Trek week. Every day we would prepare ourselves to leave, pack our bags and wrap ourselves up, and then something new would happen to the cars to force us to stay. Fez's brakes were the biggest problem and no amount of tightening or bleeding seemed to work.

Ulaanbaatar was the destination for the famous Mongol Rally, and the race or-ganisers put us in touch with some mechanics. Along with the Mighty Tony P they tried a variety of fixes, but it took days. Because we always thought we were about to leave, we didn't really do much in the city. We did get a look at the local charity, the Lotus Children's Centre. But other than that, we sat around using internet and trying to find western food. Progress was slow, it was too cold to go outside, and we watched as our China visas ticked away.

OJ's girlfriend told him over the phone that their relationship was fin-ished. I didn't really get into the ins and outs of it, but he had promised her he would be home for the end of November, and clearly he wasn't going to be. It was tough on the Slav, but it did mean we got to keep him, which was good for us.

For the hundredth time Zsofi's parents told her she should head home. They really weren't being very supportive.

"This time I said that I would," she told us at a meeting by the cars. She was nearly out of cash, she explained. She planned to fly home from Beijing.

Then there would be five.

At least Zsofi's health had improved, as had her relationship with Tony. She was brighter and happier after the darker days of Siberia.

We left Ulaanbaatar on Monday 19 November, about the time Tony thought he would be getting home to Washington DC. The only thing between us and China was the Gobi, the biggest and most extreme desert in Asia, with temperatures ranging from summer highs of 40C to winter lows of - 40C. As far as we knew, no one had ever attempted the crossing in Trabants.

GOBI: THE END OF THE ROAD

About a hundred and fifty kilometres south of Ulaanbaatar the paved road ends.

Like a river petering out in the desert it splits into streams, which divide into rivulets, then trickle out into the sands.

There is no single path from Mongolia to China. Instead there are a million tracks beaten into the desert by a million vehicles, a web of trails criss-crossing the plains for 500km. The better-worn paths may be better travelled, but that doesn't mean they are quicker or more direct. It is a lottery.

We had all sorts of advice about crossing this maze.

Some of the more vague being: "Just head south."

Some of the more reasonable being: "Follow the train track."

But the unifying theme of the advice was simple: "Don't drive at night."

Carlos, OJ, Tony, Lovey and Zsofi in the Gobi desert

So I guess when, deep into the night, we lost the railroad and stopped using the compass, we were bound to get into trouble.

Lost in the desert after sunset there are no discernable landmarks. We may as well have been at sea, and I hadn't thought to bring a sextant. By 1.30am we had been doing circles for an hour and things were getting a little desperate. It gets seriously cold out there and no one especially wanted to sit in the cars waiting for the sun, which wouldn't rise until 7.30am.

We grasped how perilous the situation was when the lead car inadvertently led our convoy onto a frozen lake. I only realised when I touched the brakes and the car skidded away. Cue mass panic as all three cars desperately tried to pull to a halt and reverse, wheels spinning on the ice and everyone freaking out in the cabins. None of us knew how deep the lake was, or how thick the ice, but it got the adrenaline pumping. We had a brief meeting to try and work out what was going on and where we were headed and found our two compasses were both pointing in different directions. You couldn't make it up.

Things went wrong throughout that trip, sometimes it seemed as if everything was against us, but occasionally the universe conspired to help. In the darkness we stumbled across a rough-hewn track, and at the end of it, deep in the Gobi, we found a building. Amazing.

There was nothing around it, just this large, crumbling two-storey building alone in the desert. It appeared derelict, but we could see a light on, so I went in with the Johns and stumbled around in the dark, shouting hello and opening doors. There was a large billiards table in the lobby and gaping holes in the floorboards. The scene was set for a werewolf encounter, or a room full of gun-toting desert bandits to appear.

Instead a kindly woman came out and told us we could stay. Earlier that evening we had stopped at a café by a crossing in the railway that was 150km from Sainshand, our destination. But the woman said we were now 230km from Sainshand. It doesn't sound too much, but in those conditions we were going no faster than 40kph, so we had needlessly gone a good few hours in the wrong direction when we were in a race to get to China.

We looked on our incredibly inaccurate guidebook map and saw that the train track we were following split at Airag—one branch went south-south-west to the border, the other doubling back on itself and heading north-north-east into nothingness. We'd followed that one. If ever you go that way, stick to the west side of the track, a piece of advice we had been sadly lacking. We all shared a freezing room and grabbed a few hours' kip.

In the sunlight of the next morning I got to look around the place we were staying: a very strange building, large but dilapidated—who drags a billiard table out into the desert? I couldn't help but wonder at its former glory. The woman who had set up beds for us didn't seem to want any money, but I gave her some anyway.

Round the back I found a small hamlet, five buildings in a square, all of them falling apart and looking unlived in. But the square was full of statues of curly horned goats on plinths—there must have been half a dozen along with a mysterious sitting camel. And at one end was a broken statue of someone in a veil; I couldn't work out if it was a man or a woman because part of the face had been sheered off. On the top of a dune opposite I saw a pile of heaped rocks.

Maybe it was some kind of religious site? Certainly I could see no reason for a tiny hamlet to have so many statues. Maybe the big building was a hotel? Maybe pilgrims used to go there? In the daylight the isolation of the place was even more vivid. We were nowhere.

The Gobi, which means desert in Mongolian, wasn't particularly sandy like the Sahara or Karakoum. It was mostly made up of plains, dirty, gritty, plains as far as the eye could roam, with the odd jagged rock face rising up. I don't think I've ever seen such a vast expanse of flatness, except when looking out to sea. In some places it got grassy, with thick weeds and a film of yellow. In others there were patches of treacherous sand, ripe for power slides and wheel spins. Many of the paths were scored deep into the soil so we had little choice but to follow the heavy grooves.

The absence of roads hadn't stopped people from making their homes far out in the wilderness. We passed a horseman in traditional robes held together with a bright sash and wearing tall felt boots over padded trousers, a thick skin hat on his head. The horse wore an ornate saddle of tarnished metal and well-worn straps. The combination looked bright and gaudy among the washed out yellows of the surroundings.

Mongolian horses have always been famous, but not for their size or speed; they are actually quite stumpy animals, looking more like overgrown Shetland ponies than world-conquering horses and their hair is thick and long and warm and cuddly. What makes the Mongol horse stand out from the bunch is its endurance; the beast will keep going until it drops dead from exhaustion.

A few hours into our second day's drive, and when the terrain had began to improve and we were making some decent progress, I had the audacity to tell Carlos that I thought there was a chance we could make it to China that day.

Then the front left leaf spring on Ziggy snapped, making the wheel arch sag down onto the tyre. The car was undrivable and after sending a scouting party ahead we walked it to a small hamlet by the railway. The place consisted of six large wooden buildings for living in, painted maroon, yellow and blue, and a bunch of small sheds for livestock. The whole thing was ringed by an unimposing, waist-high green metal fence. The hamlet could have been from Sylvanian Families or Hobiton. In the middle was a basketball court, and a stack of timber. It was so neat and pristine it felt like a film set.

OJ: "It's a home for railway workers. There are about twenty guys who live here. Every day they head out on these little carts and check on their stretch of the railway."

Those modern steppe dwellers lived in wooden homes rather than tents, and spent their days tending their stretch of the railway, rather than their herds. The path of progress.

There was a camel tethered to its cart near the hamlet and I went to investigate. I'd never liked camels, having spent three uncomfortable days on a one-humped monster in the Sahara a few years back. It spat and bit and sneezed, was ugly and grimy to look at, uncomfortable to ride, and needed to be constantly kept in line.

But this one was entirely different. Beautifully groomed with a long beard that turned into a flowing natural scarf down the length of its long elegant neck, it had a flowering Mohican on top of its head and thick, bushy leg hair above its knees that made it look like it was wearing knickerbockers. It was one of the famous Bactrian camels, and I guess I had unfairly lumped the two-humped variety in with their one-humped relatives. I'd heard they could go a month without water and then drink 250 litres in one sitting. That would put OJ to shame.

A few of the locals got the leaf spring out of Ziggy and stared at it for a while before agreeing that they couldn't repair it. We decided to split up. Three of us, Tony, Carlos and I, would drive to Sainshand to try and find parts. Three people in two cars, so that if anything broke on the way we could try and fix it (we had Tony) or dump the car (we had a spare). The other three were offered a floor to sleep on in the hamlet.

By the time the Sainshand party left it was dark and it took us three hours to cover the 85km, but we only lost the train tracks once.

Earlier that day, when we had left Ulaanbaatar, it felt like leaving the Arctic. It had snowed quite heavily overnight and the fall had settled deep and undisturbed on the endless flats. It looked like pictures of the North Pole rather than East Asia, but the snow slowly dappled out as it got warmer and by the time we reached Sainshand it was a giddy 4C.

It was a strange little town with some impressive administrative buildings but the whiff of desperation in the air. The focal point was a public square outside the government offices. In the square was an empty swimming pool which appeared determined to morph into a sandpit, and an unpaved, unloved basketball court with both hoops torn from their backboards. At night we watched a woman fighting a man in the street and saw the top of a large new apartment building burning down.

The kids were cute. They looked like little Ewoks with their big woolly hats and backpacks that made their arms stick out funnily. They spoke like the adults: in strange whisperings. The Mongol language sounds like a gruffly gentle fluting, coming from the back of the throat in rasping, airy grasps. Unlike anything I had heard before, it sounded rather like the murmurs of extras talking among themselves in a film, all hushed tones muttered under the breath.

The next day we got the leaf spring welded and made it back to rescue the others. In the daylight I could see just how much livestock there was in that part of the desert, where it reached the lusher plains of eastern Mongolia. Scores of horses roamed in herds, hundreds of cattle chewing absently. We ploughed through the shrubs, scattering tiny birds. There was life in that harsh environment.

We got the whole team back to Sainshand and stayed the night, then rose early to try and push for China. The welding on the leaf spring quickly began to split, so Ziggy, and therefore the rest of us, were limited to just 30kph.

Shortly after lunchtime the tracks we were following disappeared into a sand dune. Carlos thought he could cross it and pushed on, but only succeeded in getting Fez stuck in the sand, then tearing up the clutch plate trying to get us out.

The plate was destroyed and we were miles from any life, so we did the repairs in the desert. It was dark by the time we finished and some people wanted to sleep out there, though I wasn't one of them. It was so cold that all our water had frozen solid, but we made a fire out of dried camel dung and tumbleweed, then sawed down some posts from the railway fence we were following to fuel the smelly, smokey blaze.

Sitting around that fire we ate a few noodles and drank the dregs of a bottle of vodka, then one of the Americans realised it was Thanksgiving.

Tony: "This has to be the strangest Thanksgiving ever. Broken down in the middle of the Gobi, sitting around a fire made of camel shit, eating dried noodles from the packet. Man."

I slept in Fez and probably had the coldest night of my life. Whatever position I tried I got an icy draft from the uncloseable door, my sleeping bag seemed to radiate cold. "This one's really warm," my brother Tobi had told me when he handed it over. It wasn't. I could only snatch a half hour here and there before being woken by my own shivering. I came to in the night to find a chunk of ice had formed on my hat and where my breath condensed on my scarf it was frozen stiff. My feet turned to numb aching blocks. I spent most of the night muttering curses, though the others, in the tents, didn't seem much better off.

The next morning, day five of our attempt to cross the Gobi, we drove long and hard to get to the border before six. We arrived at five thirty, and initially they wouldn't let us pass, but we begged and made it through Mongolian customs as it closed.

We were a mess. Everyone had scruffy beards, even Zsofi, and we had been living in the same dirty, unwashed clothes for weeks. There was little inclination to shower when it was so damn cold, and most of us had grease and engine oil matted into hair and across our faces.

"Maybe this should have been called Trabant Wreck," Tony suggested. We were dirty, cold and exhausted. But finally, nearly four weeks after leaving Bishkek, we had completed the Northern Route. We had reached China.

7

CHINA

23 November – 23 December 2007

Q) When does a Trabant reach its top speed?
A) When it's hauled away by a tow truck.

CHINA

CHINA. The name had been on our lips for so long. Normally spat out with disdain and preceded by a vehement expletive. The stringent conditions attached to taking cars across the country had made it an expensive and irksome hassle. It had been a worry for months. But we'd made it. Walking through the border was the best feeling I'd had in weeks.

"We're in China, mate. China!" I said to OJ with a huge smile and we shook hands and hugged. Fez was the last vehicle to arrive, screeching up as night fell and the border closed. Luckily our guide was waiting for us, and he persuaded the guards to stay open late to let us in. Customs was closed so the cars spent the night at the border, while we strolled hungrily into town, reasoning that it was probably a good place to get a decent Chinese. I felt like I floated along that road, the buzz was tangible.

I tried to put in perspective what we'd achieved. We'd crossed blazing deserts like the Karakoum, freezing deserts like the Gobi, rough industrial cities in Russia and stunning cultural cities in Europe. We'd done the Turkish summer and the Siberian winter, the icy Pamir Mountains and the dusty Carpathians. We'd dealt with crooked cops, despotic regimes, withering bureaucracy, enough breakdowns to break a man and all at a gentle 80kph. It had taken four months to cross 18,000km.

From that moment it was all south. The long Northern Route was over, things would get warmer and cheaper, we were heading in the right direction for the first time in months, and every day we got closer to our goal. Closer to the beach. That piña colada was going to be awesome. Just 6,000km to go.

Chinese roads were great. Chinese food was great, and living was cheap, even if getting into the country wasn't. And once we cracked China we'd be in South East Asia—pretty much home. It wasn't the final straight, but it was the last bend on the track, the third leg of the relay. Suddenly it seemed that we could do it.

Carlos and I with Ziggy

But of course it wasn't going to be that easy. Our new guide, a prerequisite for travelling with our own car in China, sprung on us the news that we wouldn't be heading south. First we had to go 350km east to get Chinese driving licences, only issued in the provincial capital of Xilinhaote. Extra mileage we hadn't reckoned on. He told us it was going to get colder.

And our timing wasn't great. We arrived on a Thursday and got the cars through customs the following day. But government offices didn't open at weekends, so we would have to wait 'til Monday to get our new licences.

All the time the clock was ticking. Our customs papers for the cars expired on 30 November, just seven days away. There was no chance we'd be out of the country by then. But our guide spoke to a customs official and they predicted a few days leniency. Maybe five or six days leniency. So in theory we could get to the China-Laos border on 6 December. That gave us twelve days to get 4,500km on good roads. It was feasible, but we probably wouldn't see anything of China, a double disappointment considering how much we had spent getting in there. Even so, having just crossed the Gobi on dirt tracks, I felt confident that those well-paved Chinese roads would float by.

But the next day the problems began. Not the extreme but simple-to-diagnose problems like the sheered clutch plate, the broken gearbox, the snapped suspension, the seized engine, the car on fire, the bubonic plague or the outbreak of war. But the finicky, hard-to-diagnose problems.

At high revs Dante began to give up and shut down. At low revs Fez would stall. Neither car would start with the key, and both needed to be push started. With Dante this was quite easy—a decent shove from a couple of people. But the brakes on Fez seemed to be on too tight, so it was a struggle to get moving, and even then it took a few tries to force the engine to turn over. It was exhausting work, and sometimes we would get Fez started just in time to see Dante stall. It was like spinning plates—just as we got one going another came crashing down.

It is hard to get across just what an exhausting nightmare this was. Imagine you are trying to drive for twelve days, but every time you stop, two cars need to be push started. Even if you slow at traffic lights there is a high chance of a stall, and again you're push starting. It's about - 15C and icy outside, so you are wrapped up warm, but after two minutes of running you are hot and tired and sweaty. And just as you get one car going, the other one stalls again. Sometimes these episodes would last ten or fifteen minutes and they could happen every hour. I hadn't done so much pushing since my rugby days, and we were down to physically forcing the cars on. Only 6,000km to go…

I lost count of the amount of times I heard OJ shout: "FUCK. I've had it with this shit."

I told him so and he said: "If I could, I would have quit by now. But I don't have an option."

That night he kicked out at Dante, breaking a gash in the panelling. The stress was getting to people.

In Fez roles were reversed. The passenger used to sleep while the driver dealt with all the problems, but now the driver had to concentrate on keeping the engine running—he needed to be at the throttle and choke constantly—so the passenger had to get out and do all the push starting, refilling, repairing. That meant no sleep, so 24-hour driving was out of the question.

All weekend we stop-started east. All weekend to get 350km. The terrain was similar to the Gobi, but now it had long, straight, well-lit roads running through it. Once we were actually moving we could cruise nicely at 70 kph. But it was a little dull after the random adventure of crossing the desert. We literally pushed the cars the final furlong to Xilinhaote, the provincial capital, arriving late on Monday night, 26 November.

The city had a little of the communist influence we saw in Russia—grand buildings and sweeping public squares, slab-like construction—but a lot of it was sexier, better finished with nicer lighting, more subtle textures, cleaner, neater. The authorities clearly love neon lights, plenty of public buildings were outlined in them and they often changed colour, shifting red, blue and yellow. Despite how that sounds it didn't seem garish.

Food and board was cheap and high quality: $10 for a clean double room with *en suite* and a TV, though there were only state channels, and no BBC. It was $4 for a slap-up meal with a couple of beers. The standard of the food and amenities was all the more welcome after our rough experiences on the Northern Route. We liked China, and because we had a guide there were no communication difficulties. Everything was good except the cars.

The next morning we went to the Chinese version of the DVLA so they could do checks on all our cars and issue us with driving permits. The fact that we were towing Fez to a car inspection was not lost on anyone.

The car park at the DVLA was full of people, and suddenly we were back at the zoo, the latest prime exhibits wheeled out for the punters. Welcome to the Trabbi Road Show—Come And Stare. The locals were swarming. They had no shame, happy to stick their heads into cabins and have a good look around. I got my computer out to write and the swarm migrated from the open bonnet, where a crowd of locals were watching Tony and spitting, to the driver's window so they could stare over my shoulder.

A sea of faces was watching me, more people than had been to some of my gigs. I was 99 per cent sure none of them could read English, so I didn't know what they were looking at. I threw them a dummy, putting my computer away, and watched the crowd disperse then reform at the engine. A few seconds later I got the laptop out again and they returned, the onlookers. They were like zombies, no motion flickered across their faces, few words were exchanged, they just stared. They had definitely seen a computer before, but they were all over the place. Had they seen a Mac? Maybe not. But still, I was word processing, hardly a riveting display of the power of the Macintosh.

The Chinese certainly have an interesting take on privacy and personal space. Two days before, at a two-bit town en route to Xilinhaote, a guy walked into my room at a guesthouse. He just smiled at me and nodded.

"Hi," I said. Then he just walked around looking at our stuff. We had computers, cameras, tapes, hard drives, phones—loads of valuables. It felt like he was scoping us out, making me really uncomfortable. I was in my pants, which also made me a little uncomfortable, so I put my trousers back on. The clincher was when he reached out and started stroking one of my socks. He looked up at me and said something that sounded like approval and smiled.

"Good, good, so you like my socks. Great."

Very strange behaviour.

Our guide approached us. "There is a problem," he said, "we have driven here without the proper licences. We should have got the papers at the border. Now we must pay a fine. One thousand Yuan per car."

We'd paid our tour company a lot to get us though the country, and this was their blunder, so no one was too bothered by $135 per car. Lovey said: "We'll just knock $405 off the money we pay the agent."

But we went to meet "the leader" and argue the case anyway. He was understanding and agreed to waive the fee. I was really getting to like that country.

Still, the delay meant our cars couldn't be processed that day and would have to sit at the office as they were still not road legal. We would have to stay another day in Xilinhaote.

I got a lift back from the Chinese police, hoping that would be my only trip in one of their cars. I'd now been in police cars in Azerbaijan (luxurious), Georgia (budget), Kyrgyzstan (a disgrace, I had to pay for the gas), China (average) and good old Blighty (very friendly).

TRABBI DOWN

Friday, 30 November 2007, and we were meant to leaving China. But seeing as we were in a manic rush to get to the south of the country, we had travelled just 350km sideways in a week. We were still 4,500km from the border with Laos, a journey it would take a decent car a good few days to cross, but in Trabants...

As a marker, it took us nine days to drive 3,600km through Siberia with one major breakdown. So potentially we could be out of China by 10 December? Or by the 11th? Or the 12th? I just hoped Chinese customs would be understanding.

We got our neat new driving licences, but Fez was still broken. The engine had completely seized and Tony decided we needed to change the whole thing out. Our guide found a kind man who let us use the back of his workshop for free. It was not a big job—the engine only weighed about 40kg—and we were told a trained Trabbi mechanic could replace it in twenty minutes. It took Lovey and Tony two hours, a job well done.

The next day we set off for Beijing with high hopes of reaching the city. Fez started first time using a key, a big moment after so much push starting. But after completing a fitful 40km in two hours, it was clear something was wrong. We towed all the way back to the workshop in Xilinhaote, where Tony announced that the new engine was broken and we didn't have the spare part we needed to repair it.

What happened? Well, it wasn't a new engine (there's no such thing as a new Trabant engine), it was second hand like all our other spare parts. Maybe there was something seriously wrong with Fez and the little car tore up the new engine. But there was also a chance that we had carted a broken motor

Fez, boxed up, and ready for shipping

18,000km across the globe. Through mountains, deserts, swamps and cities we'd lugged a 40kg dead weight. That level of ineptitude was well within our collective capability.

That day Fez was loaded onto a truck bound for Beijing. We hoped to meet it in the city the next day and decide whether to fix it, ditch it, or ship it. So we were down from the original four cars to just two. That reduced the number of people we could carry. As Zsofi was on her way home anyway it was decided that she should go ahead to Beijing by public transport. The remaining six of us—five trekkers plus our guide—would throw all our belongings into Fez so they could be shipped and then squeeze into Ziggy and Dante.

THE FOUR HORSEMEN OF THE APOCALYPSE

Watching the slow mental collapse of our guide was fascinating. The poor chap claimed to be called Edmund, although that didn't sound very Chinese, and he was having his sanity attacked on three fronts. The horrendous car issues were taxing his patience, the looming and impossible exit date was the iceberg on his horizon, and his boss was giving him constant grief because we had yet to stump up the $6,500 we owed for his services. That was the bank's fault.

Most of us were dealing with these issues and delays pretty well (except OJ, whose outbursts of aggression were getting worse: rock throwing, screaming and kicking out at the cars. He's a teddy bear really). But after four months of what OJ politely termed "this shit", we were used to it. It wasn't the same for Eddie. Old Edmund—35, married, missing his kids—was a lovely man, who had been an invaluable guide and huge asset, patient and understanding. But I could see him starting to crumble. Although he remained polite, the stress was showing.

In our last few days stuck in Xilinhaote he had taken to regularly consulting the Bible, a faded old St James version he carried around. Searching for wisdom I imagined. But the morning after we boxed up and packed off Fez, I watched Edmund reading from the back of his book. The last chapter of the Bible is the Book of Revelation, the fire and brimstone stuff: Four Horsemen of the Apocalypse, Armageddon, the Anti-Christ, 666.

I knew we were bad, but I didn't think the end of the world was nigh. Maybe we were the Four Horsemen? Gunther, Fez, Ziggy, and Dante: Death, War, Famine and Pestilence.

Fez had waged a war against its engine. In Ziggy, OJ had eaten enough to cause minor famines. When Tony took off his shoes Dante became horribly pestilent. And Gunther was dead. For Fez at least, it felt like the final reckoning could be looming.

We tried to leave Xilinhaote for the umpteenth time, but Dante only made it a few miles before starting an ominous spluttering. Tony thought that the cold weather may have been affecting the engine, so we returned to the hotel and resolved to try again in the morning sun. We had lost a week in Xilinhaote.

Hitting the Wall

The drive from Xilinhaote to Beijing was mostly downhill and as we descended the steppe the temperature rose rapidly from a bone chilling - 15C to a pleasant 5C. For the past six weeks we had been fighting running battles with condensation in the cars, which froze almost as soon as it appeared so you constantly had to use an ice scraper on the inside of the windows. But at one point on that road south OJ turned to me.

"Watch this," and he breathed a deep, heavy lungful of warm air onto the windscreen, and instead of sticking, settling and frosting over, it melted the film of ice on the glass. We cheered that one for a long time.

What a stupid place to put a wall. Skirting the steep, pyramid hills north of Beijing, the crumbling, turreted Great Wall of China rises and dips across the horizon as our noisy, angry convoy stop starts down the motorway. What a stupid place to put a wall. If I'd bothered leading an army up those vertiginous slopes I wouldn't get to the top and go: "Oh bollocks, someone's only gone and built a wall up here. Right that's it. Turn back lads, we're not invading. Let's go home."

Surely those hills are enough of a natural barrier and don't warrant being topped by a shaky-looking heap of bricks. And it's not a continuous wall. It's a bunch of small strips, a half-formed defence, as if the labourers had stopped work during a pay dispute. What kind of barrier is that? Don't worry we've sort of walled off China. Rubbish.

The Great Wall did stop one invasion. Dante didn't make it. The little Trabbi gave up within sight of the thing, maybe scared by that epic wonder. OJ, Carlos and I hitched a lift from a passing people carrier. Lovey, Tony and Edmund used Ziggy to tow Dante into Beijing. With just one working car left, it was an ignominious arrival in the Chinese capital.

Our two parties reunited under the big Mao picture in Tiananmen Square. We went to McDonalds, then Pizza Hut and revelled in the tastes of home. Incredibly expensive Western food—sometimes you just have to do it.

We found a hostel in a grubby area of town alive with a vibrant assault on the senses. This was the China we had come to see. Narrow streets, unwelcoming for cars, filled with a giddying stream of hawkers, floggers, taxis and shoppers. Men cooking stir-fry in giant woks lined the street with women deep fat frying odd-shaped spring rolls. Buddhist candles, fighter pilots' helmets, digital cameras, wood-carved Buddhas, friendship bracelets, straw hats and memory sticks competed for attention.

At the bar of our guesthouse, the sensationally friendly Leo Hostel, I got chatting to a Dutch author and journalist who had been covering the region for 25 years. My Dutch friend was anxious. He had just published a book about Tibet, the Himalayan country that had been controlled by the Chinese since the 1950s. In it he revealed interviews with a lot of unhappy Tibetans and portrayed the Chinese involvement as an occupation. Although the book wasn't to be printed in Chinese, he was worried that someone working at the Dutch embassy would read it and report him to the authorities. The book had been out for five days, and he was worriedly sitting out the last three before his flight home.

"If they don't like what I wrote, maybe they won't let me leave," he said. I'll leave his name out of this. I asked him to describe the Beijing he first saw in 1982.

"The whole city was mostly *hutongs*."

A *hutong* is a traditional neighbourhood of low-rise buildings with narrow lanes and alleys.

"It was great, lots of character," he continued, "but every fifty metres you have a communal shit house. So it stank. And people used communal kitchens or cooked on the streets, so everywhere there is this smell of cooking and shit. There weren't many proper roads, and the streets were full of bicycles, there were almost no cars—just a few trucks. Everyone was riding bicycles.

"Tiananmen Square was full of young lovers. They would set their bikes up with blankets and do what young lovers do. Not like now: it is all police now. To me everyone looked the same, because everyone dressed the same. They had the Mao tunic, and the short trimmed hair. I couldn't tell the boys from the girls. I remember coming back in 1988, when things had moved on a bit, and thinking 'wow, where did all these tits come from?'"

The next day I went into the city and tried to compare it to the Beijing Old Dutchy had portrayed. There were certainly cars now, and driving around the city was as much of a nightmare as in any other—it was a bustling, heaving metropolis—and there were plenty of proper roads, some controlled by solar powered traffic lights.

We were staying in a *hutong*, but most of the city showed signs of redevelopment: skyscrapers, sprawling malls and shopping districts, neat, glassy office blocks and flashing neon. And the people certainly weren't sexless. It seemed a fashion-conscious society, particularly among the younger generation: teenagers in bright stockings and denim mini-skirts with furry boots. Guys in hip-hop leather jackets with baggy pants and baseball caps. "Shopping is not a sin," one advert gleefully shouted out in bright English. So much for the communist mantras. Our cultural leaders—David, Jodie, Kate—pouted down at us from billboards that rivalled even Mao's.

Mao. His portrait hung, not smiling, but still looking benevolent, at one end of Tiananmen Square, the square made famous by the violent quashing of a student demonstration in 1989: an event immortalised by the iconic photo of the student standing in front of a tank.

On emerging from an underpass into the square I was greeted by a line of five cops, four grunts standing stock-still and a senior, eyeing the passing crowd. A little over the top I thought, but not too sinister.

I strolled around it and felt the little Dutchman had been a bit harsh. It was busy, filled with tourists and guides, hawkers selling Chinese kites and Mao watches. The centre of the square had the obligatory monument, though that one had no statue on top, and at one end were some impressive statues depicting idealised Chinamen rising up in the revolution of the 1950s. A pleasantly nationalistic scene, just like Trafalgar Square.

But as the square opened up before me, and I could see the subtle scale of the military presence, it dawned on me: the place was under lockdown. Guards in sharp cut uniforms stood at attention every fifty metres, remaining so still they faded into the background, almost invisible, but omnipresent. They were everywhere, but you would only notice if you looked.

It was the same at the zebra crossings, where eagle-eyed officials stared warily at visitors as they filed through a narrow gap in the perimeter fence. CCTV cameras ringed most of the lampposts, there were scores of them, and there must have been hundreds of military and police. I even felt self-conscious walking around with a notebook out, looking at uniforms and cameras and scribbling. I didn't imagine there would be too many protests there in future.

The Cars Are Broken: Episode 302

The cars broke: all three of them—kaput. We towed Dante to the transport depot to join Fez, reasoning that we might as well ship both of them south. But the next day Ziggy succumbed to whatever affliction had downed his comrades. He, too, was sent off to the depot for shipping and we watched as the three Trabbis had boxes built around them and were loaded onto trucks.

It was frustrating. We'd crossed blazing deserts, the icy steppe, some of the world's highest roads, some of the world's worst roads. We'd dealt with a Siberian winter, a Turkish summer, and always, always managed to scrape the cars forward. But we hit China and what messes it all up? A couple of tanks of dodgy petrol. That's what Tony reckoned anyway, and it made sense. What else could have brought down all three cars like that?

We didn't have enough spare parts left, as over the previous four and a half months we'd gone through or ditched so much that we were down to the bare minimum. We were going to need new parts shipped to us, but we had already overstayed our car permits and couldn't really stick about any longer. So we had little choice but to ship all the cars out of the country and into Laos as fast as possible.

The cars were loaded onto trucks bound for Kunming, about 3,000km south of Beijing. They would be there in a week, then we would have to try and get them trucked the last 900km to the border. Personally I didn't think we'd get them out of the country for another ten days, maybe by 17 December? Seventeen days late. I was interested to see what customs would have to say about that one. Probably a lot of arguing and some fines. But so far the Chinese officials had been great, so there was hope.

In the meantime the gang was splitting up again. The plan was to get the parts we needed shipped to Bangkok. Lovey would fly there to collect them then he would head back through Laos to meet us at the China border. The remainder of us, OJ, Carlos, Tony and I, would head down to Kunming and find a way of getting the cars to the border. Hopefully we would reconvene there, us with the cars, and Lovey with the parts. Once again the stage was set for separation and here was another crazy plan involving dividing up and spreading across the region. The last time that happened, in Khorog, Tajikistan, we didn't see each other again for three weeks.

That night Lovey, OJ, Carlos and I went out for a drink, and a few home truths came out. The Americans had been talking about another trip, loosely called Trabant Trek 2, a planned drive across the States with whatever was left of the cars. I hadn't been invited and I mentioned it.

"Well we just thought you're kind of a liability," OJ told me.

Oh, right, cheers.

"Mostly just because of the drinking."

Fair enough, a liability. I've been called worse.

Lovey followed up with one of my favourite lines: "For most of this trip I have fucking despised you."

How do you respond to that one? Despised. It was all put across in a friendly way, and we had a good night, but I wasn't quite sure what to say.

China. It's all south from here, right? The final leg, yeah? Easy now, ok? Not a bit of it. The cars were in the worst state they had been—completely undrivable. It should have been our lowest ebb. But strangely, morale was high.

"I've been clean for two weeks now," said Tony, clearly enjoying not being elbow deep in grease. We were in an amazing city, we were staying at a great place and surrounded by travellers who thought what we'd done was awesome. The cars were broken, but not our spirits

From Six to Four

Our group was shaved from six to four. Lovey flew to Bangkok as planned, definitely to collect the spare parts, ostensibly to arrange press contacts, and possibly to meet women.

His departure was temporary, but on 7 December Zsofi left for good, flying home to Budapest to a world of exams and studenting. It seemed like she'd been saying she would have to go home for months, so it was no great palaver. We walked her to her cab and waved her off. It was pretty sad. I guessed it would affect the Mighty Tony P the most, they had been driving Dante together for five months, so it would surely be strange for him.

Before she left I chatted with her about the trip. Her highlight was Central Asia, her lowlight was being unwell in Siberia. Her best friend was Tony, but she got on with everyone. Yes, she was disappointed not to finish the trip, but she felt she had done as much as she could—she had to go home for exams.

When we got back to the hostel, I looked around and for the first time it was just the boys. Just the elite who planned to finish the job. In a way that felt good—the final team assembled for the final push.

By the end of my week in Beijing I had grown too familiar, too comfortable in my little niche, to notice the city. I woke up every day in the same place, in the same part of town. I began eating at the same joint, choosing my favourite thing off the menu, drinking the same beer and generally feeling comfortable. Familiarity didn't breed contempt—I loved Beijing—but the excitement of the first few days dwindled into apathy, and the ink stopped flowing as the bizarre became the usual.

First impressions are best, at the time when you don't yet understand your surroundings and wander intrigued by the little differences. After five months on the move those changes were so quickly assimilated that Beijing's early romance and novelty were too quickly taken for granted. So I was pleased to get out and try something new.

We took the overnight train, Beijing to Xian, twelve hours. The air con went off in the night and for the first time in months I remembered what it was like to be too hot to sleep.

XI'AN

The city of Xi'an exists in a cloud. At least it did when I was there, a thick fog obscuring the sky and the tops of buildings. Smog or moisture or maybe both, our two days were spent walking in a damp hundred-metre wide bubble, so it was impossible to grasp the scale of the place.

We passed a McDonalds and a smart-looking Starbucks to get to our hostel (the more time I spent in those Chinese cities, the less different they appeared from their Western counterparts). It could have been one of those strange, misty London mornings when the city's grey stone sits camouflaged and disorienting in the opaque air. Only Chinese faces stared back at me, but even so, it could still have been home—but then, from the gloom, like a Polaroid developing, would emerge a pagoda or temple, unlike much outside Soho or the tower at Kew Gardens.

For a while in Xi'an it felt like I'd been transported back to Central Asia. We'd stumbled into the Muslim Quarter, a strange and ancient place that owed its existence to the Silk Road. Xi'an was the first big Chinese city Western merchants would get to and plenty of Arab traders decided to settle there to make their fortune.

It was an interesting walk. Although most of the people looked Chinese, I could see the odd Arabian among the stalls. People wore little Arabic touches: a man wearing a fez, women with headdresses. Little birds sang from cages that lined the main road, like street lamps. A girl with club feet crawled around after us, clattering along a paint tin with a few bills in. Every now and again we would stop long enough for her to catch up and she'd start banging her tin. She could only have been eleven or twelve. She wore gloves on her hands like shoes as she dragged her lame, bare feet behind.

A man sang traditional songs at the top of his nasal voice as he sliced up a great rice cake, a huge yellow thing the size of a bedside table. He skewered thick, moist pieces and barbecued them. Next to him whole carcasses hung from butchers' hooks, dripping blood into congealing pools.

We stopped for something to eat and the menu was straight out of Central Asia: *shashlik*, *manti*, *naan* bread, even *pismaniye*, a sort of candyfloss-like sweet we'd had in Izmit in Turkey almost four months before and hadn't seen since.

THE TRAIN TO SPRING

The thing about long train journeys is the smell. As is the way with odour, it builds up around you, slow, subtle and unnoticed, like carbon monoxide poisoning or senile dementia.

But you step off the train to fight over a satsuma with a bunch of cabin-fevered commuters, return to your cot, and then it hits you. Piss, eggs, wine, fart, sweat, rice, coke, beer, perfume, shit, bleach, noodles, effluent, chicken, hair, feet, feet, feet, feet and more feet—a heady brew of satanic spices concocted in a cauldron previously used as a dustpan when Beelzebub swept out hell's charnel house.

Overpowering, stomach-turning revoltingness on a chemical weapon scale: expect pre-emptive action by a US-led multinational force acting under the auspices of the UN.

There were no windows on the Xi'an to Kunming train. I imagine we couldn't be trusted to regulate our own temperature to aroma ratio, and the only draught came when someone opened the toilet door, wafting a port-a-loo breeze of acrid disinfectant and sewage through our carriage.

We didn't have a cabin, just three storeys of bunk beds arranged along an open and busy corridor. Every half hour a man with a trolley would dash through shouting in Chinese, but disappear before we could see what he was wheeling. Thirty-five hours in those conditions was always likely to be testing.

There were a few other inconveniences. The freak show fame attached to being Westerners in the East: aren't we funny, aren't we strange, come and have a look. Fair's fair—we were only there because they're funny and strange and we wanted a look. But we didn't watch them crapping.

The Chinese have a penchant for the art of throat clearing. Never have I seen a nation attack the issue of phlegm with such vehemence. True connoisseurs of the clearance—huge, racketing, barking, choking hocks that are enough to make innocent bystanders gag while dogs howl at the moon and gnash at their ears. I sometimes expected cranial chunks or nasal cavity to come roaring out with the gob: oh, look, that's his frontal lobe, that was a good spit.

And it isn't just the men; communism is non-discriminatory, a truly equal form of suppression, so women too can hurl vile slime balls down as they adjust their make-up. Nor is the practice restricted to the outdoors. Our train was something of a haven for spitters, the beat to our journey the rhythmic expulsion of snot.

What could make that paradise of sight and smell complete? Throw in the tantrum-prone youngster. A perfect wake up call for day two on the Nifkin Express. She must have been nine or ten, not the screaming baby who knows no other way to express her wants, but a young girl with command of language taking out a vicious yet unknown grievance on a train full of folk who were not her tormentors. Hours of it, lung-bursting, head in hands shrieks—not even crying, just wailing. And her guardian, in what I imagine was an attempt to discipline the brat, sat stony, silent and impassive. Just give her what she wants, I thought, we shouldn't all have to be involved in this terrible lesson. But on it went 'til she seemed to forget what she was screaming about.

Time decided to relax and spread out, the only punctuation to its mindless passing the decision to have a pot of instant noodles. A little treat for having coped with another six hours and a rare chance to do something gratifying and rewarding. I got hot water. I made noodles.

The red wine we brought as our Valium went too quickly and the night was restless, sleep hindered by the jagged progress of our driver, who had a sixth sense for passengers nodding off and gleefully hit the breaks to put a stop to such weakness. Isn't sleep deprivation a form of torture?

On the second morning everyone was ratty, but the mood lifted when we peeled back the curtains. Outside all was green and yellow. True, vibrant, healthy, vegetable green dowsed in a wash of eastern yellow from a heavenly body long lost to us, but now reintroduced—the sun. Rolling fields bathed in sunshine. We cast our collective minds back to the last time we'd seen such simple glory. Tajikistan? Mountains. Turkmenistan? Desert.

We placed it in Azerbaijan, the long drive to Baku, 25 August, nearly four months ago. I greedily absorbed the view, and tried to snatch a look at what the farmers were wearing as they flew past my little screen. Is it sandal weather? Shorts?

Kunming means the City of Eternal Spring, and we stepped off the train into a beautiful spring day. T-shirt weather. It seems strange to hark on about the weather. I am English, and in a country with such an unpredictable climate commenting on the clouds is an understandable national pastime. But for us it was more than that.

Since Bishkek, when we'd plumped for the long, cold and difficult route north, we had spent seven weeks in sub-zero temperatures, which had been severely trying. Even in Tajikistan, where we broke down relentlessly, it felt like a bit of a holiday because you could always relax in the sun. But when you have to slide under the car at night time in two feet of snow it really doesn't feel like a vacation. When two of the cars need to be push started every time they stop and it is so cold that even touching the back windows with gloved hands freezes your fingers so they hurt, then things can get to you.

I'd done seven weeks of wearing thermal underwear, three pairs of socks, huge jackets, scarves, gloves, layer after layer giving me a sumo wrestler physique. Having to take everything off when you got in somewhere, and putting literally everything on in the evening to spend another night in a Tupperware box with no heating and doors that didn't close so that the outside was very much inside. It had been a real test of endurance. And it was over. We made it. We did the Northern Route. We beat the Kazakh steppe, the Siberian winter, the Gobi Desert, and now we were safe. Whatever happened, the threat of exposure and frostbite was overcome.

Our hostel had a terrace, no, a *sun* terrace. From it I could see palm trees. South East Asia here we come.

THE CUSP OF SOUTH EAST ASIA

Kunming was beautiful, and I felt very much at home. Busy, warm and vibrant with a large university population, it was a modern city, but with a distinctly Chinese twist. The huge government buildings could have come from the New York skyline, except they had subtly curved roofs, a little nod to a pagoda.

Walking back from watching the United-Liverpool game at 2am on a Sunday night, the streets were still busy. A little oasis of stalls around a street lamp was filled with fruits and foods I didn't recognise. Dozens of people were sitting out in the night, eating and chatting. A patrol of policemen passed, about half a dozen all swinging long clubs as they sauntered by. The back two cops were arm-in-arm, laughing.

The cars were meant to arrive in Kunming and be shipped out to the border on 14 December. But the delivery company must have been infected by Trabbi

Dante attracts attention

Time, as the last car, Fez, didn't arrive until Wednesday and didn't get shipped 'til Thursday, 20 December, another week-long delay.

When Carlos and I went down to the shipping company to pay them and check on the cars we found Ziggy surrounded by a swarm of men. They had the windows down, the doors open and were rifling the inside playing with the walkie-talkies. Three men had the boot open and were going through the stuff inside, waving our 8mm camera about.

We approached by stealth and I shouted a loud English greeting in an attempt to scare them. But they just looked up, shameless, and waved our stuff at us. I gave them a tour of the engine, to much laughter.

We got a night bus south to a town nearer the border to wait for the cars. There were three rows of double beds on the bus, which was nice, except that Carlos, Tony and I were in a five-person bed at the back, sandwiched between two Chinamen. A sweaty and frustrating night—sleeping with five men was everything I'd imagined it to be.

The cars were again delayed, so we relaxed in the town of Meng La, about 50km from the border. We needed a few hundred pounds to pay the shipping company, and, although Carlos had sorted out the European money, none of the ATMs in town would accept the Americans' cards. They had to take a four-hour bus ride to the nearest city to withdraw the cash. OJ broke a pen in protest.

That afternoon I went to check out a basketball court I had seen the following evening. There were a couple of guys playing and a load of seven- or eight-year-old girls in school uniform. It was about 4pm so I guessed they were on their way back from school, and I joined in. I was getting a lot of funny looks, which I expected, being a pasty, sweaty white man, but after ten minutes a woman came out.

"What are you doing here?" she asked.

"Well, I'm on my way to Laos."

"But what are you doing here?"

"Just passing through, I've driven here from Germany, actually, we're trying to get to Cambodia. Oh yes, we've had quite an adventure."

"No, no. What are you doing here? This is a school. This is a PE lesson."

I'd inadvertently wandered into a playground and started shooting hoops during a class. Oops. The lady was the school's English teacher who had been summoned to sort me out.

I wonder what would happen if a pot-bellied Chinaman turned up at an English girls' school and joined a basketball lesson. He would probably be arrested. But they were ok about it and I ended up playing a proper, hour-long game of full court with the PE teachers, complete with scoreboard, referee, floodlights and refreshment table. Exhausting.

The next day the Americans returned from their ATM mission and Edmund, our guide, texted us to say the last car was at the border. We headed down to Mo Hoa but they couldn't get Fez off the truck before the crossing closed, so we were stuck another day.

Edmund had been pretty awesome throughout our stay in China, sorting out all the paperwork, officialdom and shipping, and going beyond the call of duty. He had a five-day journey home, but we were running so late that the poor chap wouldn't make it back to be with his family for Christmas. He was a devout Christian, and we all felt terrible about it.

Carlos found out about his distinctly un-Chinese name. Apparently he'd once worked at a hotel, and the manager told him he could pick his uniform. Each one had a name stitched on and he chose one with Edmund. I think all people deserve a similar opportunity at birth—take the parents out of the equation.

It was a shame not to have driven the length of China. It would have been some road trip and was a real missed opportunity, especially considering how much we paid to get the cars into the country. Instead, all our driving was limited to the dull northern desert. It would have been interesting to watch that dry, dirty, grey landscape develop into the humid, lush, greenery that we'd seen in the south.

Looking outside the window on our long journey south—65 hours of trains and buses—I had seen the ebb and flow of city to countryside. Rural wooden shacks and chocolate cake hills drifting to suburbs, mixing old thatched homes with light industrial, low-rise factories, then the neck craning city centres, thirty- and forty-storey apartment blocks and offices, filthy decrepit estates near shining new glass and metal skyscrapers.

The image would rebound as we left the centre, returning through the fading development and arriving back at hillsides carved into terraces, sweeping like grand colonial staircases down to sun-kissed green fields and heavy streams topped with a head of floating mist.

It was sad we couldn't drive, but driving the Trabbis was a double-dged sword. On the one hand we never knew when we were going to stop, as we could break down at any point. So the little cars took us to places we would never normally have visited, places that didn't make the guidebook, that weren't even on the map, that few Westerners have visited. That was a great experience: no guesthouses, no internet, no restaurants—we had to rely on our wits and the hospitality of locals.

On the other hand, we never knew when we were going to stop, as we could break down at any point. So the little cars took us to places we would never have normally visited. Places that we didn't want to visit. So we ended up staying five days on the Turkmen-Uzbek border, instead of getting to know Ashgabat. We lived a week in tiny Tajik villages, instead of exploring the Pamirs.

In China we spent a week in Xilinhaote when we could have used the time doing anything: Three Gorges Dam? Shanghai? Without the cars we had seen China in a completely different manner to all the other countries we visited. We were on the tourist trail. It was refreshing in some ways, but still, a missed opportunity.

Where we cheating? Did shipping the cars for 3,500km invalidate the whole trip? Not in my mind. We did everything we could to get them going, and pushed them and ourselves to our limits. And what other choice did we have? Because of the issues with our permits we either had to ship the cars out of the country or just dump them and abandon the whole thing. No, for me we did all we could.

Now we were limping in, stumbling across the border with the cars wrecked. None of us really knew if we would be able to get them working on the other side, but we were well used to living with such uncertainty.

We were nearly there, the home straight, South East Asia. I could already smell it in the food, see it in the foliage and feel it in the air: sticky and humid and home.

8

SOUTH EAST ASIA
Laos, Thailand and Cambodia
23 December 2007 – 4 January 2008

Q) What do you use to measure the speed of a Trabant?
A) A calendar.

A Sad Humiliation on Entering Laos

A more humiliating arrival in a country would be difficult to imagine. To get the cars across the China-Laos border we enlisted the help of a local tuk-tuk driver. We thought he might tow them into Laos one-by-one. But no, his little tuk-tuk, with its tiny motorbike engine, was powerful enough to tow all three cars at once. Our three Trabbis, pride of our lives, towed across the border in convoy by a single tuk-tuk. Shameful. Passers-by pointed and laughed, officials stopped and stared, motorists gawped and swerved. Trabant Trek hits South East Asia.

In a rare moment of group co-ordination Lovey returned from his Bangkok mission to meet us on the Laos side of the border as we crossed. Our tuk-tuk had dropped us off just before the frontier, but luckily it was downhill into Laos so we released the handbrakes and freewheeled into the country. What an arrival.

It was good to see Lovey again and get ourselves back up to five. He was tired after a couple of days on buses, but in good spirits, and he had with him the valuable box of bits that we hoped would rescue the Trek.

It was 22 December: more than three weeks after the expiry of the Trabbis' Chinese customs papers, just a day before the end of our own Chinese visas, six weeks behind the original schedule, and three weeks behind the revised Bishkek timetable. Three days until Christmas, and none of the cars worked.

We'd done more than 23,000km through 19 countries, and the Trabbis were showing it. Much of the damage was superficial or cosmetic. The doors didn't close properly, none of them locked, and when they did you couldn't open them again and had to break in through the boot. The paintwork was a horrible mess and there were various battle scars from minor collisions. Back in Tajikistan, Megan had reversed Ziggy into a wall, smashing out the taillights.

Arriving in Laos with broken cars

Somewhere in Kyrgyzstan OJ had driven into a cow, cracking Dante's bonnet. He had also put a long, gaping gash in the side of the car when he threw an angry, ogre-ish foot at it in northern China.

That afternoon Carlos accidentally smashed Fez's passenger window, which was ok because before that it wouldn't open—fine in freezing Siberia, but a problem in sunny Laos. None of the cars had seatbelts, all of them had been removed to use as tow cables at some point. Wing and rear-view mirrors were a thing of fantasy. Ziggy could only indicate left. Fez's brakes were suspect, the stereo had been broken for months and he didn't even have a passenger seat.

All those things we could, and had, been dealing with. The cars were rubbish, we knew that. They'd been lived in for five months and were trashed. But we had less idea about what was going on under the bonnet. None of them worked, that was clear enough, and a lot was resting on the box of parts Lovey had brought with him.

We ate, caught up, rifled through the box and discussed our plans. I was keen to have the cars towed all the way south to Vang Vien, a traveller's town where we hoped to spend Christmas. That way we could relax for a few days, fix the cars and enjoy the festivities with some other Westerners. I was very afraid that we might get the cars going and begin the drive, only to break down in the middle of nowhere and spend Christmas by the side of the road.

But the others were confident we could fix the cars quickly where we were. So, on a dusty patch of concrete by the side of the road, 160km from the border with China, we removed all three engines and began rebuilding them.

It turned out we hadn't requested the correct parts for the job. But Gabor was smarter than to send us what we requested. As Tony said, "I love Gabor. He didn't send us what we asked for. But he did send us what we need."

Everyone got burned in the blistering heat, but we loved it after the cold of the last few months. By nightfall we had Fez and Ziggy back together, but all the cars had flat batteries. We tried push starting them, to no effect. I managed to find someone with leads to give us a jump start, but Fez only ran for a few minutes, making a terrible racket and sounding distinctly unwell, before the engine just died. Tired and getting ratty, we turned in at what we later learned was a house of ill repute.

The next morning I found a garage where we could charge the dead batteries.

We could only do them one at a time, so it took all day, but by lunch Fez was working. We hoped to make it to Luang Prabang, about 300km away, but as the day drew in that seemed less and less likely. It was 23 December. I just wanted to make it somewhere by Christmas.

That afternoon I rested my sunburn in a shady restaurant and wrote up what had happened to us. Earlier, when I had returned from the mechanics, I found the Americans drinking Beer Laos. They excitedly told me they were going to make Dante into a convertible. From my perch in the restaurant I could see them on the other side of the road. They were going at the roof with a saw. It doesn't rain in Laos, does it?

Big Trouble in Little China

I was often bored with Christmas back home—those jingles, that shopping, the decorations. I often wished to be somewhere completely away from it all and, inadvertently, I think I found it: Boten on the Laos-China border. A one-road town trapped in a terrible struggle for identity. You see, we were in Laos. We had crossed the border; the little barrier that divided Laos from China was visible from all over the village. But somehow China had crept over that fragile demarcation. Cultural seepage or cultural creepage I didn't know, but the locals didn't seem to realise where they were. It was Little China. All the clocks were set to China time, all the signs were in Chinese, all the prices were in RMB, the Chinese currency.

In fact, we were having a tough time trying to use our Laos Kip. When I handed some over the locals stared uncomprehendingly as if I had just passed them, well, a foreign note.

"It's Kip. It's Laos money," I would say.

A shake of the head, "Renminbi," they'd reply.

We were able to exchange, but we were getting royally screwed every time, and rapidly running out of cash.

And Christmas. What Christmas? There wasn't a shred of tinsel in sight, not a whiff of mistletoe or a tinkle of jingle bells. I don't think they'd heard of Slade. No Santa hats, roast chestnuts, crackers, stilton or port, and the surrounding forest had been spared the shame of being chopped down, dressed-up like a kitsch, pantomime drag queen, sprinkled with ribbon and glitter, and topped by a winged bimbo with a wand.

When setting out on that adventure, I never thought that I would wake up on Christmas Eve 2007 in a tiny room with plywood walls in a house of ill repute. The cheapest joint in town and thankfully, unlike the previous morning, I wasn't woken by the moans of the single member of staff doing her job. Someone had a happy ending.

We'd made some progress with the cars. Fez and Dante were working. But Ziggy wasn't and, more worryingly, Tony was still unable to diagnose the problem. It had never taken that long to solve a Trabbi riddle before.

So it was day three on a patch of dust by the side of the road. There was some life there: it was a free trade zone, and there was a big new casino up the road with a $50 a night hotel, and there were a few little boutiques with some trendy Chinese fashion, all well out of our price range. There was also the best internet café I had seen in South East Asia, although I hadn't been to the region for six years. There must have been fifty PCs, all pretty new with a good connection and gangs of boys and girls, the boys playing *World of Warcraft* and *Counterstrike*, the girls on a dancing game and social networking sites. In that part of the world the *interwang*, as it was called, was the place to be. Whenever I walked in the girls just cracked up. Occasionally it prickled to have a few dozen teenagers giggling at me, but mostly I just took a deep breath.

Dante had a new skylight stretching over the driver and passenger seats. Which was interesting. Because Dante was now terminally insecure, we took the passenger window and put it in Fez to replace the one Carlos broke. But it only took a light tug to open the passenger door anyway, so Fez wasn't especially safe. The Americans had tried pretty much everything to get Ziggy going, with no success. It had got to the stage that we were considering ditching it.

"It's annoying if we have to dump a car just because we don't know what's wrong with it," Lovey told me.

"I agree—it could be something really simple."

Ziggy had always been the strongest car and it would have been a shame to leave it there when it could be fixed. By the evening Ziggy still didn't work, but Dante was broken too. Carlos and Lovey needed a tow back after a 20km trip to the petrol station. Tony thought he knew what the problem was but was in no mood to tackle it. We were resigned to another day in Boten. Christmas Day.

As a group we had $100 left. There was no ATM and when we waved a credit card at the manager of the hotel he looked very confused. We were dirty and smelly, having spent the days deep in engine grease and two nights alternating between a brothel and a tent. So we wanted a hot shower and fresh sheets as our Christmas present. We found a hotel that would do it, but it was $35—a fair chunk of our money. After some debate we went for it, just so we didn't wake up on Christmas Day in a whorehouse. That only left us $65 to try and get to Luang Prabang, where there was an ATM. There was a chance we'd be stuck somewhere in northern Laos with cars that didn't work and no money. In fact it seemed quite likely.

I didn't feel like we were in a rush anymore. We weren't going to make Vang Vien for Christmas, nor Cambodia for New Year. So why hurry? I was resigned to the trip not being over 'til 2008, so why bother rushing through the last few weeks at a frantic pace, getting stressed out and not enjoying it?

We've made South East Asia, I reasoned, it's warm, it's cheap, I'm happy to settle into a more gentle rhythm, and if that means we sit here for the whole of Christmas trying to get Ziggy going, then so be it.

I'd only be whinging about Christmas at home anyway. Those jingles, that shopping, the decorations. Ever wished to be completely away from it all? Try Boten, Laos.

Dante's Infirmity

I have never woken up with a man on Christmas morning and, other than hoping to catch out Santa, I never expected to. We could only afford four beds at the hotel, and the Mighty Tony P and I drew the short straws. But at least it was a room with clean sheets and a hot shower, not the crab-infested plywood brothel. And Tony is a gentle lover.

Christmas Eve back home is spent down the pub with scores of old friends I haven't seen for a year. I spent Christmas Eve 2007 with a gerbil-like Mexican-Italian-American watching a Japanese slapstick in Chinese in Laos.

I'll be home for Christmas. I'd told that to a lot of people, and although I knew months ago that I wouldn't, it still felt strange.

Christmas lunch was fried noodles with squid and coffee. God knows where the squid came from. There were a few closed shops in Boten—maybe they knew something of that Christian holiday—but otherwise no signs of festive cheer. And though we'd been living in the village for four days, and everyone had noticed us, no one wished us season's greetings. I'm not sure what the locals thought of the strange white people with their funny cars.

Someone must have been celebrating something because I watched a man cooking a giant hamster with a flamethrower. He was just out on the street with

Christmas Day, Boten, Laos

some gloves, a jet of flames and this enormous rodent. What are you up to?

"Just flamethrowering this here hamster."

Okay.

Round the back of the restaurant they had a crazy-looking owl and three bears in cages. The bears were a few feet tall, with thick dark hair and powerful arms. I asked two of the boys where they came from and they gestured towards the surrounding forest. They told me they got them when they were very small, and when they were very big they would eat the paws and heart. One of the boys was playing slaps with a bear through the cage, trying to palm the back of its paw before getting clawed.

We spent the afternoon successfully repairing Dante and unsuccessfully working on Ziggy. Everything was tried, every piece taken apart and rebuilt, every component tested. But it wouldn't start. The starter would whir and whir, and then, just when you thought the engine was going to catch, a loud ominous clunk, and nothing. It was the same sound as back in Beijing, and four days of work had not fixed it.

By late afternoon OJ was plying Ziggy's engine apart with a chisel. I think at that point we knew it was the end. Christmas Day 2007, one-hundred-and-fifty-six days since we set off from Germany, 23,000 kilometres down the road, in our nineteenth country, we were going to have to dump a Trabant.

The decision to ditch a car was pretty much made for us: one engine didn't work. But which Trabbi to get rid of? We had two working engines that could go in any of the cars. The victim would be cannibalised for parts, butchered for spares, and it would take a lot of work, so really it didn't matter which car went—it didn't have to be Ziggy.

We decided the time was right to sit around with a beer, discuss the situation and vote. But there wasn't much agreement or discussion, more argument and contradiction. People became sentimental about their Trabbis and didn't want to see them dumped, and they admitted it. Carlos wanted to keep Fez because he loved it, Lovey wanted to keep Ziggy because he loved it, Tony wanted to keep Dante because he loved it. Only OJ and I remained impartial. I had no problem with losing Fez. I'd spent a lot of time in the little car, but it was a pile of rubbish. It'd probably had more problems than any other car and ran terribly.

"This is not the time for sentiment," I said, "let's make a decision which gives us the best possible chance to get to Cambodia."

Everyone agreed. Then continued to let their sentiment cloud their judgement.

We thought about the car's pluses and minuses:

FEZ

Cons: no passenger seat, front right bearing and transaxle dodgy, passenger door doesn't lock and swings open, brakes dodgy, rear control arm welded, history of problems, exhaust welded to the floor (extra noisy), headlights dim, speakers broken.
Pros: It looks good (subjective), currently works so we could just drive away. In theory three people could squeeze in.

ZIGGY

Cons: It's in pieces all over the floor, broken front leaf spring, rear control arm welded, only Lovey can open the door, hand brake broken, shocks too big on the back (damaging rear tyres).

Pros: The only car that locks, hasn't had too many problems, seats four people.

DANTE

Cons: A giant hole has been cut into the roof (wet, cold, insecure). Passenger window missing, driver window stuck open. Passenger door broken (sealed shut). Trunk door broken (sealed shut). Can only seat two people.

Pros: Currently works so we could just drive away. Big trunk.

It was too tough to call. Not being particularly in on the mechanical side of things, which I felt should be the only consideration, I had no idea how to vote. But this is how it went:

Tony wanted to ditch Ziggy as it was in pieces. He also loved Dante.

Carlos voted Dante, because there was no roof so it was terminally insecure. And he loved Fez.

Lovey voted Dante for the same reason (and he loved Ziggy), and so did OJ.

So when it came to my turn the decision was already made, Dante by three votes, with the main reason being the giant hole in the roof, which the Americans had cut out just the day before. Ooh, the bitter irony.

Tony was pissed. That's an American pissed, which I have learned means angry, not a British pissed, which means drunk. But soon he spanned the linguistic differences by downing a mini bottle of rice wine. Then he was really pissed.

Tony: "I'm not annoyed at anyone for the decision, I just think it was the wrong one. I don't see the point in tearing apart a perfectly good car, when we could just take the drum and the transaxle from Ziggy and go before it gets dark."

But the car is insecure.

"So is Fez, the passenger door doesn't close."

Personally I didn't really care about the time it would take to rebuild Ziggy and strip Dante. It would be better to get the job done properly than to rush it. "We're here now," I said, "we should just get the job done as best we can."

But Tony was right. It took ages, it got dark, the job got harder and we'd scattered our tools across a mechanic's forecourt. It was midnight by the time we'd finished testing Dante's engine in Ziggy, switching the leaf springs over,

191

Dante's end

harvesting the best tyres from Dante, taking the drum, transaxle, speakers, stereo and anything else we might need.

When we'd finished gutting Dante it really was a sad sight—sitting on bricks, shocks hanging loose, roof gaping open. We left it there, by a garage, and told the owner we were going to Vientiane to get parts. The Americans talked about returning to pick it up after the Trek. They wanted to ship it to the States. But I was pretty certain we had seen Dante for the last time.

We set off in convoy, if you can call two cars a convoy. Really we were just following each other. "How far do you think we're gonna get?" I asked Carlos, who was driving.

"I don't care. I just want to make it out of this town."

The battery in Fez was dead, but we were on a hill so we roll started down, back towards the Laos border. The engine kicked in, the loud, raucous vibrations, the exhaust filling the cabin. Fez hadn't been properly driven for a month, but now, on Christmas Day, after a complete refit, he was ready to take us the last leg. Carlos clicked him into gear and slipped the clutch.

And we went... nowhere.

He turned to me: "There's no gears."

We looked at each other in silence as he shifted the gear stick about. He had that flicker of a grin he grows around the corners of his mouth when he knows something's gone horribly wrong. He tried slipping the clutch, but nothing.

"Clutch?"

I stepped out the car and looked around. We were still in Boten.

"So on that attempt we actually managed to go backwards?" I said. We'd roll started towards China, not Cambodia.

"Nice work. So we've lost one car and scored minus fifty metres today."

We set up the tent for our fourth night in Boten. Lying in Fez, where I had made a bed, I heard that infuriating sound of a mosquito buzzing about in the dark, looking for a target. I couldn't remember the last time I'd heard a mosquito. South East Asia, we're here. Five of us, with two cars. But we're here.

"Happy Christmas," I shouted towards the tent, and squashed the midge.

Parasols and Elephants

Culture shock. The way we meandered slowly across the world we completely avoided it. It's all very well flying in from cold, stony London to sticky, clingy Bangkok—that's culture shock territory. But driving so slowly you get over-taken by cyclists is a different prospect. The changes are slower, more gradual, so you see a hint of China in southern Mongolia, a whisper of Turkey in eastern Bulgaria.

But driving into Laos proper for the first time, I felt stunned by the sur-roundings. The little villages that exist in the northern mountains could not be more different from the Chinese mega cities we had come from. It was a dif-ferent dimension, an old way of life. No concrete, glass and steel, it was town planning *au naturel*. Bamboo houses on wooden stilts with woven wicker walls, thick thatched roofs topping sun shelters, where locals sat around cooking sticky rice in bamboo canes over open fires.

Pretty, idyllic, backwards, mesmerising, remote and unmistakably Laos. It was unlike anywhere else we had visited, from Slovakia to Mongolia, from Romania to Russia—nowhere looked like Laos.

I watched a tiny little girl, she couldn't have been more than nine or ten, walking around with a baby strapped to her hip in a papoose. She cuddled and nurtured the infant while the family's elder females beat rice into a paste with heavy sticks of bamboo. We tasted the congealed pulpy grain, which the locals chewed from leaves. It had the texture of rubber and was declared "completely flavourless" by OJ.

Before that day I would probably have put Tajikistan down as my favourite drive—the five days trying to get to the foot of the Pamir Mountains, when we hugged the rugged Afghan border.

But the mountains of northern Laos could not be more different. Tajikistan was all bare cliff faces and sharp, jagged outcrops reaching up straight and spiky, with a few shrubs and grasses. Northern Laos was all curves and lumps, soft lines clothed in thick jungle and blooming, exploding colours from all types of tropical wonder. The mountains rolled up in a swell, steep but rounded like camels' humps, and where the Pamirs were thick and slab-like, those mountains seem to spurt up like little nipples leaving ample room between peaks for rangy, eye-watering views.

There were dangers. Just a few years before we arrived the government had rounded up hundreds of bandits who terrorised traffic along Route 13, the same road we were travelling, and the north was rich in opium and its associated villains. On three or four separate occasions I saw men walking the road with AK47s over their shoulders. One of them was in khaki green and could feasibly have been military. But the others were in faded T-shirts and grubby trousers, looking every inch the jungle mercenaries.

As we moved further south it felt like we were heading west. More and more signs of tourism—a couple of Spanish motorcyclists shared lunch and offered us a smoke, while a whole car full of Germans were delighted to see Trabants so far from home and donated $20 on the spot. We passed a lone English cyclist and a fleet of Thai Volkswagen enthusiasts. There were more Chinese and Japanese tourists than I remembered too.

We spent two nights trying to get to Luang Prabang, the first camped on the side of the road, the second in a seedy transfer hub after a Fez breakdown. Fez kept playing up and people began getting a little frustrated with it, especially since we had just decided to ditch Dante.

"Maybe I should have voted for Fez", Lovey said. Tony looked angry.

We weren't in Luang Prabang for long, but we were greeted by a new sight. Hordes of Westerners, mostly couples in their mid-thirties to late-sixties. I hadn't seen so many white people since Europe and it was a little off-putting. The whole town was based on tourism, it was a world heritage sight, and the sort of place retired French couples visit. It was odd, like going to an all-inclusive resort after months in places that couldn't attract a traveller with all- day happy hour, *en suite* bathrooms and free internet.

Carlos and I spent a relaxed day working on Fez, drinking, smoking and lapping up the sun. Since the previous week's work on the engine it had dawned on the little Catalan that he actually knew what he was doing. He could take out the engine and gearbox to replace the clutch plate himself. He even managed to put the engine back in, a heavy and finicky job normally left to the muscles of the Slav. Although not as confident as Carlos, I too felt far more comfortable taking apart the car. It was a good feeling after months of terminal ineptness, and the Americans left us to it.

NEW YEAR'S EVE LAOS STYLE

I don't know if the sport of tubing would be allowed in England. Mixing one of the world's great rivers with a bunch of piss-heads screams health and safety. And we don't really have the climate. But I can't really think of a better way to spend New Year.

30 December was another drive of epic beauty from Luang Prabang to the little river town of Vang Vien. We'd been told it was a haven for Westerners and we had hoped to spend Christmas there. We were, of course, well behind schedule on our 78th revised Trabant Trek plan, but at least we made it to a party town for the New Year. I may have snapped spending another holiday on the roadside.

The drive through the mountains continued where the rest of northern Laos had left off—awe-inspiring scenery dotted with thatched villages and bathed in sunshine.

Fez did his best to ruin things, struggling up the hills and eventually breaking down agonisingly close to our destination. Carlos and I were so desperate to reach Vang Vien we pushed the car up a hill, hoping to freewheel down the other side and roll into town. It didn't work, but we got a tow from some laughing Japanese tourists and, in typical Trek style, announced ourselves at our new home by taking apart and rebuilding one of the cars on the main drag.

Fez had chewed up another cylinder, he was going through them quickly. But the warmth in the air, the elation at reaching the town and the constant attention of young tourists added to a party atmosphere around our impromptu street side workshop.

We heard there was a party at a beach a few kilometres away so headed down. It was more of a campfire affair, a mix of nationalities sitting round and sharing a skin of moonshine, but it was cool to chat with other Westerners, relax and loosen my tongue ahead of the big day, which Carlos had insisted we would spend tubing.

The essence of tubing is this: you pay some entrepreneurial locals to lend you a giant, over-inflated lorry tyre. They then drive you five kilometres upstream and lob you into South East Asia's biggest river, the Mekong. You spend the day lapping up rays and drifting through the idyllic riverside, flanked by jungle and overlooked by palm-peaked mountains. All very tranquil and relaxing.

However, the serenity has been compromised by the building of dozens of bamboo bars along the route. These roar out ear-splitting tunes, which are mostly rubbish, and provide regular pit stops for refreshments, which are mostly cheap.

As you float along, a boy with a long stick will catch hold of your tube and pull you onto his bar's bamboo decking, which is built along the banks and over the river like a jetty. It's obligatory to down at least a shot of Laos Laos, the local moonshine, before heading to the well-stocked bar for Beer Laos and the lethal Buckets of Joy—a combination of vast quantities of local rum mixed with the deadly Asian Red Bull and a dash of Coke. Depending on the bartender, some of these are knee-wobblingly strong, and according to popular legend the Red Bull contains amphetamine. The whole concoction is served with ice and straws in a children's beach bucket. What a beverage.

To add to the pandemonium caused by large doses of sun and booze, many of the bars have built giant rope swings, zip lines and tall jumping platforms. These ensure an acrobatic spectacle is provided for drinkers by inebriated Westerners throwing themselves into the water from great heights. What more could you ask for?

In England, where you're not allowed to operate a pond without a qualified lifeguard, I'm sure this whole event would be banned. But in Laos, which according to one guidebook has fewer than a hundred written laws, plying tourists with dangerous levels of home-made alcohol and launching them down a major river is a minor industry.

It was awesome fun, a giant adult water park in the most beautiful of settings, literally hundreds of people laughing, dancing, splashing and playing like kids. And it being New Year's Eve, all the revelry was attacked to the power of ten.

My favourite bar had multiple decks, an enormous rope swing, two stratospheric diving platforms and a couple of volleyball courts, where I picked up a few minor sprains and some serious grazes—not that I noticed at the time.

Of course, I spent far too long at the bars socialising, and not enough time actually floating downstream. So, a long way from home, night fell. The blazing sun gave way to a brisk chill, and I was lying in a three-foot rubber hoop with my arse in the Mekong.

Luckily this was a pretty typical fate and taxis patrolled the road near the riverfront to pick up hypothermic tubers and drop them back into town for a small fee. Like I said, it is a minor industry.

I didn't get back to the hotel till gone ten, happily drunk, and found the others sleeping off their excesses. I woke them, showered, and headed down to a large island in the river that was hosting the parties. There we did all the things you'd expect on New Year's Eve. The only regret was a running and unnecessary argument with Lovey that tainted the evening.

The partying took a terrible toll. With the longest hangover of my life, I think the moonshine may have been some kind of poison. I couldn't drink for days but resisted the urge to indulge in a reckless and unsustainable New Year's resolution.

One Night in Bangkok

Diverting to Bangkok was a controversial decision. It meant a longer route, but on better roads, and it would add another country to our hit list and let us pull the cars into the traveller's Mecca of Khao San Road. I had no particular desire to go, since I was worried about driving into and out of that sprawling, congested city and concerned that we could easily lose a few days. But Lovey had pretty much forced the decision by leaving his bags there when he went to collect the box of spare parts a few weeks before.

We made the drive from Vang Vien to the Thai capital in one hit, stopping off in Vientiane to eat and collect a parcel of car stickers we'd been sent from the States.

The drive was straightforward, but we weren't sure how we would get on at Laos customs. We'd brought three cars into the country but, having dumped Dante, we were only leaving with two. In many countries that would result in a fine of thousands of dollars, but we didn't know how organised the Laotians were.

We arrived at the border, the Friendship Bridge that links Laos with Thailand across the Mekong River, and began the process. Laos customs didn't ask any questions, but getting into Thailand was more of a problem. After a lot of searching, emptying cars out and swearing, it became clear that the Americans had lost the car papers for Ziggy, and the guards weren't going to let the car across without them. We stalled and stalled, but OJ and Lovey couldn't find them.

Although we no longer had Dante, we did have Dante's old papers and Dante's old plates. So, right at the border, in full view of guards, police, military and passers-by, the Ziggy crew began switching the plates.

"Very Bond, right?" Tony asked.

I couldn't help but laugh. Kind of Bond. It took twenty excruciating minutes, though I'm sure in films it's over in a flash. Now the car plates matched the papers, although the model, year, and engine numbers didn't, but luckily the guards didn't check. We made it across and entered Thailand, our twentieth country.

The whole journey took about 26 hours. Carlos did most of the work on day one, driving an epic shift from 10am till 3am while I slept and whimpered and complained about the quality of Laotian moonshine. Then I got to take over for the last six hours of highway and three hours of traffic. I hated that early morning shift, from dark through sunrise into the blazing noon, and I felt ropey, so it took it out of me.

The long drive also took its toll on Fez, which broke down three times in the Bangkok traffic: brakes seized, spark plug popped, cylinder head smashed up. So close to our destination, these trifling stoppages were easily dealt with, and repairs swiftly made.

Thai petrol stations are a wonder of cellophane-wrapped indestructible snacks, so pumped with e-numbers and preservatives that only they and cockroaches will survive WW3. Hot dogs, microwave burgers, instant noodles, frozen meals and dried out pastries compete with chocolate, crisps, coffee, tea and every soft drink under the sun thankfully kept chilled to a Siberian cool. If these treats had been available along our whole journey the trip would have been considerably more comfortable.

The big camera we'd been using to film our whole debacle broke at some point in Vang Vien, so we found a Sony repair shop in Bangkok. It would take about a week to fix, so we decided to leave it behind and OJ would collect it when he flew out of Bangkok later in the year. We still had the mini-cam so, although it wasn't ideal, we could still film the end of the Trek.

As expected, Bangkok traffic really was shocking, worse than Beijing, worse even than Budapest. The only way to avoid it was to pay a hefty fee to join the elite on the toll roads—a rollercoaster circuit of swerving overpasses built above the maelstrom. Unfortunately Carlos and I managed to get thoroughly lost on this racing circuit (Carlos: "I know the way." He didn't). We paid repeated tolls, lost the Americans and had to return to the underworld to get to our destination anyway.

Parked at one end of Khao San waiting for Ziggy, we attracted quite a lot of attention, handing out fliers and telling our story. It felt good to sit there with our battle-scarred Trabbis after all we'd taken them through, though the police didn't seem to think so. But we were good with police by then. In fact, it was a joy to be pulled over for the first time in months. I'd lost my driving licence, but we managed to wing it.

Khao San seemed to have gone a little upmarket since I was last there. The bars looked a little trendier, a little better decked out. There was more English football, more internet at the pubs and a bit of wifi floating about. There were still pirate CDs, but now pirate computer games and even Mac programmes. It wasn't so filthy and there were more ATMs as well as a McDonalds and a Burger King. They were still selling Pad Thai and fried grasshoppers though.

I almost wasn't allowed into Thailand. My passport was three months from expiring and it was Thai policy that your passport must be valid for six months. The border guard eventually stamped it, but gave me a telling off and warned that I wouldn't be allowed into the country like that again, adding that Cambodia wouldn't let me in either.

I got in touch with the UK embassy, who said it was impossible to extend my passport. I would have to apply for a new one, which would take a week. No one was willing to wait in Bangkok that long, so I had a few options. I could try to get a new passport, then fly out to meet the others. But that would put me behind by a week and mean I would probably miss the end of the trip. Or

I could go to the Cambodian embassy first thing and beg for permission to enter the country. But what if they refused and made a note of my passport number, guaranteeing I wouldn't make it into Cambodia?

If I just went for it, then there was a chance the border guards wouldn't notice and I'd sail in. But there was also a chance I could be refused entry into Cambodia. By that point I would already have been stamped out of Thailand and unable to return. So I'd be caught in no-man's-land with a valid but expiring passport and no country that would take me in.

That would not be the best conclusion to the Trek.

In the end I decided to go for it; we'd blagged plenty of borders up until then, and there was just one crossing left.

Carlos' mum had flown to Phnom Penh on 1 January to meet him. He was already four days late, so we planned to leave at 5am the next morning in order to make the border before it closed. I was still feeling pretty terrible and got an early night, as did Carlos, but the Americans stayed out drinking 'til the early hours and didn't enjoy being woken up at 4.30am.

"I'm still drunk. There's no way I can drive," Tony told me when he made it down. I felt rubbish, too. Whatever I had was more than a New Year's hangover, it surely couldn't last four days, so I just lay down in Fez hoping I wouldn't wake up again until the border.

But we'd only been driving for twenty minutes when Ziggy pulled over. The Yanks shouted out the window at us, "Have you seen the mini cam?"

Shit.

We raced back to the hotel, but the mini cam had gone and no one there knew anything about it. Tony thought he might have left it on the floor of the hotel when we drove off. So suddenly we were in a race against time to find a video camera, cross the border and reach Carlos' mum.

We phoned the Sony Centre, but the camera we dropped off wasn't repaired yet. We looked at buying a new one, but it was too expensive. Lovey then phoned a contact at the Foreign Correspondents Club and they put us in touch with a company that loaned professional quality cameras. For $500 a week we could borrow one identical to the awesome Sony that was being repaired.

It seemed the only option and we went to grab it, but by the time we'd waded through the thick Bangkok traffic, collected the camera and got out of the city, there was no way we were going to make the border before it closed. Sorry, Carlos' mum.

We drove to Aranyapratet, six kilometres from Cambodia, found a hotel and slept. It felt peculiar being so close to our goal. If all went well, the Trek would be over in just a few days. But first I had to make it across the Cambodian border with an invalid passport.

The Final Frontier

The signs on arriving at the border weren't promising. OJ was filming quite blatantly, and the Thai border guards weren't happy. One guy was a real prick and seemed determined to give us shit. He was a shouting little man in an immaculate uniform that looked like it'd been picked up at an illegal eBay auction of SS memorabilia. Maybe the kit had rubbed off on him, as he kept shouting, "Papers. Show papers."

He looked through my passport, but I managed to divert his attention when he was on the expiration details. And for some reason he made me unpack a fold up chair in front of his cronies, but didn't ask to look in the boot. They spent half an hour questioning us, photocopying passports and poking around in the cars.

The only non-uniformed personnel who seemed to have the freedom to roam the border were the kids, ragged little urchins who tapped on car windows and asked for money. They looked sweet, but you wouldn't want to leave your thoughts unattended, never mind your car.

We attracted a lot of stares, large crowds pointing and laughing. Watching is a big hobby in the East. Since we'd left Europe the rules on staring engagement had shifted more and more. It was now open stare warfare, with laser-guided looks constantly locking onto us. I noticed the cultural differences when we parked the Trabbis on Khao San Road. The Westerners sidled up to the car, often adopting a blasé approach to conceal their interest. They'd fake a look at a nearby stall, then swivel and cast a glance at the car. I had to greet them to show it was ok to come and have a look.

"How's it going?" I'd break the ice.

"Oh, oh," mock embarrassment, he wasn't really looking at my car, "yes good, thanks."

"You recognise the car?"

And there we go, then they were free to explore. But with your typical countryside East Asian there was no such charade. He would see the car from his perch in the shade, walk straight up to it, tap the hood, peer in through the window, push on the spare wheels, pluck at the wipers, then stare me up and down, sometimes laughing, sometimes looking troubled.

Maybe it was because a lot of the places we visited were pretty light on entertainment—computer games, cinemas, theatres, clubs, TVs, radios, music. So people took advantage of any form of fun they could get, and watching Westerners drag a brightly coloured plastic car down their High Street was about as good as the scheduling got that day.

I often wondered how much conversation we caused on dinner tables across the world. Not that they used dinner tables in a lot of the places we went. At all those little villages we passed and caused a stir I'm sure people were talking about it afterwards.

"Hey did you see those stupid white people earlier? What was that all about?"

We were probably victims of all sorts of speculation and gossip. The proud father boasting that he knew the name of the car, the grandfather claiming we were Russians, the old woman thinking Tony was from Pakistan.

After the Nazi border guard was satisfied, and we'd got our stamps, the Thais waved us through and we drove down to the Cambodian side of the border. The Thais and Cambodians had made full use of the 150m stretch of no-man's-land between them. The untaxed zone had become a haven for duty-free trading, with people selling everything from clothes to blocks of ice, and a plush casino cashing in on the tax break. Maybe it wouldn't be such a bad place to be stuck, I thought.

Thankfully the Cambodian border guards were friendlier and less organised than their Thai counterparts. We filled out our forms, paid our dues, got in line and I got my stamp. Elation. We still didn't have the required permission from Phnom Penh to bring cars into the country, so there was a small altercation at customs. Luckily the official was easy going and let us in: "As long as I don't get in trouble."

"We never cause any trouble," we told him and made a prompt getaway.

The Cambodian border town of Poi Pet was not a pretty place. It stank of the decomposing rubbish that littered the streets, a treasure hunt for wild kids and wild dogs questing for morsels of food and money. The architecture was grubby and crumbling, the streets were unpaved, pot holed and dusty, and the 50km stretch of road out of the town was the worst we had driven since Mongolia.

But we were in Cambodia—our twenty-first and last country: the final frontier. Six months and one day since I flew out of London, eight time-zones and 15,500 miles later, we were nearly there.

VICTORY PARADE

There were days on the trip that I would rather forget. But others I know I will remember forever. Driving the cars to Mith Samlanh Friends, the Phnom Penh charity that we were raising money for, was one of those days.

I had no idea what to expect. A cup of tea and a pat on the back? An informal chat with some volunteers? But as we pulled up to the gate I could here clapping and drumming, and see photographers and a cameraman, and it gave me butterflies.

The reception was astonishing. A corridor of 400 screaming, cheering kids were led by a band in traditional costume beating drums and dancing. We stepped out of the cars into a bubble among the throng and just stood there while hundreds of people applauded and waved at us and cameras flashed.

None of us were quite sure what to do. We probably should have jumped on the roofs of the cars and raised our hands like triumphant Grand Prix drivers lapping up the crowd's adulation. But instead we all got a little emotional. It was lump in the throat stuff seeing all those little kids and what our trip meant to them. We stumbled about, hugging each other and smiling so broadly we got cramp.

Eventually, after an age of cheering, a head of house appeared with a microphone and a translator and gave a speech basically saying that we were awesome. Then a representative from the kids spoke and expressed his gratitude, talked about how much the money meant to them and how they'd been following our progress. It was very emotional and I didn't really want it to end.

"I was welling up," said OJ, "I was pleased to have the camera so no one could see me."

"I almost cried," admitted Tony.

The kids all swarmed to the cars. We opened them up so they could sit in and play with the wheel and we posed for photos. I was literally wading through children, hundreds of these tiny, smiling kids staring up, waving and holding hands. "Helloooo... helloooo," they would shout and cling onto me. I couldn't stop laughing. We spent an hour with them, so many smiling faces. We were told they were expecting us to arrive in big cars, that they thought it was hilarious that we'd crossed two continents in tiny Trabbis.

After the kids had been called back to class we were given a tour of the facilities. It is truly a stunning project. At the city centre base the organisation takes more than 800 disadvantaged kids a day, aged 0-24, and puts them through informal education and vocational training. Most of the kids would otherwise be living and working on the streets, involved in everything from petty crime and drugs to prostitution.

As part of the core curriculum, everyone learns numeracy, literacy, English and health education. On top of this the centre provides training for aspiring hairdressers, seamstresses, mechanics, welders, beauticians, electricians and cooks.

There was so much laughter in that place. The kids were ridiculously cute and friendly. Everywhere the children did the hands clasped greeting, like a little prayer—it is such a sweet and respectful hello. In nursery the toddlers greeted us as "father", and wouldn't stop waving till we were well out of sight. They made me a little origami car, painted like Fez with the word "Trabantterk" on the side. Tony, as team mechanic, was given a paper hammer.

Tony: "I've been smiling so hard for so long now that my cheeks are hurting. I don't think I can smile anymore."

At the end of the day two giant trucks turned up to take all the kids home. About 500 of them lived around the city, mostly in the slum areas. Another 300 lived in the charity's two houses, a boys' house and a girls' house. They kept waving and shouting as they boarded the truck; it was hugely touching.

After saying goodbye we went to the excellent Friends restaurant just by the school, and treated ourselves to the most expensive meal we'd had in months. Tapas and cocktails. We were all exhausted from a long afternoon, but elated, absolutely on top of the world.

Lovey: "That has to have been the best day of Trabant Trek. I'm not kidding."

OJ: "That really has made it all seem worthwhile, that was just awesome."

Everyone agreed.

It felt like the closure we needed. After six months on the road, arriving in Phnom Penh was weird. I'd sat down with a beer and thought, well is this it? Is this what we did? I was still suffering from my New Year excesses and didn't feel like celebrating. It was a bit of an anticlimax.

But the welcome we got from the kids, who made us feel so special, and seeing the work Mith Samlanh does, and how we'd been able to help, really put it in perspective. What a day. The only disappointment was that Carlos hadn't been around to see it. He had gone ahead to Sihanoukville to meet his mum. I felt bad for him.

FINALE

How do you finish a trip like that? Where is the end? Well, Sihanoukville, that is the finish line, right? Actually no, it's when we've visited the last charity. That'll be the end. But then there's an interview the following day, so maybe that's the end? Actually I still need to write the last blog, once I've posted it, then we'll say it's over, ok? Well maybe, but I'm hanging around for a few weeks, what about once I'm home?

I think I just didn't want it to end.

We'd hoped to arrive in Sihanoukville early evening, but a series of press interviews delayed our departure from Phnom Penh. The Americans had replaced a missing screw in Fez, restoring the pressure in a cylinder and solving the car's power issues, but the brakes were still broken.

OJ, who was my new driving buddy following Carlos' departure, refused to let me drive after witnessing me collide with a scooter in the city that afternoon. It was the only accident I had in 16,000 miles of driving and it was entirely my fault. I'd attempted a tight u-turn at Hamilton pace on a major road, but we didn't have any wing mirrors and I hadn't checked my blind spot. As Fez neared a right angle with the flow of traffic, a scooter with three people on board slammed into the driver's door. Oops.

Luckily no one came off, nor seemed hurt, but OJ, who had never been comfortable with my roadside manner, was not prepared to take any further risks. He insisted on driving.

It was only four hours from Phnom Penh to Sihanoukville, but the BBC reporter we'd spent much of the afternoon with was adamant that driving in the dark was a bad idea. "You really shouldn't drive at night. The road is terrible. It'll be pitch black. I wouldn't do it, seriously, why put yourselves in danger?"

He obviously didn't know what we were made of. When you've crossed the narrow, winding Anzob Pass at night, flanked by sheer drops and dodging unstoppable lorries, then driving to the beach holds few fears.

We were right to go for it—the road was beautiful—and in Fez we were able to stay close enough behind Ziggy to use the spread from its headlamps to light the way. Fez's lights hadn't worked for some time.

I was happy to let OJ drive, but disappointed that after six months of driving Fez I wasn't going to be able to take him over the finish line. Luckily OJ is a kind and noble gentleman. A few miles out of town we stopped to take a last photo of Trabant Trek on the road, and he handed me the keys.

"Do you wanna drive Fez in?"

Hell, yeah. What an odd feeling of nervous energy and excitement, tempered by loss and regret, as we stood there, the last four of us, posing for photos with our arms round each other. "This is it, the final stretch," Lovey said.

But it still didn't feel real.

Shortly before midnight we pulled up at Monkey Republic, the bar-guesthouse where Carlos had booked rooms for us. The Spaniard was there with a small crowd of fans. Some sort of fireworks were set off, and there was a banner and lots of cheering. Characteristically we were about four hours late, so everyone was pretty merry, and the excitement in the air was palpable:

"We did it."

"I can't believe we actually made it."

"We're here."

What else is there to say?

"How do you feel?" people would ask.

"Very strange."

I don't think I ever doubted that we would make it, and pretty much since we reached South East Asia it felt like we were nearly finished.

"I'll feel like it's over once we've visited the charity," I told people, and myself. The emotional party moved on to a beach bar for intensive celebrations. The alcohol flowed, but the night was again sullied by running arguments with Lovey, who had it in for me about something. This time there was a violent culmination—I lamped Lovey square in the mouth, putting him on his arse and getting myself thrown out of our leaving party. What a way to finish the trip, decking the team leader.

Lovey surrounded by the kids of M'Lop Tapang

The next morning I woke feeling terrible, hung-over and gut-wrenched. Lovey and I weren't talking. In fact we never really spoke again.

With sore heads, we headed to our second charity, M'Lop Tapang. The wonderful children there put on a show for us, with traditional Khmer music and dancing complemented by more modern moves, break dancing and theatre. The kids were great fun, and were obviously having a laugh dancing around on stage. There was plenty of hand holding and waving and jumping on the cars.

I'm not sure what it is about Cambodian children, they are so sweet, friendly and quick to smile, it's touching. I'm not sure either what they thought of us though, giant and pale with those odd cars.

We were given a tour of the school. It wasn't as big as Mith Samlanh, but followed the same educational principles, minus the vocational training. It was another group of people doing fantastic work for children with few opportunities and a worthy cause if ever there was one.

The last official engagement of Trabant Trek drew to a close, and we headed back to Monkey Republic.

"How do you feel?"

It still didn't feel over. Maybe it would once I'd said goodbye to Carlos, who was leaving the following day to go to Canada and continue his travels. Nutter.

I didn't like saying goodbye to Carlos. I'd only really known the little Catalan for six months, but it was a pretty intensive six months. We spent a lot of it together in a little plastic box—I must have slept with Carlos more than any other man in my life. Despite what could have been a suffocating proximity, we remained good friends throughout, and other than a few weeks following a brief falling out in Ulaanbaatar, I always felt like he had my back.

Carlos drove Fez to the bus station, then handed me the keys, which felt pretty symbolic. You know those moments that will never come again? You try to absorb everything about them, the smell, the sound, the feel.

This is definitely the last time my co-driver will hand me the keys.

I remember everything about it.

It felt like the end.

EPILOGUE

"Come to Cambodia, he said. We'll have a good time, he said. We'll be home for Christmas, he said."

A favourite ditty of The Mighty Tony Perez.

SIHANOUKVILLE

If I lived in a place like Sihanoukville, I'd be smiling too. It was pretty much paradise and the locals' natural expression was a wide, toothy grin.

But we were firmly in tourist land. Where people used to help us out of genuine kindness and hospitality, now they just saw dollar signs. It was an unwelcome but understandable shift.

There were plenty of Westerners out there, searching for the dream. I met a couple of English guys who were running a beach bar called Zion's Den. The premises were empty when they found it, so they just moved in and bought some booze from the supermarket to flog. They lived and slept there, "Like squatter's rights," they said.

They were all wasted most of the time, and in fact the sanest member of staff seemed to be the dog, Zion, a beautiful little Andrex puppy who could attract the coos of the most hardened traveller.

"Did you find the dog on the beach?" I asked innocently.

"Nah, man. We got her free with some acid."

Fair enough.

We Trekkers had become a family, but a terribly dysfunctional family. I hadn't exchanged more than a couple of words with Lovey since our falling out. While on the road, you couldn't really afford to fall out with anyone; you knew you were with them for the long haul. But the end of the Trek had severed those bonds. The incident didn't affect my relationship with Tony or OJ. In fact, sitting on the beach, talking about old times, we realised we'd never had an argument.

There was a lot of sitting around on the beach. We were minor celebrities; most people had seen the cars parked up outside Monkey Republic and wondered who they belonged to. And we had a story that was far better than most of the other travellers, so at least our answers to the Sacred Three Questions of Backpacking were vaguely interesting.

"Where You From?"

The last five trekkers who made it to Cambodia, (l-r) Carlos, Dan, OJ,
Tony and Lovey

England.

"Where've You Been?"

We drove here from Germany.

"And Where You Going... what? You drove here from Germany?"

That normally wiped the complacency off the face of the half-hearted, un-original plebeian who claimed to give a toss about my itinerary.

Most people expressed genuine amazement when we showed them the route map on a flier, and it did give me a sense of pride. I'd tell a few stories—stuck in the Gobi, trying to cross the Pamirs, Turkmenistan—and it was clear that what we did was pretty far from most people's ideas of travelling. It had been funny to follow the slow shift in people's reactions from "you'll never make it" via "I can't believe you've made it this far" to "I can't believe you did it".

We did a rough estimate and reckon we broke down more than 300 times—an average of twice a day, for six months. A stunning achievement, and I genuinely think it helped me to become a more patient person (either that or brain dead to delays).

I told our story to a British guy at Zion's Den. "Travelling overland like that must give you a real sense of distance," he said, "You know, you can step on a plane and be here in fourteen hours. But driving here. Then you really get to understand the scale of things."

I hadn't really thought about it before, but he was absolutely right. Going overland you get a feel for the size and shape of Eurasia, its bumps, dips, puddles and curves. But, oddly, the landmass felt far smaller to me than it did when we set off. I could look over large sections of the map and recognise the pitfalls, po-tential hazards, things that might slow you down and places you could race through. Having crossed deserts, mountains and forests, cities, seas and tundra, nowhere felt remote anymore.

"Slovenia? Hop in I'll give you a ride. It's only a week in that direction."

And I used to bitch about picking my mates up from across town.

Although the world had shrunk since I set off on the Trek, the trip also gave me a feel for how people travelled before cars. I know what it's like to spend a week trying to cross a mountain range, or pack the wagon with the knowledge that there won't be any supplies *en route* for a few days. I know the awkwardness of stumbling about in the dark in a tiny hamlet trying to beg a place to stay and something to eat, or waving down passers by to ask for a lift into town.

I had often wondered whether the world was being homogenised by the forces of progress and globalisation. But on my journey I realised that people are probably as polarised as ever. The differences between the way of life I'm used to and some of the ones we experienced are huge, so much so that the Tajikistan I visited was probably more different to me than to Marco Polo when he arrived 700 years before. The bustling, congested streets of London couldn't be further from the rutted donkey trails of the Tajiks. My mod-con-filled home, my electronic gadgets and my way of urban living would be bewilderingly un-recognisable to some of the old men we met living with their entire family in Mongol *gers*.

People always ask me what the best parts of the Trek were. There were many, some man-made like Budapest or Beijing, some natural like the Pamirs or Gobi. But for me, the main highlight was the hospitality of strangers. It sounds corny, but I was genuinely struck by how many people went out of their way to help us. People who gave us a tow, helped find a part, gave us a push start, provided food or a bed, acted as translator, forgave our misdemeanours or pointed us in the right direction. They must number in their hundreds, the people whose acts of genuine and selfless kindness made the whole Trek work.

Tim Slessor, who in the 1950s was part of the first expedition ever to drive from London to Singapore, pointed out to me that he drove back again after-wards. Not a chance. Although I can honestly say I never felt like quitting, and I'd do it all again, road trips are off my agenda for a while.

We Trekkers gradually returned to our lives. Carlos headed to North America before returning to Barcelona, via a weekend in London. Tony, OJ and Lovey relaxed in South East Asia for another few months.

I was determined to sit still for a while, and stayed in Cambodia for four weeks. I got back to England on 5 February 2008, seven months after setting off.

Home for Christmas? I was only six weeks late.

The cars would never make it home. None of us know what has happened to Dante, though I wouldn't be too surprised to find him fixed up and trawling the roads of northern Laos. Fez didn't make it much further. The Americans dumped him near the Cambodian border after a failed attempt to get back to Bangkok a few weeks after I left. OJ saw a Cambodian farmer eyeing up the little East German, and thinks he may well have been converted into a plough.

A few weeks after Fez's demise, Ziggy blew two tyres on the way to the beach. Tony and OJ didn't have the tools to repair the car and were forced to abandon him on the side of the road. The pair had to fly home before they could rescue old Ziggy, so they left the keys with a friend in Sihanoukville. But by the time the rescue party had arrived Ziggy had already been raided by bandits, the engine stolen and spirited away. Who would steal a Trabant engine? I guess it is a mark of how far the Trabbis were from home—far enough to escape their woeful reputation. Tony tells me Ziggy was towed to a secret location to await our return.

Though the paintwork will fade, the plastic wont rust, and it's entirely conceivable that Fez, Dante and Ziggy will hang out in South East Asia for years to come, curious locals wondering where the odd little cars have come from. But who would ever guess what those Trabants had been through for their retirement in the sun?

Lightning Source UK Ltd.
Milton Keynes UK
UKHW011619010321
379592UK00003B/807